THE RIGHT TO BE LOVED

THE RIGHT
TO BE LOVED

S. MATTHEW LIAO

OXFORD
UNIVERSITY PRESS

OXFORD
UNIVERSITY PRESS

Oxford University Press is a department of the University of Oxford.
It furthers the University's objective of excellence in research, scholarship,
and education by publishing worldwide. Oxford is a registered trade mark
of Oxford University Press in the UK and in certain other countries

Published in the United States of America by Oxford University Press
198 Madison Avenue, New York, NY 10016, United States of America

© Oxford University Press 2015

Library of Congress Cataloging-in-Publication Data
Liao, S. Matthew.
 The right to be loved / S. Matthew Liao.
  p. cm.
 Includes bibliographical references and index.
 ISBN 978–0–19–023483–6 (cloth : alk. paper) 1. Children's
rights—Philosophy. 2. Children—Philosophy. 3. Human
rights—Philosophy. I. Title.
 HQ789.L53 2015
 323.3'5201—dc23
                    2015001733

9 8 7 6 5 4 3 2 1

Printed in the United States of America on acid-free paper

For Wibke, Caitlin, and Connor

Contents

Acknowledgments

I embarked on this project more than twenty years ago when I first became acquainted with Susan Moller Okin's seminal work, *Justice, Gender and the Family*, in which she criticized John Rawls for not applying his principles of justice to the family; in particular, Okin had in mind the relationship between men and women inside a family. Okin made a powerful case that if Rawls had applied one of his principles of justice, namely, the principle of equality, to such a family, he would have come to the conclusion that men and women should share household responsibilities equally in a family. When I reflected further on Okin's criticism of Rawls, it occurred to me that the family often also consists of the relationship between parents and children. However, the principle of equality seems less applicable to this relationship. I became interested in finding out what kind of moral principles would govern the parent-child relationship.

Given the prominent status of rights language in our moral, legal, and political discourses, a good starting point seemed to be rights. I then came across a number of international declarations, bills of rights, and the mission statements of various charitable foundations that claim that children have a right to be loved. This claim is intriguing for a number of reasons. For one thing, a number of philosophers such as James Griffin and L. W. Sumner have expressed concerns that rights are often claimed without sufficient consideration as to whether these claims can be justified. So there is the worry that this claim is merely empty rhetoric. In addition, feminists and the then-in-vogue communitarian critics of liberalism often argue that the liberal language of rights is incompatible with affection, care, and love. If they were right, the right of children to be loved would appear to be an oxymoron. My aim in this book is to show that the claim that children have a right to be loved is coherent and that its justification can and does hang together as a whole.

When I began this project, there were only a handful of philosophers working on the topics of human rights and family ethics. In the last ten years or so, both of these fields have experienced rapid growth, and the arguments in these fields have increased tremendously in their level of sophistication. I enjoyed working through this literature as I wrote up the book-length version of my arguments.

As it is bound to be the case with a long-term project, I am greatly indebted to many people. I am particularly grateful to James Griffin, my DPhil supervisor at Oxford, whose rigorous philosophical standards I have strived to conform in my work. I am also indebted to Geoffrey Marshall and Nick Bunnin for their support and encouragement of my ideas, especially in the early stages of this venture. On the overall direction of the project, I have also been helped by David Archard, John Tasioulas, Wibke Gruetjen, Joseph Shaw, Jeff McMahan, John Broome, and Roger Crisp. Tremendous thanks also go to Roy Lam for helping me with photocopying at a time when the Internet did not exist and books could not be taken out of the Bodleian Library, and to Rotem Herrmann for her assistance with the index.

An article version of my arguments was published in the *Journal of Political Philosophy* in 2006. On various drafts, I was greatly aided by the people I mentioned above, as well as by Nir Eyal, Douglas Wolfe, Peter Singer, Harry Frankfurt, Hugh LaFollette, David Wasserman, Agnieszka Jaworska, David Rodin, and Gerald Lang. The Greenwall Fellowship Program at Johns Hopkins University and the Kennedy Institute of Ethics at Georgetown University also provided generous research support when the article was written.

Chapter One is partly derived from "The Basis of Human Moral Status" and "The Genetic Account of Moral Status: A Defense" in the *Journal of Moral Philosophy* (© Koninklijke Brill NV, Leiden, 2010) and (© Koninklijke Brill NV, Leiden, 2012), respectively. I am grateful for valuable inputs from Jeff McMahan, Peter Singer, David Wasserman, Nick Shea, David DeGrazia, Joseph Shaw, Nick Bostrom, Nic Southwood, Agnieszka Jaworska, Nathan Nobis, Michael Walzer, Clifford Geertz, Chris Grau, Anders Sandberg, and Steve Clarke.

Chapter Two is a reprint of my chapter in Rowan Cruft, S. Matthew Liao, and Massimo Renzo (eds.), *Philosophical Foundations of Human Rights* (Oxford: Oxford University Press, 2015), and draws on my articles "Agency and Human Rights" in the *Journal of Applied Philosophy* (2006), and "Political and Naturalistic Conceptions of Human Rights: A False Polemic?" co-written with Adam Etinson in the *Journal of Moral Philosophy* (© Koninklijke Brill NV, Leiden, 2012). I received helpful advice from John Tasioulas, Fabienne Peters, James W. Nickel, Jonathan Quong, Samuel Scheffler, David Velleman, Joseph Raz, Matt Smith, Japa Pallikkathayil, Paul Bloomfield, Ben Saunders, Rowan Cruft, Massimo Renzo, Rob Shaver, Daniel Khokhar, Carolyn Plunkett, Andrew Franklin-Hall, Nic Southwood, Collin O'Neil, Christian Barry, Daniel Nolan, Rachael Briggs, Rahul Kumar, Kerah Gordon-Solmon, Meena Krishnamurthy, Christine Sypnowich, Adrian Currie, and Adam Etinson.

Chapter Three contains material from "Why Children Need to Be Loved" in *Critical Review of International Social and Political Philosophy* (2012). I was aided by valuable observations from David Wasserman, Daniel Khokhar, and Wibke Gruetjen. Chapter Four is derived from "The Idea of a Duty to Love" in the *Journal of Value Inquiry* (2006). I received helpful comments from Nick Bunnin, David Archard, Joseph Shaw, Karin Boxer, Wibke Gruetjen, Bernard Williams, Justin Oakley, and Julie Tannenbaum. Special thanks are due to Daniel Khokhar for his various insightful suggestions regarding Chapter Five. For Chapter Six, I benefited greatly from comments from Andrew Franklin-Hall, Collin O'Neil, Daniel Khokhar, Ralf Bader, Joseph Millum, and Magdalena Hoffman. I am grateful to the *Journal of Moral Philosophy*, *Journal of Political Philosophy*, *Journal of Applied Philosophy*, *Journal of Value Inquiry*, and *Critical Review of International Social and Political Philosophy* for their permission to include material from these articles.

Much of the new material for this book was written while I was at New York University. I am particularly grateful to Bill Ruddick, the founding director of the Center for Bioethics, and to members of the Department of Philosophy for providing such a congenial place to complete this book. I am also greatly indebted to Collin O'Neil and Dan Khokhar, who generously read, and commented on, the entire manuscript.

I am also particularly grateful to Peter Ohlin at Oxford University Press for his enthusiasm and encouragement of this project and to Emily Sacharin, Sabrina Hill, Elina Sluzhman Carmona and their team at Oxford University Press for their care in the production of this book. I would like to thank the two anonymous referees for Oxford University Press for providing me with over fifteen thousand words of valuable comments. This book has significantly improved as a result of these observations.

Thanks are due to my parents, Yi-Chen and Susan, and my grandparents, Ting-Fai and Chuen-Duan, for all their love and support, which I shall never be able to repay.

Lastly, I would like to thank my family for their patience, support, and encouragement while I completed this book. My wife, Wibke Gruetjen, has shared a life with me since before the inception of this project. I am very fortunate to have run all the core ideas in this book by Wibke, and my confidence in an idea invariably grows when I learn that Wibke also endorses it. Our children, Caitlin and Connor, have been great sources of pride and joy for us. Participating in their growth and development has reinforced my view that children indeed have a right to be loved. I dedicate this book to my family.

Introduction

1. Foundational Issues

That children have a right to be loved is a claim that can be found in many international declarations, bills of rights, and in the mission statements of various charitable foundations. For instance, the Declaration of the Psychological Rights of the Child (1979) states that children have "the right to love, affection, and understanding." The Declaration of the Rights of the Child in Israel (1989) describes every child as having "the right to a family life—to nourishment, suitable housing, protection, love and understanding." According to the Declaration of the Rights of Mozambican Children (1979), children have "the right to grow up in a climate of peace and security, surrounded by love and understanding." The Children's Charter of Japan (1951) declares that "All children shall be entitled to be brought up in their own homes with proper love." In the United States, the Bill of Rights of Children in Divorce Actions (1966) mandates that children have "the right to the day by day love, care, discipline and protection of the parent having custody of the children." The LIFT Foundation (2003) aims to promote "the basic human right of children to be loved."

In addition, there are many other international declarations and bills that can be interpreted as claiming that children have such a right. For instance, in the United States, the Joint Commission on Mental Health of Children (1969) proclaims that children have "the right to continuous loving care." Likewise, according to the Bill of Rights for Foster Children (1973), every foster child has "the Inherent Rights . . . to receive continuous loving care." Principle 6 of the United Nations Declaration on the Rights of the Child (1959) states that "The child, for the full and harmonious development of his personality, needs love and understanding. He shall, wherever possible, grow up in the care and under the responsibility of his parents, and in any case in an atmosphere of affection." The Children's Bill of Rights of the New York State Youth Commission (1949) lists children's having "the right to the affection and intelligent guidance of understanding parents." The Children's Bill of Rights as formulated by the White House Conference on Children and Youth, USA (1970) affirms children's "right to grow up nurtured by affectionate parents." Charter on the Rights of the Arab Child of the League of Arab States (1984) aims to "confirm and guarantee the right of the child to grow up in the family where there is family stability coupled with affection and warmth." In 2014, the United Kindgom announced the so-called "Cinderella law" that would jail parents who fail to show love and affection to children for up to ten years in prison.[1] Given the sheer number and variety of sources from which the idea of a child's right to be loved has issued, it seems without a doubt that the idea that children have a right to be loved is cross-cultural, widely accepted, and enduring.

Some people will think that it is obvious that children have a right to be loved. For example, the legal philosopher Neil MacCormick says:

> Let me start from what seems to me a simple and barely contestable assertion: at least from birth, every child has a right

to be nurtured, cared for, and, if possible, loved, until such time as he or she is capable of caring for himself or herself . . . I should regard it as a plain case of moral blindness if anyone failed to recognize that every child has that right.[2]

However, there are other people who are likely to be skeptical that there is such a right. One reason is that in recent years, there has been a proliferation of the language of rights in our moral, legal, and political practices. A number of people are concerned that rights are often claimed without sufficient consideration as to whether these claims can be justified.[3] Hence, L. W. Sumner warns that "Like the arms race the escalation of rights rhetoric is out of control . . . The proliferation of rights claims has devalued rights by eroding their argumentative power."[4] Or, James Griffin speaks of the "debasement" of the language of human rights in public life and in philosophy.[5] As these writers correctly point out, inappropriate use of the concept of rights can have the effect of diluting the important status of rights generally.

In fact, there are a number of *foundational* concerns regarding whether children have a right to be loved. For example, can children, especially very young ones, have rights? That is, are they rightholders? Rightholding, according to a popular view, should be ascribed only to beings that are actually capable of acting rationally and/or morally, that is, to actual agents. Are children, and in particular infants, actual agents? A number of philosophers have argued that very young children cannot have rights precisely because they are not actual agents.[6] For example, Carl Wellman writes: "I propose the hypothesis that only those kinds of entities who are agents could be moral rightholders . . . If moral agency really is necessary for the possession of rights, as I have argued, and if infants lack agency, as scientific psychology and everyday observation attest, then infants, at least, cannot be rights-holders."[7] Similarly, after arguing that only actual agents can have rights, James Griffin concludes that "human rights do not extend to infants."[8] If children cannot have rights, it would follow that they cannot have rights of any kind, including a right to be loved.

But even if children can be rightholders, one might doubt that they have a right to be loved. The interests of children in nutrition, shelter, and education may be important enough to ground rights, but is a child's interest in being loved comparably important? What is the kind of love at issue and why do children have an interest in this kind of love? Why would this interest be important enough to ground a right to be loved and justify holding someone else to be under a duty to love a child? Although many international declarations and bills of rights have proclaimed that children have a right to be loved, as far as I am aware, none of them say how this right is to be justified.

Indeed, there are duties corresponding to rights[9] and it is far from obvious that someone could have a duty to love someone else. Many people believe that love as a duty is absurd because love is an emotion and is therefore not something that we can bring about at will, that is, love is not commandable, while duties require an action to be commandable. For instance, Kant expresses this commandability objection as follows:

> Love is a matter of feeling, not of willing, and I cannot love because I will to, still less because I ought to (I cannot be constrained to love); so a duty to love is an absurdity."[10]

Similarly, Francis Schrag says that

> [T]here may be something wrong with this entire approach [of using rights] to the problem of securing for children that which they need to develop into healthy human beings . . .

[because] it does not seem that one can have a duty to love someone inasmuch as loving someone is not something which one can determine to do or not.[11]

Also, is love that is required still love? One might think that if one loves another out of a sense of duty, then one does not really love that person. As Bernard Williams famously warned, this may be one thought too many.[12] If there cannot be a duty to love, then it would seem to follow that there cannot conceptually be a right of children to be loved. Indeed, even though MacCormick seems to think that children's right to be loved is self-evident, he does not say that "every child has a right to be nurtured, cared for, and loved." Instead, he says, "every child has a right to be nurtured, cared for, and *if possible*, loved" (my italics). Is Mac-Cormick less confident that children have a right to be loved because love might not be an appropriate object of a duty, and therefore of a right?

Furthermore, an adequate account of this right should tell us who the dutybearers are. A natural response might be that this duty belongs to the biological parents. But are biological parents the sole dutybearers? What happens if the biological parents of a particular child are dead? Also, how demanding should the duty to love a child be? What are we required to give up in order to ensure that a child is adequately loved?

Moreover, there is ample evidence that some biological parents are grossly inadequate parents. Each year, child protection services in the United States alone receive an estimated 3.4 million reports of abuse and neglect concerning approximately six million children.[13] Should we license parents, that is, require biological parents to demonstrate certain competence and character before they are permitted to parent their biological children? Relatedly, UNICEF estimates that more than two million children are in institutional care.[14] This estimate is likely to be low, as many institutions are unregistered and many countries do not regularly collect and report data on children in institutional care.[15] In the United States, there are over four hundred thousand children without permanent families in foster care.[16] Is there a duty to adopt and provide love for these children without adequate parents? If so, who has this duty?

2. A Plan Forward

The issues mentioned above can be grouped into seven main questions:

1. Can children have rights?
2. If they can, what grounds a child's right to be loved?
3. Is love an appropriate object of a right?
4. Who has the corresponding duty to love a child?
5. How demanding should the duty to love be?
6. Should biological parenting be licensed to ensure adequate, loving parents?
7. Is there a duty to adopt children who do not have adequate, loving parents?

In this book, I shall argue that children have a right to be loved by answering these seven questions. I shall also consider some policy implications of this right.

To begin, I address the issue of whether children can have rights, that is, whether they are rightholders. As mentioned earlier, a number of prominent philosophers have argued that very young children are not rightholders. To a lay audience, it might seem surprising that it has to be shown that children are rightholders. After all, the Universal Declaration of Human Rights (1948) explicitly states that "all human beings are born free and equal in dignity and rights," which would seem to include children as rightholders. However, the claim that all human beings are rightholders is in fact surprisingly difficult to defend. When philosophers try to explain how all human beings are rightholders, they end up adopting what Peter Singer calls a "speciesist" position, where speciesism is defined as morally favoring a particular species—in this case, human beings—over others without sufficient justification. In Chapter One, I develop a new account of rightholding, what I call the "genetic basis for moral agency" account of rightholding, and I propose that this account can allow all human beings, including infants, to be rightholders without being speciesist. I defend this account against potential objections and I explain how this account is different from a potentiality account and why it is preferable to an actual moral agency account of rightholding, which writers like Griffin and Wellman hold.

Next I consider what grounds the right of children to be loved. In my view, the various international declarations cited earlier provide a clue to this question. Many, if not all, of these declarations are declarations of human rights, that is, rights that all human beings have in virtue of being human. I propose the following: the right of children to be loved is a human right. Specifically, my argument is that human beings have human rights to the fundamental conditions for pursuing a good life. As human beings, children therefore have human rights to the fundamental conditions for pursuing a good life. Being loved is a fundamental condition for children to pursue a good life. Therefore, children have a right to be loved. In Chapter Two, I defend the idea that human beings have human rights to the fundamental conditions for pursuing a good life. The fundamental conditions for pursuing a good life are certain goods, capacities, and options that human beings *qua human beings* need whatever else they *qua individuals* might need in order to pursue a characteristically good human life. As this is a new approach to the question of what grounds human rights, among other things, I shall explain how this Fundamental Conditions Approach is better than James Griffin's Agency Approach and Martha Nussbaum's Central Capabilities Approach, and I also show how it can be compatible with the increasingly popular Political Conceptions of human rights defended by John Rawls, Charles Beitz, and Joseph Raz.

In Chapter Three, I explain why being loved is a fundamental condition for children to pursue a good life. Some will find this claim intuitive and obvious, perhaps because of their own reflection on their childhood, their experience with child-rearing, and/or their observation of the practice of child-rearing. However, our personal experiences can be mistaken. Also, some people have questioned whether children really need to be loved.[17] Psychologists have long theorized about the importance of early relationships for all aspects of children's later development. Drawing on their theories, I shall offer some theoretical explanations of why children need to be loved. Also, there is a vast array of ongoing scientific research devoted toward understanding why children need to be loved, both at the psychological level and at the biological level. To support further the claim that children need to be loved, I shall present some of the key findings and detail some of the latest results from this research.

In Chapter Four, I consider some objections against the possibility of a duty to love. In response to the objection that a duty to love is an absurdity because love is an emotion and is therefore not commandable, I respond that in fact, love is commandable *even if* it is an emotion. I also consider other objections to the idea of a duty to love such as the concern that true love cannot be motivated by a sense of duty (the motivation objection); and the concern that the duty to love may only promote loving behavior and not genuine love (the pretended love objection). I argue that these objections also do not undermine the possibility of a duty to love.

In Chapter Five, I examine the issue of who has the duty to love a child, supposing that there is a right to be loved. Here I make the striking claim that everyone has this duty, *even when the biological parents are available.* I argue that everyone's having this duty does not mean that everyone has to do the same thing, and that biological parents should be given the status of primary dutybearers while others have associate duties to assist the primary dutybearers in carrying out this duty, and I explain what some of these duties require. I also consider how demanding the duty to love a child should be and I propose that while there are limits as to how much we are required to sacrifice to fulfill this duty, we may be required to sacrifice more than what common sense morality supposes.

In Chapter Six, I address the issue of whether we should institute some kind of parental licensing scheme, that is, require biological parents to demonstrate certain competence and character before they are permitted to parent their biological children. Existing concerns regarding parental licensing tend to be practical concerns such as whether there can be a reliable way of determining who is a competent parent and whether the parental licensing scheme can be enforced. These practical concerns leave open the possibility that parental licensing is a good idea in theory. In this chapter, I present a new, theoretical case against parental licensing. In particular, I argue that biological parenting should not be licensed because biological parenting is a fundamental (human) right and fundamental rights should not be licensed.

In Chapter Seven, I argue that there is a duty to adopt children without adequate parents, and that we can derive this duty straightforwardly from the right of children to be loved. I begin by considering a related view, which draws on Peter Singer's idea of a duty of easy rescue, according to which those who want to have children have a duty to adopt rather than have biological children.[18] I argue that there are problems with grounding the duty to adopt on this Easy Rescue view. I then argue that what I call the Human Right view is a better way to justify a duty to adopt. I conclude this chapter by proposing a potential, practical way of encouraging more people who are motivated to adopt actually to adopt.

If these arguments are successful, we have strong reasons to believe that children have a right to be loved. I do not claim that this is the only way to defend this right. My aim here is to show that the claim that children have this right need not be merely empty rhetoric and that in fact this right can be justified in the same basic way as other rights that we intuitively take to be central. Moreover, I believe that the arguments for this right can hang together as a coherent whole. This should go some ways toward satisfying those who are concerned about the proliferation of rights claims and who believe (correctly) that rights should not be claimed without considering whether these rights can be justified. This may also serve as an example of how other purported rights claims can and should be justified.

1

Can Children Have Rights?

1. The Speciesism Challenge

At first blush, it might seem puzzling that anyone would argue that children cannot have rights, that is, that they are not rightholders. After all, the United Nations Convention on the Rights of the Child would not make much sense if children were not rightholders. Similarly, the Universal Declaration of Human Rights (1948) states that "*all* human beings are born free and equal in dignity and rights" (my italics). This seems to recognize that children are rightholders. However, as we have pointed out, many prominent philosophers have argued precisely that children are not rightholders. For instance, James Griffin and Carl Wellman have both claimed that infants are not rightholders.[1] For our purpose, if children are not rightholders, it would follow that they cannot have rights of any kind, including a right to be loved. Hence, to show that children have a right to be loved, we first need to show that they are rightholders.

To do this, let us consider in greater detail why some philosophers hold that children are not rightholders. A reason may be that the Universal Declaration of Human Rights' claim that all human beings are rightholders is surprisingly difficult to defend.

When philosophers assess this claim, they tend to find themselves either accepting that some human beings such as infants are not rightholders or adopting what Peter Singer and others have called a "speciesist" position, where speciesism is defined as morally favoring a particular species—in this case, human beings—over others without sufficient justification.[2] Why is this?

Many philosophers believe that when we assess who can be a rightholder we must meet what might be called the Species Neutrality Requirement.[3] The Species Neutrality Requirement says that an adequate account of rightholding must provide some criterion for rightholding that in principle does not exclude any species and where the criterion can be assessed through some objective, empirical method. The reason for the latter condition is that there does not seem to be an a priori way of knowing who the rightholders are. For example, if we meet some alien beings and we want to know whether they are rightholders, it seems that we would not be able to know a priori whether they are rightholders. If so, the only way to find out is to investigate empirically what attributes they have and to consider if these attributes are relevant enough to make them rightholders.

However, supposing that the Species Neutrality Requirement is valid, there does not seem to be a relevant empirical attribute that would apply to all human beings. A number of the attributes that philosophers have considered and proposed, such as actual sentience and actual agency, do not apply to all human beings. For example, some human beings such as anencephalic children and comatose persons lack actual sentience and many human beings such as infants lack actual agency. These human beings would not be rightholders on these accounts. Indeed, the fact that infants lack actual agency is the reason why philosophers such as Griffin and Wellman believe that they cannot be rightholders. Hence, Wellman writes: "I propose the hypothesis that only those kinds of entities who are agents could be moral right-holders . . . If moral agency really is necessary for the possession of rights, as I have argued, and if infants lack agency, as scientific psychology and everyday observation attest, then infants, at least, cannot be rights-holders."[4] Similarly, Griffin argues that only agents can have rights, and concludes that "human rights do not extend to infants, to patients in an irreversible coma or with advanced Alzheimer's, or to the severely mentally defective."[5]

Given this, those who wish to defend the claim that all human beings such as infants are rightholders typically reject the Species Neutrality Requirement. For example, some argue that all human beings are rightholders because they have intrinsic worth or because they have dignity.[6] Neither notion is an attribute that one can empirically identify and assess. Others assert that it is just self-evident that all human beings are rightholders, and that it is not necessary to find out the particular attributes that make them so.[7] Although justification for any moral principle must end at some point, if being human is a sufficient but not necessary condition for rightholding, it seems problematic that this approach is not able to help us determine whether the beings with which we presently live and the beings we might encounter in the future are rightholders. If being human is a necessary condition for rightholding, this approach would have the seemingly counterintuitive implication that all non-human beings that we presently know as well as those we might meet in the future cannot be rightholders.

Still others have argued that all human beings can have rights, not in virtue of the actual attributes they possess, but in virtue of belonging to the kind of beings that typically have the relevant attributes for rightholding. For example, John Finnis says that "to be a person is to belong to a kind of being characterized by rational (self-conscious, intelligent) nature."[8] Or, T. M. Scanlon says that "the class of beings whom it is possible to wrong will include at least all those beings who are of a kind that is normally capable of judgment-sensitive attitudes."[9] Indeed, Scanlon believes that severely mentally handicapped human beings can be wronged, "even though they themselves do not and will not have the capacity to understand or weigh justifications." For convenience's sake, we can call this account the species-norm account.[10]

The species-norm account faces the following kind of objection advanced by Jeff McMahan. McMahan describes a Superchimp who has rational capacities as a result of gene therapy, but is a chimpanzee.[11] Since the Superchimp does not belong to a kind that is characterized by having rational capacities, it seems to follow, from the species-norm account, that the Superchimp is not a person. According to McMahan, this seems absurd if the Superchimp indeed has rational capacities. Moreover, suppose Superchimps come to outnumber the normal chimpanzees. The norm for the species would have changed. It would follow, on the species-norm account, that we would now need to treat the normal chimpanzees as persons. As McMahan argues, this also seems absurd if the normal chimpanzees do not have rational capacities at all.

In this chapter, I shall defend the idea that children, including infants, are rightholders by proposing an account of rightholding that meets the Species Neutrality Requirement and that at the same time allows all human beings to be rightholders. I am assuming, therefore, that there is some merit to the Universal Declaration of Human Rights' claim that all human beings are rightholders, and that when trying to justify this claim, one should try to meet the Species Neutrality Requirement so as to not be speciesist. I also assume that the methodology employed by adherents of the Species Neutrality Requirement is valid, namely, it is possible to identify an empirical attribute relevant for rightholding, and, *pace* G. E. Moore, it is possible to derive moral claims such as claims about who can have rights from empirical attributes.[12]

The account I shall develop can be called the "genetic basis for moral agency" account of rightholding. I do not claim that this account is the only way to explain why children are rightholders, but, as my remarks below will suggest, I do think that this is a plausible account of rightholding generally. Here it is worth noting that every plausible account of rightholding comes with certain "theoretical baggage." That is, each account will face difficult issues particular to it that it must address. For example, on a sentience account of rightholding, according to which beings that have the same level of sentience have the same moral status, it seems that one would have to address the issue of how to treat a human being and a non-human animal, when both possess the same level of sentience.[13] Similarly, an account of rightholding according to which all human beings are rightholders may imply that fetuses and embryos are rightholders, supposing they are human beings.[14] If so, this would seem to require discussions about issues such as abortion and embryonic stem cell research. Typically, plausible accounts of rightholding would have responses to such issues. For example, suppose that one believes that all human beings are rightholders and that fetuses and embryos are human beings. One can follow Judith Jarvis Thomson and hold the view that even if fetuses were rightholders, abortion would still be permissible.[15] It is beyond the scope of this chapter to discuss all the theoretical issues that can arise from the belief that all human beings are rightholders. Still, I shall respond to some of the more serious objections to the genetic basis for moral agency account, and I shall explain how this account is different from a potentiality account and how it is preferable to an actual moral agency account.

Before moving on, it will be helpful to say something about the relationship between moral status and rightholding, since I shall be using both terms in the ensuing discussion. To explain their relationship, we can begin with an observation about the kinds of entities that could be, or that are, of moral concern for moral agents—the kinds of entities that have moral status. A (non-exhaustive) list might look like the following:

1. normal functioning human beings with full physical, cognitive, emotional, and social capacities (normal adult human beings);
2. human beings with impairments (the comatose, those with mental disorders, those with developmental disabilities);
3. human beings at the beginning of life (infants, young children, fetuses);
4. possible or future human beings (future generations);
5. non-living human beings (dead human beings);
6. non-human terrestrial living things (animals and plants);
7. non-human extraterrestrial species of living beings— should there be any such beings (beings from outer space);
8. artificial life forms (androids, robots, computers);
9. inanimate objects (rocks, artworks, buildings, the environment).

It should be clear that some of these entities have greater moral status than others. For example, confronted with the choice between saving an ordinary rock or saving a turtle, it seems that one should save the turtle. One way to explain this intuition is to appeal to the notion of welfare (or some other similar terms such as well-being, flourishing, or interest) and to say that those with welfare have greater moral status than those without. The notion of welfare would explain why we should save the turtle rather than the rock, because only the former has welfare.

However, among entities that have welfare, arguably, some have still greater moral status than others. For instance, confronted with the choice between saving a turtle's limb or the limb of a normal functioning adult human being, and assuming that the loss of a limb to either is equally devastating, it seems that one should save the human being's limb. A way to explain this intuition is to appeal to something like the notion of a rightholder and to say that entities who are rightholders have greater moral status than entities that are not rightholders. The notion of a rightholder would explain why we should save the human being's limb rather than the turtle's, because the former is a rightholder while the latter is not a rightholder.

On this picture, the relationship between moral status and rightholding is such that rightholding is a special kind of moral status, which at least some human beings purportedly have. The aim of the genetic basis for moral agency account of rightholding that I shall now defend is to explain why all human beings have this special moral status—why they are all rightholders.[16]

2. The Genetic Basis for Moral Agency Account of Rightholding

My proposal is as follows: all human beings are rightholders because they all have the genetic basis for moral agency; and it seems that having this genetic basis is sufficient for one to be a rightholder.

By moral agency, I have in mind the capacity to act in light of moral reasons.[17] Moral agency can be contrasted with rational agency, which involves the capacity to know something about causality such as if one does x, then y would happen, and the capacity to bring about something intentionally. It can also be contrasted with autonomous agency, which involves the capacity to determine one's life course (autonomy) and the capacities to pursue these courses (liberty). Moreover, a moral agent need not act morally all the time or at all.

The genetic basis for moral agency is the set of physical codes that generate moral agency. In human beings, this set of codes is located in their genome. We know this because a lot of complexity is needed as the developmental basis for a complex adaptive phenotype like moral agency, and the genome contains a significant proportion of this complexity. Also, the capacity for moral agency is grounded in psychological capacities such as rationality and empathy that uncontroversially have a genetic basis. Indeed, rationality and empathy, two essential components of the capacity for moral agency, develop in all normal human beings according to a fairly predictable schedule.[18] If the capacity for moral agency did not have a genetic basis, the development of its essential components would not be so regular.

At present, we do not know exactly which set of genes is necessary and sufficient for the genetic basis for moral agency. This said, rapid advances in genomic technologies might mean that we could have this knowledge sooner than we think. Also, it seems that some genes may be necessary not only for the genetic basis for moral agency but also for some other general capacities. But we can talk about a genetic basis for moral agency as long as there are genes that definitely play no role in forming the genetic basis for moral agency. For example, the genes for my toe nails or a gene whose expression serves only to produce pigment in the eyes probably play no role in the formation of the genetic basis for moral agency. Moreover, I shall shortly draw a distinction between genes that make up an attribute and genes that undermine the development of an attribute, a distinction that could help us further narrow the set of genes that is necessary and sufficient for the genetic basis for moral agency.

It should be mentioned that some people are hostile to the idea of a genetic basis for human behavioral traits. A reason for this hostility is due in part to the fact that historically, there have been racist and sexist attempts to show that human beings of a certain race or gender have the genetic basis for higher intelligence than human beings of another race or gender; and these attempts typically fail to consider seriously the role that non-genetic factors play in the development of intelligence. Hence, by association, these people might also be hostile to the idea of a genetic basis for moral agency.

However, the genetic basis for moral agency, as I understand it, gives rise to a capacity and not a behavioral trait. Thus, the fact that human beings have the genetic basis for moral agency does not mean that they will act morally. Also, nothing I have said precludes the idea that non-genetic factors are also necessary for an adequate development of moral agency. Indeed, the idea of a genetic basis for moral agency is compatible with the idea that much of the complexity needed for the development of moral agency is located in the developmental environment, a developmental resource that has been specifically adapted to afford the development of moral agency (in a niche construction-type way).

Here it is worth making two further points regarding the genetic basis for moral agency. First, the idea of a genetic basis does not mean that there is only one way this genetic basis can be sequenced or realized. In fact, this genetic basis could be multiply realizable. That is, it could be the case that in certain environments, certain genes, A, B, C, might be the genetic basis for moral agency for a particular being, while in certain other environments, genes D, E, F would be the genetic basis for moral agency in the same being.[19]

Second, to have the genetic basis for a certain attribute, the genes that make up that attribute must be activated and be coordinating with each other in an appropriate way. A being does not have the genetic basis for a certain attribute if a being just possesses somewhere in its genome the genes that could make up the attribute, but these genes are either not activated or are scrambled such that they do not coordinate with each other in an appropriate way. To illustrate the point about coordination, consider the following: Suppose there is a book containing many random words, which if put together in the right way, would result in a Shakespeare play. That book would not be a Shakespeare play just because it contained the correct words; those words must be organized in the right way.

How do we know that all human beings have the genetic basis for moral agency? We know that all normal functioning human beings and those at the beginning of life (e.g., infants, young children, fetuses) who will develop normally have this genetic basis, since they exercise moral agency or will exercise it; and after conception, the genetic codes of a human being do not change very much, if at all. We also know that most comatose human beings have this genetic basis, because they have exercised moral agency. Most cases of anencephaly are the result of environmental factors such as folic acid deficiency; undiagnosed diabetes; hypervitaminosis A; high temperatures of 102 degrees or higher for more than five hours; anticonvulsant medication, especially valporic acid (valporate); or environmental/chemical exposure.[20] Scientists know that some genetic disorders such as Waardenburg syndrome seem to have a higher incidence of anencephaly (they seem to share the pax3 gene mutation, which controls some aspects of the development of the face and inner ear). But this is far from establishing that anencephaly has a genetic cause. Since it is not clear that anencephaly even has a genetic cause, it is even less clear that anencephaly would be the result of a defect of the genes that make up moral agency. Hence, we can assume that most of those with anencephaly also have the genetic basis for moral agency.

Moreover, those with mild mental impairments, such as children with Down syndrome, typically exhibit some moral agency. This suggests that they also have the genetic basis for moral agency.[21] Finally, to see how those severely impaired human beings whose conditions are the result of genetic defects rather than environmental factors would also have this genetic basis, it is useful to distinguish between genetic defects of the genes that make up an attribute and genetic defects that undermine the development of an attribute. For example, consider a human being born without a hand. This may be because this human being lacks the genes to form the hand, or it may be that certain conditions needed for the genes to form the hand—prenatal nutrition, for instance—were blocked or lacking. In the former, this human being would not have the genetic basis for having a hand, since this human being lacked the genes that make up the hand. In the latter, this human being would still have the genetic basis for having a hand, because the genes that make up the hand were there and active, but they were blocked from developing because of certain conditions.

On this distinction, the genetic defects that we are likely to encounter in these severely impaired human beings are not defects in the genetic basis for moral agency but at best defects that undermine the development for moral agency. For example, consider phenylketonuria (PKU), Tay-Sachs, Sandhoff disease, and a whole cluster of about seven thousand other kinds of genetic disorders, which are caused by the mutation of a gene. The gene is typically necessary for producing a certain protein or enzyme, which is then needed to change certain chemicals to other chemicals or to carry substances from one place to another. Mental impairments and other defects are typically caused by abnormal buildups of certain amino acids that become toxic to the brain and other tissues, because the cell is unable to process these amino acids owing to the mutation. But with treatment of a low enzyme diet as soon as possible in the neonatal age, normal growth and cognitive development can be expected in many cases. For our purpose, this shows that the brain tissue has initially developed normally and would have continued to do so except for the abnormal buildup of the amino acids. Therefore, following the distinction between genetic defects that make up an attribute and genetic defects that undermine the development of the attribute, single gene defects seem to be cases of the latter rather than the former. Given this, one can say that human beings who have these kinds of genetic defects most likely possess the genetic basis for moral agency.[22]

Even if all present cases of deletions are not cases in which human beings lack the genetic basis for moral agency, might it be theoretically possible for a human being to lack such a genetic basis? In particular, owing to advances in genetic engineering, perhaps it might be possible artificially to create a human being who lacks this genetic basis.[23] If so, would this theoretical possibility not undermine my claim that all human beings have the genetic basis for moral agency? In response, it is important to question whether a being that is created without the genetic basis for moral agency would be a human being at all. Presumably, the genes for moral agency are not just some minor genes such as the genes for toe nails.[24] Indeed, the genes for moral agency may be necessary for the development of a brain generally, and/or for the various capacities necessary for moral agency, such as rationality and empathy. Given this, suppose someone tried to create a human being without the genetic basis for moral agency. The resulting entity, if it could survive at all, might turn out to be one without a brain and/or one without the capacities for rationality and empathy. If so, would the resulting entity still be a human being? It is not obvious that it would be. If so, it is not clear that there could be human beings who lack the genetic basis for moral agency. In any case, whether it is even a real possibility to create a human being that lacks the genetic basis for moral agency, we can still conclude that for present purposes, all living human beings that we have encountered and are likely to encounter in the foreseeable future will have the genetic basis for moral agency.

The claim that the genetic basis for moral agency is sufficient for rightholding is attractive for several reasons. First, as this account supports the widely held intuition that all human beings are rightholders, for many, this would be a reason in favor of it. Second, the genetic basis for moral agency is an identifiable, actual, physical attribute. This means that this account meets one of the primary conditions of the Species Neutrality Requirement. It also means that this account avoids speciesism. Indeed, if we were to learn that chimpanzees or some other animals have the genetic basis for moral agency, then they would be rightholders.

Third, this account captures what is intuitively appealing (at least to some) about the species-norm account, namely, it, too, is motivated by the thought that "the kind of being that is typically characterized by moral agency" should be a rightholder. However, the genetic basis for moral agency account offers a more adequate interpretation of this claim, because on this account, one possesses an identifiable, actual, physical attribute and is not just a member of a group that has this attribute. In fact, this account can handle the kind of objection posed by McMahan against the species-norm account. If a Superchimp has a rational nature as a result of gene therapy, this account can accommodate this case by locating this nature in the genetic makeup of the Superchimp. Or, if Superchimps come to outnumber the normal chimpanzees, this account can explain how the two groups can be treated differently, if, for example, the Superchimps have the genetic basis for rational nature while the normal chimpanzees do not.

Finally, since the genetic basis for moral agency is only a sufficient condition for rightholding, it avoids the intuitive cost of denying the status of rightholding to those non-human animals or other beings who may plausibly qualify as rightholders but who may not have the genetic basis for moral agency. For example, even if a dog does not have the genetic basis for moral agency, the dog could still be a rightholder on other grounds. Or, despite the doubts I have previously expressed, suppose it were possible to genetically engineer a being to lack just one gene for the genetic basis for moral agency and still to be human. Although this human being would not have the genetic basis for moral agency, this human being could still be a rightholder on other grounds.

Here it is worth mentioning that it is possible that some beings—some alien being or some super artificial intelligent being, for example—could be made up of non-genetic, that is, non-carbon-based, isomorphic material, and still possess something functionally similar to the genetic basis for moral agency. In my view, they would also be rightholders, given that they have the physical basis for the development of moral agency even though they do not have the genetic basis for moral agency. Hence, a more precise name for this account should be the "physical basis for the development of moral agency" account of rightholding. However, since most of the living beings we know are genetic-carbon-based life forms, to keep things simple, I shall continue to refer to this account as the genetic basis for moral agency account.

The intuitive appeal of the genetic basis for moral agency account of rightholding should be easy enough to grasp. Some people might of course not share these intuitions and might demand that one produce an independent argument as to why one should believe this account. In response, I am inclined to think that a non-circular, independent justification is not possible. As far as I am aware, those who advance other criteria for rightholding typically do not offer non-circular, independent arguments for why their preferred criterion is relevant for rightholding. To give just one example, suppose one holds the view that if X has actual sentience, then X is a rightholder. It might be asked, why is this so? Asserting that "pain is bad" does not seem to be providing an independent argument for this account. Arguably, this is just a circular way of restating that actual sentience is relevant.

Earlier I gave several reasons why the genetic basis for moral agency account is an attractive account of rightholding, including the fact that it explains why all human beings are rightholders without being speciesist. To make this account even more attractive, I shall consider some possible objections to it and respond to them.

3. Just a Potentiality Account?

To start, some might wonder if the genetic basis for moral agency account is just a potentiality account of rightholding in disguise. That is, it might be thought that having the genetic basis for moral agency is just having the potential for moral agency. As such, so the argument goes, the genetic basis for moral agency account contributes nothing new to the debate and inherits all the problems that have been attributed to the potentiality account.

First, even if the genetic basis for moral agency account were just a potentiality account, this may not be a problem, because the arguments against the potentiality account are not conclusive. I do not want to defend the potentiality account here, but let me present two oft-rehearsed arguments against the potentiality account. One goes as follows:

1. According to the potentiality account, if X is a potential F, then X has the same rights and interests as an actual F, where F could be a rightholder, human being, person, and so on.

2. However, potential Fs typically do not have the same rights and interests as actual Fs. For example, a potential president does not have the same rights and privileges as an actual president.
3. Therefore, the potentiality account is mistaken.

Clearly, proponents of the potentiality account would deny premise 1. No such proponent would hold the view that a potential rightholder has the same rights and interests as an actual rightholder. A more plausible interpretation of the potentiality account is something like "If X has the potential for V, where V denotes attributes such as moral agency, sentience, and so on, then X is an F, where F could be a rightholder, human being, person, and so on." For example, A. I. Melden has proposed that if X has the potential for moral agency, then X is a rightholder.[25] If so, a proponent of the potentiality account need not be making the kind of mistake that this argument attributes to her.

The other oft-rehearsed argument against the potentiality account is that if the potentiality account were correct, then sperm and ova would be rightholders, because on some notion of potential, they would be regarded as having the potential to be rightholders.[26]

However, the term "potential" has different meanings. It can mean "possible." For example, flour, water, eggs, and raising powder have the potential to become a cake, which means that it is possible for these ingredients to become a cake.[27] "Potential" may sometimes also mean "probable." For example, one may say that the Lakers have the potential to win the NBA Championship. By this, one may mean that there is some probability that the Lakers will win the NBA Championship. Finally, "potential" may mean that an entity, which has a certain nature, has an inherent capacity to realize its particular nature. For example, one may say that an acorn has a potential to become an oak. This may mean that the acorn has the inherent capacity to realize its nature of being an oak.[28]

On the most plausible reading of potential, namely, in the third sense, sperm and ova do not have the inherent capacity to realize the nature of being an agent. At best, they have the inherent capacity to realize their nature of being functioning sperm and ova. Indeed, as Joel Feinberg has pointed out, critics who continue to insist that the potentiality of the sperm and ova is identical to the potentiality of the zygote are vulnerable to a reductio ad absurdum, namely, "[a]t the end of that road is the proposition that everything is potentially everything else, and thus the destruction of all utility in the concept of potentiality. It is better to hold this particular line at the zygote."[29] Hence, the argument that sperm and ova could be rightholders is also not a problem for the most plausible potentiality account.

In any case, having the genetic basis for the development of a particular attribute is not the same thing as having the potential for a particular attribute. Consider a human being, Joe, with hands. We would say that Joe actually has hands and that Joe had the potential to have hands. But suppose Joe's hands were accidentally sawed off in a wood factory. We would say that Joe no longer actually has hands and that Joe does not have the potential to have hands. However, we can still say that Joe has the genetic basis for the development of hands, because Joe still has the genes for the development of hands in him. Indeed, if Joe has a child, the child will most likely develop hands. Or, consider another example. Friends of the potentiality account typically would accept that anencephalic infants do not have, and individuals in irreversible coma no longer have, the potential for moral agency.[30] As I have argued earlier, though, anencephalic infants and individuals in irreversible coma both still have the genetic basis for moral agency. If so, having the genetic basis for the development of a particular attribute such as moral agency is not the same thing as having the potential for a particular attribute such as moral agency.

4. Only Actual Agency Matters

As another possible objection, other people might argue that surely moral agency matters only if one can actually exercise it. On this view, the possession of the genetic basis for moral agency does not matter. What matters is that one actually has the capacity to act in light of moral reasons. As we have seen, Griffin, Wellman, and others hold this view and, as a result, believe that infants cannot be rightholders.

But actual moral agency cannot be a necessary ground for rightholding. The reason is that if rightholding served any function at all, one would be the following:

> If and when the rightholder's interest is in conflict with the same kind of interest, that is, with the comparable interest, of a non-rightholder, the rightholder's interest should prevail.

A corollary of this is that if one were to give the interest of a non-rightholder priority over the comparable interest of a rightholder, then one would be acting wrongly.

For example, normal adult human beings are typically regarded as rightholders, whereas normal adult turtles are not. (Those who believe that all animals have rights may be unhappy with this example. If so, I suggest that they substitute the turtle with whatever they would regard as a non-rightholder. The general point would remain valid.) Suppose this is correct, and suppose rightholding has the function I suggested. This means that if and when the interest of a normal adult human being conflicts with the comparable interest of a normal adult turtle, one should give the interest of the human being more weight. Hence, to use an earlier example, suppose that the limb of a normal adult turtle and the limb of a normal adult human being are both in danger of being cut off and suppose that it would be equally devastating to either to lose a limb. Suppose further that one can only help one of them. It seems that one should help the human being, because the turtle is not a rightholder while the human being is. If one did not do this, it seems that one would be acting wrongly. This does not mean that one does not have any duties at all regarding non-rightholders. For example, if a turtle's limb needs to be saved and it would cost one little effort to save it, it seems that one would have a duty to save the turtle's limb. It also does not mean that any interest of a rightholder would be more important than any interest of a non-rightholder. Supposing that the turtle's limb needs to be saved and it would cost one little effort to save it, and I, a rightholder, am having a cup of tea at the moment, it seems that I may have a duty to save the turtle's limb even if my tea may become cold.

If actual moral agency were a necessary ground for rightholding, though, adult human beings would be rightholders, while human infants would not be, as the latter do not have actual moral agency. If rightholding has the function I suggested, it would mean that an adult human being's interest should be given priority over the comparable interest of an infant. And, if one were to give an infant's interest priority over the comparable interest of an adult human being, then one would be acting wrongly. Yet, it is often permissible to give the interests of infants priority over the comparable interests of adult human beings. For example, suppose a human baby and a human adult are drowning, and one can only save one of them. It seems permissible to save the baby rather than the adult. Or, in a high sea when a ship is sinking, it seems permissible to give infants the priority to be in the lifeboat instead of the adults.[31] These examples suggest that either we are wrong to think that it is sometimes permissible to give infants preference over adults, or actual moral agency is not a necessary ground for rightholding. Our intuition is that it is at least permissible and not morally wrong to give infants preference over adults. This suggests that actual moral agency is not a necessary ground for rightholding.

Some might say that the human baby versus human adult case is not a case in which comparable interests are at stake. In particular, it might be said that from the perspective of a whole lifetime, the baby has more at stake, because all things being equal, the baby has more years of good life to lose.[32] However, suppose that the choice was between the same adult and a turtle that will live much longer, such that the turtle would lose many more years of good life as a result of death than the human adult. It would not be permissible to save the turtle just because the turtle has more years to lose. So the fact that the baby may have more years of good life to lose cannot be the reason why it is permissible and not morally wrong to save the baby.

Moreover, we can stipulate that the baby and the human adult both have the same number of years to live. Even so, it still seems permissible to save the baby at least some of the time. For example, it certainly seems permissible for a mother to save her baby instead of a stranger. One might add that this is so not just because it is *her* baby. To see this, suppose that the mother was instead faced with the choice of saving her turtle or a stranger, both having comparable interests at stake. Even though it is *her* turtle, it would be wrong for her to save the turtle, given that the turtle is not a rightholder. In any case, even if the choice is between saving an infant who is not one's own and a stranger, it often still seems permissible to give preference to the infant.

Others might question whether the status of rightholding really has the function I proposed. They might point out that sometimes non-rightholders' interests are given priority over the comparable interest of a rightholder. For example, suppose that to rescue an adult human being, one must blow up a gigantic planet that contains many wonderful life forms, none of which are rightholders. One might decide against blowing up the planet. If so, it seems that non-rightholders' interests can sometimes be given priority over the comparable interest of a rightholder.

However, the claim above is not that the interest of a rightholder can never be outweighed by any amount of non-rightholders' interests. The proposal, instead, is that the comparison should be one to one—that is, one rightholder's interest versus a comparable interest of a non-rightholder—and not one to a much larger number. On a one-to-one basis, I cannot think of an example where it would be permissible to give preference to a non-rightholder's interest over a comparable interest of a rightholder. At the same time, there are many instances where it seems permissible to save an infant's life over the life of an adult human being, even if the infant does not have more to lose.

Still others might suggest that perhaps we save the infants not because the infants are rightholders but because in doing so, we would be promoting the interest of some rightholders, namely, the interest of the parents. This argument may have some plausibility if the choice is between saving an infant and the infant's parent, and the parent wishes for the infant rather than himself to be saved. But, as noted previously, even when the choice is between saving an infant and an unrelated adult human being, it often still seems permissible to give preference to the infant. If all of this is right, this suggests that actual moral agency is not a necessary ground for rightholding.

5. Actual Agency Matters More

At this point, some people might accept that the genetic basis for moral agency matters somewhat for moral status, but they might insist that actual moral agency always matters more, and therefore, only those with actual moral agency should be right-holders. For example, suppose that an in vitro fertilization (IVF) clinic is burning and one could either save an embryo, which has the genetic basis for moral agency, or a five-year-old child, who has actual moral agency.[33] It seems that one should save the five-year-old. If so, according to this argument, this seems to show that actual moral agency matters more.

However, this case does not show that actual moral agency always matters more. Imagine a variant of this case in which another IVF clinic is burning, and there is another embryo and another five-year-old child. This time, however, the five-year-old child has inhaled too much smoke, has temporarily passed out, and will die soon (in a few days' time), and the embryo happens to belong to you. You have been desperately trying to have a child for years and the doctors tell you that this time there is a very good chance you will succeed, but that this is your last chance to have your own biological child. Is it so intuitively clear that you should save the five-year-old? It does not seem so clear in this case. Indeed, it seems that you may be permitted to save your last embryo. Notice that if the alternative is between saving the five-year-old and saving, for example, your beloved Picasso painting, it seems clear that you should save the five-year-old. This suggests that the reason why you may be permitted to save the embryo in this case is not just because the embryo is *your* embryo, since the Picasso is also *your* Picasso. If this is right, there may be certain circumstances in which saving someone with the genetic basis for moral agency matters more than saving someone with actual moral agency.

In any case, we can accept that often an actual moral agent will matter more than a being with just the genetic basis for moral agency. This, though, would not show that the two beings have different moral status. When a stranger and one's partner are both drowning, other things being equal, one's partner typically matters more than the stranger. This does not mean that the two therefore have different moral status.

Does the genetic basis for moral agency account imply that we should always save an embryo rather than a child, given that an embryo typically has a greater future potential than a grown child? This implication need not follow. First, just as there could be agent-relative reasons for choosing one's embryo, there could also be agent-relative reasons for choosing one's grown child, even if the embryo indeed has a greater future potential. Second, there could be agent-neutral considerations for choosing the grown child over the embryo. In particular, it could be argued that the embryo will have little or no *time-relative interests*, while the grown child may have very strong time-relative interests.[34] To have time-relative interests is to be able to stand in some psychological relations to one's future and past selves. The strength of one's present time-relative interests depends on how strongly one is psychologically connected to those future and past selves. For example, an infant will typically have weaker time-relative interests in continuing to live than a grown adult, since an infant has little or no awareness of his or her future self. Similarly, the embryo will have little or no time-relative interests, since the embryo will not have the required capacities to be able to stand in some psychological relations to the embryo's future and past selves. The grown child, on the other hand, may have very strong time-relative interests, since the child would typically have fully developed psychological capacities. If so, this could provide an agent-neutral reason to choose the grown child over the embryo—namely, although the grown child may have less future potential, the grown child may have stronger time-relative interests. This said, the fact that there is a difference in time-relative interests between the embryo and the grown child does not mean that there is also a difference in moral status.[35]

6. Anencephalic Infants and Embryos Cannot Have Interests

It seems reasonable to assume that if a being is a rightholder, then the being has at least one right. Since the genetic basis for moral agency account implies that anencephalic infants and embryos are rightholders, it seems reasonable to assume that they have some rights. Some people might ask, though, in what sense can anencephalic infants and embryos have interests that can ground rights? Following Feinberg, some people hold that to have an interest is to be interested in something, which requires that a being has the capacity to desire and want things and to be self-aware.[36] Given that anencephalic infants and embryos lack brains, they lack the capacity to desire and want things and to be self-aware. Consequently, on this view of interest, it would seem to follow that they cannot have interests that can ground rights. But if they cannot have interests that can ground rights, then it would seem to follow that they cannot have any rights. If so, one might question whether it still makes sense to regard them as rightholders.

First, it is worth pointing out that healthy newborn infants would also not be able to have this kind of interest, given that newborn infants are hardly self-aware. Indeed, some people are led to conclude that infanticide is permissible precisely because newborn infants cannot have this kind of interest.[37] But rather than accepting that infanticide is permissible, it seems that one should question instead whether rights are necessarily grounded in this kind of interest.

Second, there is an alternative view of interest that is equally common and plausible, namely, one can have an interest if something is in one's interest, even if one is not able to be interested in it.[38] For example, as a number of writers have argued, it is in the interest of a plant to be watered, as the plant will die if it does not receive adequate water, even though the plant is not able to be interested in being watered.[39] Or, an individual in a deep coma can have an interest in being fed, even if the individual cannot desire to be fed. If plants or individuals in deep coma can have this kind of interest, then anencephalic infants and embryos can also have this kind of interest. For example, it may be in their interest not to be destroyed or mutilated, not to be used as food or objects of experimentation or play, and possibly not to be used as sources of organs. Some people might insist that plants cannot have interests because according to them, plants are merely valuable insofar as they are valuable to us, and not for their own sake. But from a biological perspective, a plant certainly needs water for its own sake. In any case, there is no reason to think that anencephalic infants and embryos cannot be valuable for their own sake and cannot have interests in this sense.

Third, Feinberg defends the more restrictive notion of interest because he holds that entities such as plants cannot be rightholders and that being able to have interests is a sufficient (as well as a necessary) condition for rightholding.[40] However, one can reject the idea that being able to have interests is a sufficient condition for rightholding. If so, there would be less pressure to have this restrictive notion of interest. On a view according to which having an interest and having rights are two different matters, the fact that a plant can have interests would not mean that it is a rightholder. Indeed, on the genetic basis for moral agency account, anencephalic infants and embryos are rightholders because they have the genetic basis for moral agency, and not just because they can have interests.

7. A Reductio?

Finally, some might think that the genetic basis for moral agency account faces a possible reductio ad absurdum. According to this line of thought, it seems that every human cell has the genetic basis for moral agency, since theoretically it is possible to produce a human being from any human cell. But if every human cell has the genetic basis for moral agency, would it not follow that every human cell is a rightholder? Clearly, human cells are not rightholders. So there must be something wrong with this account.

This argument fails, however, because human cells are not beings; they are parts of a being. It is not so easy to distinguish a being from parts of a being, but it seems that the kind of being at issue is some sort of a self-contained organism that is ready to develop into an individual or that is developing as an individual *as long as nutrients and normal developing conditions are provided*. On this view, a human cell is not a being, because it is not a self-contained organism ready to develop into an individual or that is developing as an individual as long as nutrients and normal developing conditions are provided.

Moreover, for a human cell to become a human being, its nature must be significantly changed—to the extent that it would stop being a human cell. Specifically, given present technologies, one must de-differentiate the genetic material of a human cell, that is, make the cell unspecialized, such as changing a skin cell into an unspecialized cell, and transfer the genetic material to a viable egg. As I noted before, for a being to qualify as having the genetic basis for moral agency, it is not enough just to have the genes for the genetic basis for moral agency located somewhere in the being; these genes must be activated and be coordinating with each other in an appropriate manner, which is not the case with normal human cells.

This last point allows us to respond to some hypothetical examples involving injecting or integrating the genes for the genetic basis for moral agency into non-human entities. For example, suppose we injected these genes into a cabbage; would the cabbage be a rightholder?[41] To answer this question, we should inquire whether these genes are integrated into the cabbage or not. If they are, then the cabbage would no longer be a cabbage, since its nature would have changed. In such a case, the resulting being may be a rightholder, given that it has the genetic basis for moral agency. A real-life parallel may be transplanting human genes into a rabbit egg and creating an embryo with human characteristics.[42] Arguably, such an entity may be a rightholder. On the other hand, suppose that the genes for the genetic basis for moral agency are not integrated into the cabbage, but instead these genes just sit inside the cabbage. In such a case, the cabbage may not have the kind of moral status that a cabbage with integrated genetic basis for moral agency may have. (Consider a fictitious example from comic novels. Upon being bitten by a radioactive spider, Peter Parker would still be Peter Parker, because although the genetic materials from the spider were in Peter, they were not coordinating with Peter's genetic materials in the right way. Peter Parker became Spiderman only when the genetic materials from Peter and the spider were coordinating in the right way.)

8. Conclusion

In this chapter, I argued that the genetic basis for moral agency account of rightholding can meet the Species Neutrality Requirement and at the same time accommodate the Universal Declaration of Human Rights' claim that all human beings are rightholders. I explained how the genetic basis for moral agency account is different from a potentiality account and how this account is preferable to an actual moral agency account of rightholding, and I defended this account against possible objections. If what I've said is correct, we also have an account of rightholding that can explain why children are rightholders, namely, because children have the genetic basis for moral agency.

However, even if children are rightholders, this only means that they can have rights. It does not mean that they have a right to be loved. I now turn toward providing a justification for this right.

2

Human Rights as Fundamental Conditions for a Good Life

1. The Need for a Substantive Account of Human Rights

In the previous chapter, I argued that children are rightholders, but this alone does not show that they have a right to be loved. To establish that children have this right, we need a *substantive account* of human rights, that is, an account that tells us what human rights we have and why we have these rights.[1] But what gives content to a substantive account of human rights? In this chapter, I offer a new answer: human beings have human rights to what I call the fundamental conditions for pursuing a good life. I refer to this as the Fundamental Conditions Approach. As we shall see, this approach will enable us to justify children's right to be loved.

To articulate and defend this approach, I shall do five things. First, I shall explain what I mean by the fundamental conditions for pursuing a good life and why human beings have human rights to these fundamental conditions. Second, I shall demonstrate how this approach can explain many of the rights found in the Universal Declaration of Human Rights (UDHR). At the same time, I shall illustrate how this approach can explain why some of the claims in the UDHR are not genuine human rights. Third, James Griffin has argued that the notion of agency should ground human rights.[2] I shall explain how Griffin's Agency Approach differs from the Fundamental Conditions Approach and why the Fundamental Conditions Approach should be preferred. Fourth, my appeal to the notion of a good life will prompt others to think of Martha Nussbaum's Central Capabilities Approach, which, like the Fundamental Conditions Approach, is in part Aristotelian in spirit.[3] My complaint against the Central Capabilities Approach as a substantive account of human rights is that it cannot adequately explain a significant number of human rights.

Finally, the Fundamental Conditions Approach (along with Griffin's Agency Approach and Nussbaum's Central Capabilities Approach) assumes that human rights are those that we have simply in virtue of being human. It therefore belongs to what might be called a Naturalistic Conception of human rights.[4] In recent years, a new and purportedly alternative conception of human rights, the so-called Political Conception of human rights, has become increasingly popular. The Political Conception has been defended by, among others, John Rawls,[5] Charles Beitz,[6] and Joseph Raz.[7] According to the Political Conception, the distinctive nature of human rights is to be understood in light of their role or function in modern international political practice.[8] Proponents of the Political Conception believe that the Naturalistic Conception "tend[s] to distort rather than illuminate international human rights practice"[9] and should therefore be rejected in favor of its Political counterpart. Since my aim here is to develop what I take to be the correct substantive account of human rights, it will be helpful to discuss the Political Conception of human rights. On behalf of the Naturalistic Conception, I shall argue, among other things, that the theoretical distance between the Naturalistic Conception and the Political Conception is not as great as it has been made out to be.

Here it is worth making explicit an assumption that I make but do not defend, namely, I assume that there are positive rights. A person has a positive right if the person is entitled to the provision of some good or service, such as a right to welfare assistance; and a person has a negative right if the person is entitled to non-interference, for instance, a right against assault. Although some people have claimed that there are only negative rights,[10] many others have put forward strong arguments in favor of positive rights.[11] Given this, and given that what I take to be the main competitors to the Fundamental Conditions Approach such as Griffin's Agency Approach and Nussbaum's Central Capabilities Approach all accept that there are positive rights, I shall not try to defend this assumption here.[12] My argument can therefore be understood in conditional terms, namely, conditional on the existence of positive rights, human rights should be seen as grounded in the fundamental conditions for pursuing a good life.

2. The Fundamental Conditions Approach

To start, let me explain what I mean by a good life and the fundamental conditions for pursuing it. I shall then explain why human beings have human rights to these fundamental conditions.

As I see it, a characteristically good human life, or a good life, for short, is one spent in pursuing certain valuable, basic activities. "Basic" activities are activities that are important to human beings qua human beings' life as a whole. Sunbathing, for example, is an activity, but is not a basic activity, because a human being qua human being's life as a whole is not affected if a human being does not go sunbathing. In addition, activities that are very important to an individual human being's life as a whole may nevertheless not be basic activities, because these activities may not be important to human beings *qua human beings'* life as a whole. In other words, it is important to distinguish between activities that are important to human beings *qua individuals'* life as a whole and activities that are important to human beings *qua human beings'* life as a whole. Only activities that are important to human beings qua human beings' life as a whole qualify as basic activities. For instance, being a professional philosopher is very important to my life as a whole. But being a professional philosopher is not a basic activity because it is not an activity that is important to human beings qua human beings' life as a whole. Similarly, an individual may devote her entire life to the betterment of those in need. This is without a doubt a very moral activity and may also be very important to this individual's life as a whole. But it is not a basic activity, as I understand it, because, again, it is not an activity that is important to human beings qua human beings' life as a whole. Finally, basic activities are ones that if a human life did not involve the pursuit of any of them, then that life could not be a good life. In other words, a human being can have a good life by pursuing just some, and not all, of the basic activities. Some of the basic activities are as follows: deep personal relationships with, for instance, one's partner, friends, parents, children; knowledge of, for example, the workings of the world, of oneself, of others; active pleasures such as creative work and play; and passive pleasures such as appreciating beauty.[13]

It is worth noting that a good life, as I understand it, is not the same thing as an excellent life. An excellent life may require one to have certain accomplishments such as discovering a cure for cancer or having climbed Mount Everest, whereas a good life, as I understand it, does not. My understanding of a good life is closer to what might be called a "minimally decent life." But whereas the idea of a "minimally decent life" is often not explicated, I explicitly understand a good life in terms of pursuing the basic activities and I detail what some of these basic activities are.

From these basic activities, we can derive the contents of the fundamental conditions for pursuing a good life. The fundamental conditions for pursuing a good life are various goods, capacities, and options that human beings qua human beings need, whatever else they qua individuals might need, in order to pursue the basic activities. For example, the fundamental goods are resources that human beings qua human beings need in order to sustain themselves corporeally and include such items as food, water, and air. The fundamental capacities are powers and abilities that human beings qua human beings require in order to pursue the basic activities. These capacities include the capacity to think, to be motivated by facts, to know, to choose an act freely (liberty), to appreciate the worth of something, to develop interpersonal relationships, and to have control of the direction of one's life (autonomy). The fundamental options are those social forms and institutions that human beings qua human beings require if they are to be able to exercise their fundamental capacities to engage in the basic activities. Some of these include the option to have social interaction, to acquire further knowledge, to evaluate and appreciate things, and to determine the direction of one's life. The difference between the fundamental goods and the fundamental options is that the former focuses on the internal, physical conditions for pursuing a good life whereas the latter focuses on the external, environmental conditions for pursuing a good life.

Having the fundamental conditions for pursuing a good life of course cannot guarantee that an individual has a good life; no condition can guarantee this. Rather, these goods, capacities, and options enable human beings to *pursue* the basic activities. Also, these fundamental conditions are intended to provide human beings with an *adequate range* of fundamental goods, capacities, and options so that they can pursue those basic activities that are characteristic of a minimally decent human life.

Now, many of the fundamental conditions are all-purpose conditions in that they are needed regardless of what basic activities one aims to pursue. For example, all human beings need food, water, the capacity to think, and the capacity to determine the direction of their lives, whatever basic activities they aim to pursue. But it is possible that some fundamental conditions are needed just for pursuing particular basic activities. For instance, it is possible that the capacity to develop deep personal relationships is needed only if one aims to pursue deep personal relationships. Suppose that this is the case. We can leave it open whether a particular individual will make use of all the fundamental conditions when pursuing a particular kind of good life. This individual's having all the fundamental conditions means that this individual would still have access to an adequate range of goods, capacities, and options to pursue those basic activities that are characteristic of a minimally decent human life. This could become important if, for instance, this individual changed his/her mind about pursuing a particular kind of good life. Finally, owing to space, I shall not be able to expound upon *how much* of the fundamental conditions human beings need in order to pursue the basic activities and what one should do when one can only promote some, but not all, of these conditions in a given society. All too briefly, my view is that human beings need *enough* of these fundamental conditions in order to pursue the basic activities; that when one can only promote some, but not all, of these conditions in a given society, what one should do will depend on the context, but that there are likely to be determinate answers; and that the ultimate goal of a given society is to devise policies that would ensure that every person has enough of these conditions.

My notion of the fundamental conditions for pursuing a good life bears some similarities to Rawls's notion of primary goods, which are goods that all individuals are presumed to want, whatever else they may want.[14] So let me briefly high-light some of the differences. One difference is that Rawls is interested in *social* rather than *natural* primary goods, where, for Rawls, social primary goods include such things as rights, liberties, powers and opportunities, income and wealth, and self-respect, while natural primary goods include such things as health, vigor, intelligence, and imagination.[15] By contrast, as I conceive it, the fundamental conditions for pursuing a good life would include some natural primary goods such as health. Another difference between the two is that a person who is severely handicapped may have all the primary goods (income, wealth, liberties, and so on) and still not have all the fundamental conditions for pursuing a good life, because he may lack certain capacities necessary to pursue the basic activities.

In my view, these fundamental conditions for pursuing a good life ground human rights because having these conditions is of fundamental importance to human beings, and because rights can offer powerful protection to those who possess them. The former is true because if anything is of fundamental importance to human beings, then pursuing a characteristically good human life is; pursuing a good life is the first and foremost aim of most human beings. And it seems clear that if we attach a certain importance to an end, we must attach this importance to the (essential) means to this end. For example, if we care about making a cake, then we must care about the (essential) ingredients that would enter into making this cake, such as flour, water, sugar, eggs, and raising agents. Losing any of these essential ingredients is tantamount to losing the cake itself. Given this, since pursuing a good life is of fundamental importance to human beings, having the fundamental conditions for pursuing a good life must also be of fundamental importance to human beings.

That rights can offer powerful protection to those who possess them is well known.[16] By their nature, rights secure the interests of the rightholders by requiring others, the dutybearers, to perform certain services for the rightholders or not to interfere with the rightholders' pursuit of their essential interests. In addition, at least on certain structural accounts of rights, rights typically prevent the rightholders' interests that ground rights from being part of a first-order utilitarian calculus.[17] This means that if a rightholder has a right to something, V, then typically no non-right considerations can override the rightholder's right to V. Finally, as some writers have pointed out, because the rightholders are entitled to these services as a matter of rights, this means that the rightholders can simply expect the services without requesting them.[18] Given the strong protection that rights can offer to the rightholders, and given the importance of having these fundamental conditions to human beings, it seems reasonable that human beings have rights to these fundamental conditions. If this is correct, this provides us with an argument for the idea that human beings have human rights to the fundamental conditions for pursuing a good life.

3. Rights in the United Nations and the Fundamental Conditions Approach

The Fundamental Conditions Approach can explain why many of the rights in the UDHR are genuine human rights, and it also has the resources to exclude some of the claims in the UDHR as genuine human rights.

Consider the right to life, liberty and security of person (Article 3). Whatever else human beings qua individuals need, they qua human beings need life, liberty, and security of person in order to pursue the basic activities. If they are not alive; if they cannot freely choose to act to some degree; or if the security of their person is not guaranteed, they cannot pursue the basic activities. Given this, on the Fundamental Conditions Approach, human beings would have human rights to life, liberty, and security of person.

Or, consider the right to recognition everywhere as a person before the law (Article 6); the right to equal protection before the law (Article 7); the right against arbitrary arrest, detention, or exile (Article 9); the right to a fair and public hearing (Article 10); and the right to be presumed innocent until proven guilty (Article 11). These are things that human beings qua human beings need whatever else they qua individuals might need in order to pursue the basic activities. In particular, when we pursue the basic activities, conflicts with others are bound to arise. If and when such conflicts arise, we need guarantees that we would be treated fairly and equally. Fair trial, presumption of innocence, equal protection before the law, and not being arrested arbitrarily serve to ensure that we would be treated fairly and equally. As such, they are things that human beings qua human beings need whatever they qua individuals might need in order to pursue the basic activities. As such, the Fundamental Conditions Approach can explain why there are these human rights.

Finally, consider the right to freedom of thought, conscience, and religion (Article 18), the right to freedom of opinion and expression (Article 19), and the right to freedom of peaceful assembly and association (Article 20). As we said earlier, one of the fundamental conditions for pursuing a good life is being able freely to choose to pursue the basic activities. In order freely to choose to pursue the basic activities, one must have freedom of expression, thought, religion, and association. On the Fundamental Conditions Approach, human beings would have human rights to freedom of thought, expression, religion, and association.

At the same time, the Fundamental Conditions Approach would exclude some of the claims in the UDHR as genuine human rights. To give one example, consider the right to periodic holidays with pay (Article 24). Is there such a human right? On the Fundamental Conditions Approach, the important question to ask is whether paid holidays are a fundamental condition for pursuing a good life. That is, are paid holidays something that human beings qua human beings need whatever else they qua individuals might need in order to pursue the basic activities? There is no doubt that human beings need some rest and leisure in order to pursue the basic activities. Without time for leisure, human beings would not have sufficient time to pursue the basic activities. Given this, some amount of leisure, in the form of holidays, is a fundamental condition for pursuing a good life. However, it does not seem that *paid* holidays are a fundamental condition for pursuing a good life, because it seems that human beings can pursue the basic activities even if their holidays are not paid. It might be thought that if holidays were not paid, then some people would not be able to afford to take holidays. But this seems to conflate a person's right to certain minimum welfare, which he has, with a right to paid holidays. If a person cannot afford to take time off work unless his holidays are paid, this person has a human right to certain minimum welfare assistance. But he does not have a human right to paid holidays, because paid holidays are not a fundamental condition for pursuing a good life. Note that while there may not be a human right to paid holidays, this does not mean that there could not be a legal right to paid holidays. It goes without saying that there are other sources of normativity besides human rights (e.g., considerations of justice and/or equality) and some of them may ground social goods such as paid holidays.

4. Why Not Just Agency?

In *On Human Rights* and in a series of articles, Griffin has argued that the notion of agency should determine the content of human rights.[19] Griffin writes,

> What seems to me the best account of human rights is this. It is centred on the notion of agency. We human beings have the capacity to form pictures of what a good life would be and to try to realize these pictures. We value our status as agents especially highly, often more highly even than our happiness. Human rights can then be seen as protections of our agency—what one might call our personhood.[20]

By agency, Griffin means our autonomously choosing a conception of a worthwhile life (autonomy), our being at liberty to pursue this conception (liberty), and our having minimum material provision and education.[21]

There is much to be said in favor of Griffin's Agency Approach. For one thing, agency is clearly of great importance to human beings. Without some of it, human beings would not be able to bring about any actions at all, let alone actions necessary for a moral and purposeful life. Given this, it seems highly appropriate to protect it with human rights, which offer strong safeguards for its possessors.[22] Also, the Agency Approach does appear to be able to help us determine which human rights are real. For example, Griffin's derivation of rights such as the right to life and the right to freedom of expression using the notion of agency seems plausible.[23]

This said, Griffin's Agency Approach also faces a number of issues.[24] I shall discuss two in order to highlight the difference between Griffin's Agency Approach and the Fundamental

Conditions Approach. First, there is an issue of whether agency should be the sole ground for human rights.[25] To understand this concern, it is useful to begin by pointing out that Griffin has what might be called a *wide* notion of agency, because he holds that agency is valuable only in the context of a good, flourishing life. In contrast, a narrow notion of agency would regard agency as being valuable in and of itself regardless of how it might contribute to a good, flourishing life. As Griffin says, autonomy and liberty, the two core values that make up his notion of agency, are "elements of a good life . . . features that characteristically enhance the quality of life," but they do not exhaust all the elements of a good life—other elements include freedom from great pain, accomplishing something in the course of one's life, understanding certain moral and metaphysical matters, deep personal relations, and so on.[26]

However, given that Griffin holds that agency is valuable only in the context of a good, flourishing life and given that he accepts that in addition to agency, there are other elements of a good life such as freedom from great pain, understanding, deep personal relations, and so on, which can be used indirectly to shape agency, this raises the question of whether agency should be considered the sole ground for human rights. For example, consider the paradigmatic human right not to be tortured. The fact that torture undermines one's agency by undermining one's capacity to decide and to stick to the decision is certainly an important factor in deciding that torture violates a human right.[27] But it seems that another important factor in deciding that torture violates a human right is that it causes great pain. Griffin insists, though, that the notion of agency by itself can adequately explain such human right as the right against torture.[28] So let us consider his arguments.

According to Griffin,

> Torture has characteristic aims. It is used to make someone recant a belief, reveal a secret, confess a crime whether guilty or not, abandon a cause, or do someone else's bidding. All of these characteristic purposes involve *undermining someone else's will, getting them to do what they do not want to do or are even resolved not to do* (my italics).[29]

Griffin then offers two arguments to support his claim that the human right against torture can be adequately explained by the notion of agency alone.

First, Griffin accepts that when asked what is wrong with torture, the obvious response is that it causes great pain. However, he argues that causing pain cannot be why torture violates a human right, because there are many cases of one person's gratuitously inflicting great pain on another that are not a matter of human right violation. For example, consider

> **Callous Partner:** There is an unsuccessful marriage in which the first partner treats the second partner callously, and the suffering endured by the second partner over the years is arguably worse than a short period of physical torture.[30]

Griffin argues that in this case, the first partner, simply by gratuitously inflicting great pain on the second partner, does not thereby violate the second partner's human right.

Second, Griffin argues that undermining someone else's agency without causing great pain is sufficient for there to be a human right violation in other cases. For example, consider

> **Truth Drug:** Instead of torture, one uses truth drugs to extract secrets.[31]

Griffin argues that while Truth Drug does not involve inflicting pain, it does involve undermining an individual's agency, which he believes amounts to a human right violation. As he says,

> We could not call [Truth Drug] torture because it is essential to "torture" that the infliction of great pain be the means. But what concerns us here is whether the painless chemical destruction of another person's will raises any issues of human rights. And it does. It does because painless domination is still a gross undermining of personhood.[32]

Since causing great pain is not sufficient for the existence of a human right against torture, and since undermining agency in, for example, Truth Drug is sufficient for the existence of a human right violation, according to Griffin, this shows that the notion of agency, and not, for instance, causing great pain, is what explains the existence of a human right against torture.

Let me start with Griffin's second argument. Truth Drug may show that undermining agency sometimes violates a human right, but it does not show that undermining agency always violates a human right. Recall that Griffin understands undermining someone's will or agency as "getting them to do what they do not want to do or are even resolved not to do." But suppose that I entice you with the possibility of great pleasure in order to get you to do something that you do not want to do or are even resolved not to do. For instance, I offer you lots of money so that you would eat large worms—something you do not want to do or are even resolved not to do.[33] In such a case, I may have undermined your agency but this would hardly constitute a case of human right violation. If so, while causing great pain may not always be a sufficient condition for the violation of a human right in all cases, neither is undermining an individual's agency.[34]

However, suppose I am wrong and enticing you with the possibility of great pleasure in order to undermine your agency is a case of a human right violation. Still, this does not seem to be the same kind of human right violation as torture is, which involves inflicting great pain. In other words, the Agency Approach faces the question of explaining how undermining agency through extreme pain might be significantly different from undermining agency through great pleasure.

Griffin's first argument at best shows that causing great pain is not a sufficient condition for the violation of a human right. It does not undermine the idea that causing great pain is necessary for explaining why torture violates a human right. One significant difference between torture and Callous Partner is that in the latter, the second partner typically can leave the marriage, whereas in the case of torture, the individual being tortured typically cannot leave the torture chamber. That the second partner can leave the marriage may explain why in this case, there is not a human right violation, despite the psychological torment the second partner has to endure. Consider instead two couples whose second partners could not leave the marriages (as, for example, in some cases of forced, arranged marriages). In the case of the first couple, the second partner was treated lovingly and respectfully by the first partner. In the case of the second couple, the second partner was subjected to a long period of psychological torment by the first partner. It seems plausible that both cases involved human right violations in virtue of the fact that the second partner could not leave the marriage. But it seems that there was an additional form of human right violation with respect to the second couple in virtue of the fact that the second partner was subjected to a long period of psychological torment.

Moreover, the kind of torture that Griffin has in mind, where one causes great pain in order to undermine the victim's capacity to decide and to get the victim to give up information, is what might be called Instrumental Torture. Another kind of torture, call it Intrinsic Torture, involves causing extreme pain just for the sake of causing extreme pain. Since Intrinsic Torture does not aim at undermining the victim's capacity to decide and stick to a decision, it involves less agency-related violations. Even so, it would still be a human right violation. If this is correct, it seems that causing extreme pain would play an even more significant and necessary role in explaining why there is still a human right violation in Intrinsic Torture. Hence, Griffin has not yet shown that the notion of agency can by itself explain the human right against torture.

The second issue regarding Griffin's Agency Approach is as follows: Griffin resists allowing the other elements of a good life to ground human rights because he is concerned that permitting these elements directly to determine the content of human rights would lead to the case that all the necessary elements of a good life would determine the content of human rights, which Griffin believes would cause the language of rights to become redundant, diluting the discourse of rights. As Griffin writes,

If we had rights to all that is needed for a good or happy life, then the language of rights would become redundant. We already have a perfectly adequate way of speaking about individual well-being and any obligations there might be to promote it.[35]

Call this the Redundancy Objection.

Griffin is certainly correct that there is no human right to everything necessary for a good life. Suppose that sailing is my passion in life, and, hence, having a yacht is a necessary condition for me to pursue a good life. It would not follow that I have a human right to a yacht. However, the Fundamental Conditions

Approach also has resources to block the Redundancy Objection. To see this, note that the Fundamental Conditions Approach would include all the essential agency considerations in Griffin's Agency Approach. In addition, it would allow fundamental, but non-agency, considerations such as freedom from great pain also to determine the content of human rights. The Fundamental Conditions Approach can straightforwardly exclude as being a valid human rights claim my need to have a yacht because such a need is not a fundamental condition for pursuing a good life. Indeed, it is not something that human beings qua human beings need whatever else they qua individuals might need in order to pursue the basic activities.

Lest Griffin wish to criticize the notion of "fundamental" conditions and argue that one cannot draw a meaningful distinction between these conditions and all the necessary elements of a good life, let me explain why Griffin's Agency Approach too requires something like the notion of "fundamental conditions" if it is to be plausible.

Recall that Griffin's main concern against broadening the ground for human rights is that he believes that there is no human right to everything necessary for a good life. For example, I do not have a human right to a yacht, even if having a yacht is a necessary condition for me to have a good life. But a similar worry could be raised regarding Griffin's Agency Approach, namely, there is no human right to every *agency* consideration that is necessary for a good life. Continuing with the yacht example, developing the agentic capacity to sail a yacht may be necessary for me to have the necessary agentic capacity for a good life, but I do not have a human right that someone help me acquire this capacity. To prevent the Agency Approach from having such an implication, it seems that Griffin would need something like the notion of "fundamental" conditions, which would restrict agency considerations to only those that human beings qua human beings need whatever else they qua individuals might need.

In other words, we can distinguish between *agency interests* and *non-agency interests*, where the former kinds of interests are derived from considerations such as autonomy and liberty, and the latter kinds of interests are derived from other elements of a good life such as freedom from pain, understanding, and so on. In addition, we can distinguish between *fundamental interests* and *secondary interests*, where fundamental interests are things that human beings qua human beings need whatever else they qua individuals might need in order to pursue a good life (that is, they are the fundamental conditions for pursuing a good life), and secondary interests are things that human beings qua individuals need in order to pursue a good life. These two sets of distinctions give us four kinds of interests: fundamental agency interests, fundamental non-agency interests, secondary agency interests, and secondary non-agency interests.

	Agency interests	*Non-agency interests*
Fundamental interests	fundamental agency interests	fundamental non-agency interests
Secondary interests	secondary agency interests	secondary non-agency interests

On this typology, Griffin's claim is that only fundamental agency interests should ground human rights, whereas on the Fundamental Conditions Approach, fundamental non-agency interests could also ground human rights. One should see that Griffin's Redundancy Objection need not apply to the Fundamental Conditions Approach because the Fundamental Conditions Approach can exclude secondary non-agency interests as grounds for human rights. More pertinently, the point I am making here is that if Griffin were to criticize the notion of fundamental conditions, then he would be unable to block secondary agency interests from grounding human rights. Accepting that secondary agency interests could ground human rights would run counter to Griffin's aim to restrict the content of human rights. Hence, Griffin's arguments do not rule out the possibility of a wider account of human rights, which would draw on the notion of agency as well as other elements of a good life.

5. Why Not Just Capabilities?

Key to Nussbaum's Central Capabilities Approach are the notions of capabilities and functionings, where capabilities are an individual's real opportunities to choose and to act to achieve certain functionings, and functionings are various states and activities that an individual can undertake.[36] To illustrate, compare a person who is robbed at gunpoint and told "your money or your life" and a person who voluntarily gives money to someone on the street. The two individuals may have the same functioning, as they are both engaging in the activity of giving money away. However, they do not have the same capability, because the individual who voluntarily gives money can choose not to do so, while the individual who is robbed at gunpoint does not have the choice.

According to Nussbaum, not all capabilities are good or important. For instance, being able to be cruel is neither good nor important.[37] Nussbaum argues that the following ten central human capabilities are particularly important, as they are "entailed by the idea of a life worthy of human dignity": life; bodily health; bodily integrity; senses, imagination, and thought; emotions; practical reason; affiliation; other species; play; and control over one's environment.[38] Nussbaum believes that all human beings are entitled to these capabilities, and these capabilities form the basis of human rights.[39] In particular, to have human dignity, Nussbaum argues that each human being must have enough of each of these capabilities.[40] Moreover, according to Nussbaum, these capabilities generate constraints that political institutions must meet if they are to be minimally just.[41] Following Rawls, Nussbaum is particularly keen to argue that her list of the ten central capabilities can be the object of an overlapping consensus among citizens who otherwise have different comprehensive views.[42]

The hallmark, and indeed the strength, of Nussbaum's Central Capabilities Approach is its emphasis on our opportunities to choose to do certain things rather than on what we actually choose to do. For instance, with respect to political participation and religious practices, Nussbaum rightly argues that it is the capability or opportunity to engage in such activities that is the appropriate social goal. The Fundamental Conditions Approach, too, recognizes the importance of being able effectively to choose to do certain things. As noted earlier, one of the fundamental conditions for pursuing a good life is *being able freely to choose* to pursue the basic activities.

My concern with the Central Capabilities Approach as an account of human rights is that a significant number of human rights cannot be adequately explained in terms of capabilities.[43] For instance, capabilities do not seem adequate for explaining what might be called status rights, which are rights that protect our moral status as persons. For instance, in the UDHR, the right to recognition everywhere as a person before the law (Article 6); the right to equal protection before the law (Article 7); the right against arbitrary arrest, detention or exile (Article 9); the right to a fair and public hearing (Article 10); the right to be presumed innocent until proven guilty (Article 11) are all status rights, as they protect our moral status as persons.

Capabilities do not seem particularly well-suited to explain these rights, because if they were able to explain these rights, it would imply that one can sometimes choose not to exercise these rights, since capabilities are concerned with our real opportunities to choose. But it does not seem that one can sometimes choose whether or not to exercise these rights. For instance, it does not seem that one can sometimes choose not to be recognized everywhere as a person before the law; choose not to have equal protection before the law; choose to be arrested arbitrarily; choose to have an unfair hearing; and choose to be presumed guilty.

Nussbaum does say that

> Only in the area of self-respect and dignity itself do I think that actual functioning is the appropriate aim of public policy. Suppose a state were to say, "We give you the option of being treated with dignity. Here is a penny. If you give it back to us, we will treat you respectfully, but if you prefer, you may keep the penny, and we will humiliate you." This would be a bizarre and unfortunate nation, hardly compatible, it seems, with basic justice. We want political principles that offer respect to all citizens, and, in this one instance, the principles should give them no choice in the matter.[44]

Thus, Nussbaum might grant that capabilities cannot adequately explain status rights, but she might argue that status rights represent only a small fraction of the total number of human rights that exist. However, this response is unpersuasive because, as we have seen, a significant number of human rights are status rights; Articles 6, 7, 9, 10, 11 of the UDHR all contain status rights. Hence, once Nussbaum accepts that capabilities cannot adequately explain status rights, she must also accept that capabilities cannot adequately explain a significant number of human rights.

In addition to status rights, capabilities also cannot adequately explain many children's rights because many children's rights are concerned with functionings rather than capabilities. For example, children have rights to health care, education, name, nationality, protection from economic exploitation, and so on. These rights are best understood as rights to certain functionings rather than rights to certain capabilities. Nussbaum concedes this. As she says, "For children, however, functioning may be made the goal in many areas."[45] Nussbaum does try to minimize the impact of this point on her theory by arguing that these functionings are important for helping children to develop adult capabilities.[46] However, this response ignores the fact that some children will unfortunately not live to adulthood (e.g., children with terminal cancer). Nevertheless, it seems that these children would still have human rights to certain functionings. If so, this further supports the point that these rights are best understood as rights to certain functionings rather than rights to certain capabilities.

Here it may be useful to point out that in contrast, the Fundamental Conditions Approach can explain these rights. I have previously already shown how the Fundamental Conditions Approach can explain status rights. Here let me clarify how the Fundamental Conditions Approach can justify many of the rights that children have. I shall not attempt to be exhaustive. Consider, for example, children's right to health care and education. Children need to be healthy in order to pursue the basic activities, and to be healthy they need to have access to basic health care. Hence, having access to basic health care is a fundamental condition for pursuing a good life. Similarly, education is a fundamental condition for pursuing a good life because children need to acquire the basic knowledge to be adequately functioning individuals in their society, and to acquire such knowledge, they need some kind of education. Given that health care and education are fundamental conditions for children to pursue a good life, on the Fundamental Conditions Approach, children would have a right to health care and education.

Consider also the right to have a name and a nationality. Having a name and a nationality is a fundamental condition for pursuing a good life because to pursue the basic activities, children need to know that they are unique individuals deserving of equal respect, and to know this, they need to have their own identity. In modern societies, having a name and a nationality gives one one's own identity. Hence, having a name and a nationality is a fundamental condition for children to pursue a good life. On the Fundamental Conditions Approach, children would have the right to have a name and a nationality.

Given that a significant number of human rights cannot be adequately explained in terms of capabilities and given that the Fundamental Conditions Approach can readily explain these rights, this is a reason to prefer the Fundamental Conditions Approach over the Central Capabilities Approach.

6. Why Not the Political Approach?

As I said at the outset, proponents of the Political Conception believe that the Naturalistic Conception of human rights should be rejected in favor of its Political counterpart. I have also said the Fundamental Conditions Approach is a Naturalistic Conception. Since my aim here is to develop the correct substantive account of human rights, it will be helpful to say something about the Political Conception. Owing to lack of space, I shall not attempt to give a full defense of the Naturalistic Conception. But I shall do three things.[47] First, I shall argue that Naturalistic Conceptions can accommodate one of the most salient concerns that proponents of the Political Conception have raised about them. Second, I shall demonstrate that the theoretical distance between Naturalistic and Political Conceptions is not as great as it has been made out to be. Third, I shall point out that a Political Conception, on its own, lacks the resources necessary to determine the substantive content of human rights. If I am correct, not only should the Naturalistic Conception not be rejected, the Political Conception is in fact incomplete without the theoretical resources that a Naturalistic Conception characteristically provides.

To start, it will be helpful to offer an overview of different ways of understanding the Political Conception.

6.1 Political Conceptions of Human Rights

According to Rawls, "Human rights are a class of rights that play a special role in a reasonable Law of Peoples; they restrict the justifying reasons for war and its conduct, and they specify limits to a regime's internal autonomy."[48] More specifically, a society's observance of human rights is necessary for the society to be a member "in good standing in a reasonably just Society of People" and is "sufficient to exclude justified and forceful intervention by other peoples."[49] Human rights, Rawls tells us, are "Necessary conditions of any system of social cooperation. When they are regularly violated, we have command by force, a slave system, and no cooperation of any kind."[50] Moreover, if a society fails to observe human rights, then, according to Rawls, it cannot complain if external agents interfere in its internal affairs, for instance by means of economic or political sanction, or even coercive intervention.[51]

Raz agrees with Rawls's idea that human rights characteristically set limits to a society's internal autonomy.[52] But Raz's account differs from Rawls's in two main respects. First, Raz argues that while human rights are primarily rights against states, human rights can be held against international agents and organizations of all sorts, including individuals, groups, corporations, and other potential violating domestic institutions.[53] Second, Raz argues that Rawls fails to distinguish between the limits of sovereignty and the limits of legitimate authority.[54] Rawls holds that human rights are necessary conditions of any system of social cooperation, and he believes that conditions of social cooperation can determine the limits of sovereignty. But Raz argues that not every action that exceeds a state's legitimate authority can be a reason for interference by other states. For instance, a state can sometimes be protected from external interference even if it lacks internal legitimacy (e.g., if the external agents are themselves biased and corrupt). If so, the conditions of social cooperation alone cannot determine the limits of sovereignty.

Beitz argues that the current role of human rights in international political practice extends beyond that of the (*pro tanto*) justification of foreign interference or intervention.[55] In particular, it encompasses the broader role of guiding practical judgments about international responsibility or concern. For instance, there is a broad range of non-coercive political and economic measures that states and international organizations can use to influence the internal affairs of societies where human rights are threatened, measures that are better classified as assistance than interference. Moreover, Beitz observes that human rights are also justifications for individuals and nongovernmental organizations to engage in reform-oriented political action. In short, Beitz believes that from the perspective of a theory's attempting to explain the current international practice of human rights, it would be better to take a broader view of the international role of human rights than Rawls's narrower view.

6.2 The Concern about Timelessness

Proponents of the Political Conception have expressed a number of concerns regarding the Naturalistic Conception. The one I shall discuss here is the concern about timelessness. Beitz and others have observed that, on a Naturalistic Conception, human rights seem to be "timeless—all human beings at all times and places would be justified in claiming them."[56] However, they argue that it is not the case that all human beings at all times and places would be justified in claiming the human rights currently recognized by international practice. For example, consider the right to education, in Article 26 (1) of the UDHR, which states that:

> Everyone has the right to education. Education shall be free, at least in the elementary and fundamental stages. Elementary education shall be compulsory. Technical and professional education shall be made generally available and higher education shall be equally accessible to all on the basis of merit.

Raz points out that if people have a right to education simply in virtue of their humanity, "it follows that cave dwellers in the Stone Age had that right. Does that make sense? . . . The very distinctions between elementary, technical, professional and higher education would have made no sense at that, and at many other times."[57]

Beitz argues further that international human rights are intended to play a role in a certain range of societies:

> Roughly speaking, these are societies that have at least some of the defining features of modernization: for example, a minimal legal system (including a capability for enforcement), an economy that includes some form of wage labor

for at least some workers, some participation in global cultural and economic life, and a public institutional capacity to raise revenue and provide essential collective goods.[58]

Echoing this sentiment, Raz argues that human rights are "synchronically universal," by which he means that all people alive today have them.[59] If it is essential to Naturalistic Conceptions such as the Fundamental Conditions Approach that human rights are timeless, but if it is the case that human rights as found in international practice are not timeless, then this seems to call into question the plausibility and validity of Naturalistic Conceptions.

In response to this concern, it seems that at least some of the rights that can be found in the UDHR are indeed timeless. For example, consider the human right against torture. There seems to be good reasons to believe that even cavemen had a human right not to be tortured. The same can be said regarding the rights not to be murdered, enslaved, and so on.

Second, recall that when Beitz says that international human rights are intended to play a certain role in modern societies, he takes this to mean societies that have a minimal legal system, an economy that includes some form of wage labor for at least some workers, some participation in global cultural and economic life, and so on. However, there are over a hundred uncontacted tribes in the world today, that is, tribes that have no contact with the outside world.[60] It seems doubtful that all of these tribes have the defining features of modernization that Beitz speaks of, such as "some participation in global cultural and economic life." Should we draw the conclusion that members of these tribes do not have human rights? Such a conclusion seems dubious. If so, why should we not accept that human rights can also apply to past societies that similarly lacked features of modernization?

The same point can be made against one of Raz's reasons for rejecting the idea that human rights are timeless. Raz argues that since many of the most uncontroversial human rights appeal to institutions and make use of distinctions (e.g., the distinction among elementary, technical, professional, and higher education) that could not possibly apply in Stone Age societies, it is senseless to think of such rights as timeless. But such institutions and distinctions also fail to apply in the case of present-day un-contacted tribes. And so, by his own reasoning, Raz would have to admit that members of these tribes do not have, say, the human right to elementary education. But if Raz accepts that members of un-contacted tribes do not have some human rights, it seems that he would have to abandon his claim that human rights are synchronically universal, by which he means that *all* people alive today have them.

Third, there are plausible ways of explaining how there could be contemporary human rights such as the right to elementary education without abandoning the claim that human rights are timeless. For instance, we can distinguish between the aim and the object of a right. The aim of a human right is the goal or end of the human right, and the object of a human right is the means to achieving that goal or end. The proposal is that the aims of human rights are timeless, while the objects of human rights may vary across time, location, and society. As long as we are clear that when we say that human rights are timeless, we are referring to the aims of human rights, then the puzzle just articulated should disappear.

To illustrate, consider the human right to free elementary education. We could say that free elementary education is the object of a right. As such, it makes sense only at a specific time, in a specific location, and in a specific society. By contrast, the aim of the right to free elementary education is to ensure that human beings acquire the knowledge necessary to be adequately functioning individuals in their circumstances, and it does not seem odd to say that such an aim was relevant, important, and applied in the context of cavemen. In other words, while cavemen would not have had a right to free elementary school education, it does not seem odd to think that the *aim* of that right did have normative force in their circumstances, and that it would have generated a different, but similar, object of right for cavemen, for instance, the right to be educated (in a basic way) about how to hunt and gather, assuming that such instruction could feasibly be provided to them. Hence, the distinction between the aim and the object of a right can explain how human rights can be timeless even if many of the human rights proclaimed in international declarations do not appear to be so.

6.3 Formal Compatibility

I shall now argue that the theoretical distance between these two conceptions is actually not as great as it has been made out to be. To see this, consider the *formal* features of both conceptions. According to the Naturalistic Conception, human rights are rights that we have simply in virtue of being human. And, according to the Political Conception, human rights are rights that set limits to a society's internal autonomy (Rawls and Raz) and/or rights that the international community has a responsibility to protect in modern societies (Beitz). Are these two formal features incompatible? One way of seeing that they need not be is to notice that the formal features of Political Conceptions seem to be concerned with the issue of who is responsible for protecting and promoting human rights—that is, the issue of the *dutybearers* of human rights—while the formal features of Naturalistic Conceptions seem to be concerned with what *grounds* human rights. Since questions about the grounds and questions about the dutybearers of human rights are non-overlapping or, at least, need not overlap, it is in principle possible for one to accept both a Naturalistic and Political Conception of the formal features of human rights.

To flesh this point out, let us consider what advocates of Naturalistic Conceptions have actually said about the issue of dutybearers. For example, D. D. Raphael argues that:

> The expression a universal moral right may be used in a stronger sense or in a weaker sense. In the stronger sense it means a right of all men against all men; in the weaker sense it means simply a right of all men, but not necessarily against all men. In the weaker sense, all men may have a right which is, for each of them, a right against some men only.[61]

To keep the discussion simple, let us focus on the:

Strong Sense: Human rights are rights against all able persons and agents in appropriate circumstances.

Is Strong Sense incompatible with a Political Conception, according to which human rights first and foremost set limits to a society's internal autonomy (Rawls and Raz) and/or are rights that the international community has a responsibility to protect in modern societies (Beitz)? The two formal features can in principle be compatible given that "all able persons and agents in appropriate circumstances" can be read as an abstract statement about who the dutybearers of human rights are, and "the state and/or the international community in modern societies" can be read as a more specific formulation of who such dutybearers are. Indeed, supposing that the relevant "appropriate circumstances" are those of modernity, if one were to ask advocates of the Naturalistic Conception who the "able persons and agents" in modern societies are, it seems likely that they would accept that it is first and foremost the state and/or the international community that are the relevant "able persons and agents." But if advocates of these two Conceptions would come to the same conclusions about who the relevant dutybearers of human rights are, this suggests that the two Conceptions can be compatible in this respect.

6.4 Formal and Substantive Accounts of Human Rights

Finally, I argue that Naturalistic and Political Conceptions are not only in principle formally compatible, but that, in fact, the Political Conception is incomplete without the theoretical resources that a Naturalistic Conception characteristically provides. To see this, it is useful to distinguish between a *formal* and a *substantive* account of human rights. A formal account provides criteria for distinguishing human rights claims from those that are not human rights claims. A substantive account, by contrast, provides criteria for generating the content of human rights. A Naturalistic Conception typically provides us with not just a formal, but also a substantive, account of human rights. In this respect, the Fundamental Conditions Approach is a substantive account of human rights. By contrast, the Political Conception tends to provide us with only a formal account of human rights. This is clearest in Beitz's account. Beitz does not provide a list of human rights that we have, but instead proposes what he calls a "model" of such rights, which has three key elements:[62]

(i) Human rights protect urgent individual interests against standard threats that one might find in the modern statist global order.

(ii) Human rights apply in the first instance to the political institutions of states.

(iii) Human rights are matters of international concern. A state's failure to carry out its responsibilities may be a reason for "second-level" agents such as the international community to hold the state accountable for carrying out these responsibilities, to assist the state if the state lacks capacities to carry out these responsibilities, and to interfere in the state if the state is unwilling to do so.

Beitz's account surely provides us with criteria for distinguishing human rights claims from those that are not human rights claims. To keep things simple, consider (i). According to (i), if something is a human right, then it will protect some urgent individual interest. And if something is not an urgent individual interest, then it will not be protected by a human right. The notion of an urgent individual interest therefore tells us something about the formal features of human rights, but it is unclear what substantive human rights would follow from this notion. Similar things can be said regarding (ii) and (iii).

The same can be said about Raz's version of the Political Conception. Raz also does not provide a list of human rights that we have, but he proposes the following three steps as a way to determine whether something is a human right.[63] A human right exists if:

(a) there is an individual interest that is sufficient to establish an individual moral right;
(b) states are to be held duty-bound to respect or promote this interest; and
(c) states do not enjoy immunity from interference should they fail to respect or promote this interest.

Raz's three-step program would, for example, exclude (from the category of interests protected by human rights) interests that cannot ground individual moral rights or interests that states have no duty to protect or promote. But, again, it is unclear what human rights would follow from this program. So Raz's account also does not give us a substantive account of human rights.

Rawls does provide us with a list (albeit a very short one) of human rights, but it remains unclear whether Rawls's account offers us more than a formal account of human rights. To see why, recall that for Rawls, one of the main roles of human rights is to set limits to a society's internal autonomy. This provides us with a criterion for distinguishing human rights claims from those that are not human rights claims. In particular, it says that if something, X, is a human right, then X will set limits to a society's internal autonomy. And if an individual right, Y, does not set limits to a society's internal autonomy, then Y is not a human right. However, it is unclear what human rights will follow from this criterion. And so it does not provide us with a substantive standard with which we can determine the content of human rights.

However, Rawls also claims that human rights are "necessary conditions for any system of social cooperation." So it might be thought that Rawls intended the notion of social cooperation to serve as such a substantive criterion. But this interpretation of Rawls faces two difficulties. First, the idea that X (a set of human rights) is a necessary condition for Y (a system of social cooperation) is not equivalent to the idea that X is based on, or grounded in, Y, and it is the latter sort of relationship that is required for something to serve as a substantive criterion. Compare: the idea that air is a necessary condition for agency is not equivalent to the idea that air is based on, or grounded in, agency; the latter does not even make very much sense. Hence, the claim that human rights are necessary conditions for social cooperation is not the same as the claim that human rights are based on, or grounded in, social cooperation. Given this, the fact that Rawls has claimed the former does not mean that he has claimed the latter. And since the latter is what is required for something to serve as a substantive criterion, the fact that Rawls has not claimed the latter means that it is unclear that Rawls intended the notion of social cooperation to be a substantive criterion.

Second, even if Rawls did intend for the notion of social cooperation to be a substantive criterion, it does not seem to be a plausible one. Not all societies that fail to respect the human rights that Rawls lists command by force.[64] For instance, it is implausible to think that communities that do not recognize personal private property (one of Rawls's human rights) must command by force. Moreover, it is unclear how one derives the right to personal property from the notion of social cooperation. Hence, a substantive account of human rights based on the notion of social cooperation seems to be fraught with difficulties.

It might be said that the Political Conception was never intended to answer the sort of substantive questions that I have accused it of failing to address. However, if this is right and, in fact, the Political Conception, as a formal account of human rights, leaves the important problem of generating the content of human rights out of view, then the Political Conception is incomplete. Accordingly, it may very well look to Naturalistic Conceptions such as the Fundamental Conditions Approach as a source for generating a substantive account of human rights.

7. Conclusion

In this chapter, I argued that human rights should be grounded in the fundamental conditions for pursuing a good life. I showed how this Fundamental Conditions Approach can explain why many of the rights in the UDHR are indeed human rights, and also how this approach can rule out some of the claims in the UDHR as genuine human rights. I also distinguished the Fundamental Conditions Approach from Griffin's Agency Approach and Nussbaum's Central Capabilities Approach by arguing, among other things, that Griffin's approach cannot adequately explain the right against torture and that Nussbaum's approach cannot adequately explain status rights and many children's rights.

I further defended the Fundamental Conditions Approach as a Naturalistic Conception of human rights against the Political Conceptions of human rights by (a) arguing that the distinction between the aim and the object of a right can explain how human rights can be timeless even if many of the human rights proclaimed in international declarations do not appear to be so; (b) showing that Naturalistic and Political Conceptions can in principle be compatible at the formal level because the formal features of Political Conceptions seem to be concerned with the issue of who is responsible for protecting and promoting human rights, while the formal features of Naturalistic Conceptions seem to be concerned with what *grounds* human rights; and (c) arguing that the Political Conception tends to offer only a formal account of human rights, which means that a Political Conception is, on its own, incomplete, and may very well look to a Naturalistic Conception to provide what it is missing—a substantive account of human rights.

If all of this is correct, we have good reasons to believe that human beings have human rights to the fundamental conditions for pursuing a good life. For our purpose, on the Fundamental Conditions Approach, if children have a right to be loved, it is because being loved is a fundamental condition for children to pursue a good life. I shall now argue that this is indeed the case.

3

Being Loved as a Fundamental Condition for Children

1. A Case for Why Children Need to Be Loved

As discussed in the previous chapter, the fundamental conditions for pursuing a good life are various goods, capacities, and options that human beings qua human beings need whatever else they qua individuals might need in order to pursue the basic activities; and human beings have human rights to these fundamental conditions. The aim of this chapter is to show that being loved is a fundamental condition for children to pursue a good life, that is, children need to be loved in order to develop the fundamental capacities necessary for pursuing the basic activities. For ease of exposition, I shall use the phrase "being loved is a fundamental condition for children to pursue a good life" and the phrase "children need to be loved" interchangeably.

The claim that being loved is a fundamental condition for children to pursue a good life is a claim that many people would find intuitive and obvious, perhaps because of their own reflections on their childhood, their experience with child-rearing, and/or their observation of the practice of child-rearing. However, personal experiences can be mistaken. Also, some people have questioned whether children really need to be loved.[1] In any case, it is useful to know to what extent love can affect a child's development and the underlying biological and psychological mechanisms by which love affects a child's development, as such knowledge can have practical implications. Psychologists have long theorized about the importance of early relationships for all aspects of children's later development. Drawing on a few of the more influential theories, I shall begin by offering some theoretical explanations of why children need to be loved. Next, there is a vast array of ongoing scientific research devoted toward understanding why children need to be loved, both at the psychological level and at the biological level. To reinforce the theoretical explanations and further support the claim that children need to be loved, I shall present some of the key findings and detail some of the latest results from this research.

2. Theoretical Explanations of Why Children Need to Be Loved

To start, it is useful to have some working definitions of children and the kind of love at issue. The United Nations Convention on the Rights of the Child (1989) defines a child as a "human being below the age of eighteen years unless, under the law applicable to the child, majority is attained earlier."[2] Similarly, in most states in the United States, minors reach the age of majority at eighteen, at which time they are legally able to make their own decisions free from parental authority and control. Likewise, in Britain, a child is defined, subject to limited qualifications relating to financial support, as "a person under the age of eighteen."[3] In scientific research, children are typically divided into three groups: infants (birth to two), young and middle-aged children (two to twelve), and adolescents or teenagers (twelve to adulthood). There are interesting philosophical issues regarding exactly when childhood ends and when adulthood begins.[4] For our purposes, unless otherwise specified, we can assume that children are those who are eighteen or younger.

One way to characterize the kind of love at issue, namely, parental love, is as follows:

> To love a child is to seek a highly intense interaction with the child, where one values the child for the child's sake, seeks to bring about and maintain physical and psychological proximity with the child, seeks to promote the child's well-being for the child's sake, and desires that the child reciprocate or, at least, respond to, one's love.[5]

As one can see, an important feature of parental love is valuing the child for the child's sake. Mia Pringle, a child psychologist, writes:

> The basic and all-pervasive feature of parental love is that the child is valued unconditionally and for his own sake, irrespective of his sex, appearance, abilities or personality; that this love is given without expectation of or demand for gratitude . . . Parents communicate this unconditional affection through all their relations with him: from physical care and handling to responding to his first smile and sounds; from protecting him from, and then gradually initiating him into, the social world; and from restraining to eventually punishing him for going beyond the limits they have set for acceptable behavior.[6]

The "highly intense" aspect of this definition captures the idea that parental love is not just behavioral or attitudinal but has emotional components that permeate through all of a parent's actions with a child. Furthermore, if parents love their children, they would maintain closeness to the child, both physically and psychologically, other things being equal. Physically, parents would try to be with the child as much as it is appropriate and optimal. Psychologically, parents would try to understand the child from the child's perspective, and they would try to open their perspectives to the child, when the child is capable of such understanding. Moreover, they would try to increase the child's prospect of having a good life for the child's sake. Finally, very young children may perhaps not be able to reciprocate a parent's love. Even so, a parent who loves his child would desire that a child would love him back if the child could do so. There may be other ways of characterizing parental love, but for our purpose, this working definition should contain the important elements that we typically find in parental love.

I shall now present four theoretical explanations of why being loved is a fundamental condition for children to pursue a good life.

2.1 Love Provides Trust in Others

One explanation is that children need this love in order to develop certain trust in others, especially in those who care for them, and they need this trust in order to develop adequately the various fundamental capacities necessary for pursuing the basic activities. This idea finds support in, for example, the influential theories of psychologists such as Erik Erikson and John Bowlby.[7]

For instance, Erikson hypothesizes that a human being goes through various psychosocial stages such as "basic trust versus mistrust" (birth to one), "autonomy versus shame and doubt" (one to three), "initiative versus guilt" (three to six), and so on. At each stage, a person faces a conflict. A healthy resolution of the conflict in favor of the positive ensures that he acquires the requisite attitudes and skills that enable him to be an active member of the society. But when one stage is not fully resolved, the old patterns or the unmet needs are carried forward, affecting the individual's ability to handle later tasks or stages.

As one can see, the first stage is basic trust and mistrust. According to Erikson, this trust is important because it helps a child to feel secure about his environment. Without such security, a child is reluctant to explore his surroundings, and without such exploration, the child cannot develop the fundamental capacities required to pursue a good life. How does a child acquire such trust? Erikson argues that the behavior of the major caregiver (usually but not necessarily the mother) is critical to the child's successful or unsuccessful resolution of this crisis. In Erickson's view, children who emerge from the first year with a firm sense of trust are those whose parents are loving and who respond predictably and reliably to the child. By contrast, those infants whose early care has been erratic or harsh may develop mistrust. According to Erikson, a child who has developed a sense of trust will carry this sense with him into future relationships. On the other hand, a young adult who has developed a sense of mistrust in the first years of life may have a more difficult time establishing secure intimate relationships with a partner or friends.

Likewise, Bowlby proposes that a child develops an "internal working model" about his attachment figures, which is a set of expectations about the availability of attachment figures and their likelihood of providing support during times of stress. The internal working model begins to be formed late in the child's first year of life and becomes more complex and firmer through the first four or five years. By age five, most children have clear internal models of their caregiver. Once formed, the internal working models shape and explain experiences and affect memory and attention; the model becomes a guide for all future close relationships—through childhood and adolescence and into adult life.

According to Bowlby, the internal working model indicates the level of trust a child has for his carer, and a positive internal working model is developed when a child's attachment figure is available and provides loving care for him. Similar to Erikson's psychosocial stages, if a child's internal working model of his carer is not positive, this will affect his future relationships. Hence, that love provides a child with trust in others provides one explanation why children need to be loved. Later on, we shall see recent scientific studies showing that children who are loved do better in all aspects of development.

2.2 Love Provides Positive Conception of Self

A second explanation is that being loved is necessary for a child to develop a positive conception of himself, and having such a positive conception of oneself is necessary for one to develop the fundamental capacities necessary for pursuing the basic activities.

Among various psychological theories, it is generally accepted that every person gradually comes to have a certain view of himself—not just a self-awareness, but a certain self-conception, what might be called a "self-scheme," using Piaget's terminology.[8] This self-conception is a person's belief about how likely it is that he will succeed or fail, especially in the important activities that he may pursue. A person has a positive view of himself if he believes that on balance he would succeed more often than he would fail in these activities; and a person has a negative view of himself if he believes that on balance he would fail more often than he would succeed in these activities. As the psychologists Miller and Siegel write,

> [T]he self-concept is the gauge against which we weigh all present successes and failures. Each of us evaluates personal accomplishment against the demands or goals of the

self-concept. When we fail to measure up to these standards, we feel less worthwhile.[9]

A child needs to have a positive view of himself in order to develop adequately because without believing that he would generally succeed in his intended actions, the child would be fearful of attempting new things. But without attempting new things, a child cannot develop adequately the fundamental capacities needed to pursue the basic activities.

It is widely accepted that to have a positive view of the self, a child needs to be loved. As Pringle writes,

> The greatest impact of [parental] love is on the self. Approval and acceptance by others are essential for the development of self-approval and self-acceptance. Whether a child will develop a constructive or destructive attitude, first to himself and then to other people, depends in the first place on his parents' attitude to him.[10]

Likewise, Susan Harter argues that a major influence on a child's self-esteem is the overall sense of support the child feels from the important people around her, particularly parents and peers.[11] Children who feel that other people generally like them the way they are have higher self-esteem scores than do children who report less overall support. That love provides positive conception of oneself offers another explanation for why children need to be loved in order to develop into adequately functioning individuals.

2.3 Love Provides Knowledge of How to Love

A third explanation for why being loved is a fundamental condition for children to pursue a good life is that by receiving love, children learn how to love, and knowing how to love is necessary for them to develop the fundamental capacities required for pursuing the basic activities.

Knowing how to love is necessary for children to pursue the basic activities because, as noted earlier, one basic activity is having deep personal relationships with one's partner, friends, parents, and children. To be able to pursue deep personal relationships successfully, however, one must know how to love. To know how to love, a child needs to be loved, because love is a complex phenomenon that one can only learn by having received it and by having the opportunity to practice it on someone. This is not to deny that human beings are not born with some rudimentary capacities for love. For example, even blind children can exhibit what is called a "social smile" in order to attract others to love them. However, newly born human beings generally do not know real love because real love involves certain kinds of interactions such as having certain emotions and attitudes, and exhibiting certain appropriate behaviors; newly born human beings typically do not know how to do this. Nor is it necessary to deny that a child may be able partially to learn how to love from other sources, such as through observation. Still, part of learning how to love requires receiving love, because the type of interactions between two persons in a loving relationship is complex, and one cannot expect to learn this without experiencing this interaction. An analogy may be that one cannot learn how to ride a bicycle just through observation. The psychologists Miller and Siegel concur with this idea: "To truly love anything we must have extensive interaction with it. We must learn how to love and what to love."[12] Miller and Siegel offer a behaviorist explanation of how one learns to love, which has certain plausibility. According to them, love is learned in the same way as learning what foods are tasty and what makes us warm and cold—that is, through experience and reinforcement:

> Love is a form of approach behavior. The loved person is approached because of frequent but not entirely predictable association with many kinds of rewarding experience.[13]

Through such an interaction, one learns love as "a response to a generalized hope signal, a broad pleasurable expectancy. The love object, be it a 'thing' or a person, is a generalized secondary positive reinforce."[14] Miller and Siegel conclude that "true love cannot develop immediately. Each person must develop the ability to serve as a generalized secondary reinforce for the other. This cannot happen immediately."[15] That being loved helps one to learn how to love provides another explanation for why children need to be loved.

2.4 Love Provides a Child with a Motivation to Develop

A fourth explanation of why children need to be loved is that to develop the various fundamental capacities for pursuing the basic activities, children need to accept and obey certain commands; and for children to be motivated to accept these commands, they need to be loved.

From early days, those who care for a child are inevitably faced with the task of controlling the child's behavior through giving him certain commands and punishing him should he digress from these commands, a process commonly called discipline. Children need discipline because they initially lack knowledge of the workings of the world, and these commands help to keep them safe while at the same time enabling them to do the exploration necessary to develop adequately. There are several reasons why children need to be loved in order to be motivated to accept such discipline. One is that children whose parents are loving find the interruption in parental affection, which results from their having strayed from parental commands, to be especially unpleasant.[16] As a result, these children are motivated to obey the parental commands generally, and when they are punished for having disobeyed the parental commands, they are motivated to regain the warmth and approval of their parents as quickly as possible. In contrast, children who are frequently punished by non-loving parents soon learn to avoid such parents rather than be motivated to obey their commands. When a child avoids interacting with those who are responsible for his upbringing, he has little opportunity to learn desirable commands from them.[17] Another reason is that loving parents tend to make demands that are reasonable in terms of their child's developing capacities. Because the demands are not beyond their capacities, children are more likely to be motivated to obey them. A third reason is that loving parents tend to explain why a child is being punished. This motivates a child to accept their commands because children feel that they are treated in a fair manner when reasonable explanations have been given to them.[18]

Indeed, in a series of now classic studies, Diana Baumrind and others found that loving parents who make reasonable demands on their children have children who are best adjusted.[19] Baumrind and others use two criteria, demandingness and responsiveness, to observe the way parents interact with their preschoolers in a variety of situations. From these two criteria, four styles of parenting are identified: authoritative, authoritarian, permissive, and uninvolved. Authoritative parents make reasonable demands for maturity, and they enforce them by setting limits and insisting that the child obey. At the same time, they express warmth and affection, listen patiently to their child's point of view, and encourage participation in family decision making. Authoritarian parents are also demanding, but they place such a high value on conformity that they are unresponsive when children are unwilling to obey. Authoritarian parents often resort to force and punishment. Permissive parents are accepting and show affection, but avoid making demands or imposing controls of any kind. Uninvolved parents show little commitment to their role as caregivers beyond the minimum effort required to feed and clothe the child. Often they are emotionally detached, depressed, and overwhelmed by the many stresses in their lives and thus have little time and energy to spare for their children. The various combinations of responsiveness and demandingness and the styles of child-rearing that result from them can be represented as follows:

	Responsive	Unresponsive
Demanding	Authoritative parent	Authoritarian parent
Undemanding	Permissive parent	Uninvolved parent

Baumrind and others found that children whose parents were authoritative—demanding and loving—were self-confident in their mastery of new tasks and self-controlled in their ability to resist engaging in disruptive behavior.[20] These children were also less gender-typed. For example, girls scored particularly high in independence, and boys exhibited more friendly and cooperative behavior.[21] Subsequent studies found that these children have higher self-esteem, are more socially mature, are more independent but at the same time are more likely to comply with parental requests, and show more altruistic behavior. In late adolescence they are more likely to use what Lawrence Kohlberg calls "postconventional moral reasoning," which is reasoning based on reflection of abstract principles and values rather than reasoning based on conformity to social rules.[22] By contrast, Baumrind found that preschoolers with authoritarian parents were anxious, withdrawn, and unhappy. When interacting with peers, they tended to react with hostility when frustrated.[23] Boys showed high rates of anger and defiance, while girls were dependent, lacked exploration, and retreated from challenging tasks.[24] Baumrind found that children of permissive parents were very immature. They had difficulty controlling their impulses and were disobedient and rebellious when asked to do something that conflicted with their momentary desires. They were also overly demanding and dependent on adults, and showed less persistence on tasks at preschool than children of parents who exerted more control.[25] Maccoby and others found that uninvolved parenting disrupted virtually all aspects of development, including attachment, cognition, play, and social and emotional skills.[26]

That love provides children with a motivation to accept and obey parental commands serves as another explanation of why children who are loved develop better, since they have someone who can effectively get them to behave and learn in a safe manner.

3. The Negative Effects of Lack of Love on a Child

The theoretical explanations presented above of why children need to be loved are supported and reinforced by a vast array of ongoing scientific research. Two broad approaches can be distinguished. One, which we will discuss in this section, examines the negative consequences for a person if he or she is not loved as a child. The other, to be discussed in the next section, examines the positive consequences for a person if he or she is loved as a child. Owing to space, it will not be possible to provide a comprehensive discussion of the research being conducted in this field. My goal here will be to present some of the key findings and to detail the results of some of the latest research.

Before doing so, it is helpful to mention explicitly an assumption I am making, namely, I am assuming that the scientific studies presented below are concerned with parental love and its effects on a child's development, even though these studies do not appear to be measuring parental love directly. Parental love is a complex phenomenon involving various internal states, many of which are not directly observable.[27] Given this, researchers working in this area have had to use indirect measures such as

1. Whether a parental figure is present or absent;
2. Turnover rate of the number of carers a child has over a period of time;
3. Duration of time a parent spends with a child;
4. Whether a child is securely attached to his primary caregiver;
5. Parental attitudes toward a child;
6. Whether a child has received adequate parental touch.

Each of these criteria has advantages and disadvantages as an indirect measure of parental love. To give just one example, consider the criterion of whether a parental figure is present or absent. The rationale for it is that if a child were to be loved, then often a parent or a parent-like person would be present. An advantage of this criterion is that it is easy to set up such an experiment, especially in the case of animals. A disadvantage is that it is theoretically less useful for assessing cases in which a parental figure is present but does not love the child; or in cases in which a parent does love a child but cannot physically be with a child.

For our purpose, it is worth noting that despite its limitations, the use of indirect measures in science, especially the social sciences, is ubiquitous and necessary. For example, using quality-adjusted life years (QALYs) as a measure of the value of health outcomes and using gross domestic product (GDP) as a measure of economic progress are examples of indirect measures. This means that unless one wishes to deny the validity of any scientific study that uses indirect measures or to deny that there is such a thing as parental love at all, it seems reasonable to assume that these measures can give us some insights regarding what parental love is and how it affects a child's development.[28]

With this assumption in mind, I shall now present research that shows the negative consequences for a person if he or she is not loved as a child. It would obviously be unethical to conduct studies of this kind by performing controlled experiments on human beings. Consequently, researchers have explored other ways of investigating this issue, ranging from naturalistic studies of institutionalized children, to clinical studies of certain growth disorders of children in their own homes, to studies of monkeys in laboratories (which raise ethical issues of their own), and to more recent neuroscientific studies of humans and animals.

3.1 Studies of Institutionalized Children

The rationale for studying institutionalized children stems from the thought that children who develop normally are typically children who live in homes with people who love them. Hence, by comparing institutionalized children with children who are likely to have received adequate love, one might be able to see the effects of lack of love on a child. As William Goldfarb, one of the pioneers of this kind of study, describes it: In contrast to the experience of children in families where, among other things, "there is warm, loving contact between a specific parent person and child,"

[a]n unusual opportunity for the experimental study of deprivation during infancy is provided by the existence of infant institutions where the conditions of baby rearing are often the obverse of those prevailing families. The child is one of a large group of babies cared for by a baby nurse. The adult-child ratio is very low so that there is a minimum of adult stimulation. Ties with specific adults are casual and fleeting. Identifications are consequently relatively unformed.[29]

These studies found that institutionalized children became ill more frequently; their learning capacities deteriorated significantly; they became decreasingly interested in their environment; they failed to thrive physically by not gaining weight or height or both; they suffered insomnia; they were constantly depressed; and they eventually developed severe learning disabilities. For instance, in an early study of this kind, 37 percent of these infants died by the age of two, compared with none in the lovingly mothered control group.[30] In a later study, Tizard and Hodges studied the development of twenty-six infants reared in an institution that offered these children a generous provision of books and toys, thereby controlling for sensory stimulation.[31] However, because close personal relationships between adults and children were discouraged, and because the staff turnover rate was high (in this study, an average of twenty-four different nurses had worked with the children for at least a week in their first two years of life; by the time the children were four and a half, the figure had increased to fifty), Tizard and Hodges found that throughout childhood and adolescence these children were significantly more likely to display emotional and social problems, including an excessive desire for adult attention, "overfriendliness" to unfamiliar adults and peers, and difficulties in establishing friendships. In a recent study of children in Romanian orphanages where the staff turnover rate is also high, Kaler and Freeman found similar deficits in the institutionalized children on standardized cognitive and behavioral tests, early social communication skills with adults, and task orientation.[32] Or, in the Bucharest Early Intervention Project (BEIP), the first randomized, controlled trial of foster care as an intervention for institutionalized children, the results confirm and extend the previous findings on the negative effects of early institutional care on mental health.[33] The results also underscore the benefit of early family placement for children living in institutions.

3.2 Non-Organic Failure to Thrive and Psychosocial Dwarfism

The rationale for clinical studies of certain growth disorders of children in their own homes comes from the thought that "hospitalism" found in institutionalized children discussed previously can occur to children in their own homes for similar reasons, that is, as a result of a child's not receiving adequate love. Two kinds of growth disorders that have been identified and that may have such a cause are non-organic failure to thrive (NFTT)[34] and psychosocial dwarfism (PSD).[35]

NFTT is a term used to describe infants before age two whose weight is significantly below the expected norm but where the cause of this disorder is not primarily organic, that is, the result of malnutrition and/or illness.[36] The linear growth of the infant may also be affected, but usually to a lesser degree. Physical examination of the infant indicates that there are loss of fat and muscle wasting, commonly in the large muscle groups such as the gluteal muscles and the inner aspects of the thighs. The behavior of these infants offers clues to the diagnosis. There is often apprehensive behavior characterized by unusual watchfulness; apathetic behavior with minimal smiling, decreased vocalization, lack of cuddliness; and an inability to discriminate between parents and strangers. An abnormal persistence of infantile posture is also often observed.

PSD is a term used to characterize children after age two, who have severe retardation of linear growth, but whose poor growth is not due primarily to organic causes such as malnutrition and/or illness. These children may sometimes be underweight for their height, but this is not a salient feature. These children often have bizarre eating patterns—they sometimes steal and hoard food, gorge themselves, eat large amounts of unusual food such as condiments, and sometimes eat from garbage cans. In addition, they often have disturbed toileting and self-harming behavior, and are often defiantly hostile and acutely non-compliant. Other features may include a history of being of normal size at birth with adequate growth for a variable period of time before a diminished rate of growth developed, and disturbed sleep.

If not treated, children with NFTT and PSD are at risk of various short- and long-term developmental problems. For example, in one study of NFTT, children who were diagnosed as organic FTT or NFTT were reevaluated at the age of four for at least six weeks. It was found that while the organic FTT children displayed normalization of height and weight growth, NFTT children continued to exhibit significantly poor growth patterns.[37] In another thirteen-year follow-up study of fourteen previously NFTT infants, it was found that these individuals were shorter, performed worse on tests of intelligence, language development, reading skills and social maturity, and displayed more behavioral problems when compared to peers of the same age, sex, and socioeconomic status.[38] More recent studies continue to support these patterns.[39]

Similarly, in studies of PSD, a follow-up study of fifty-five children hospitalized for PSD after four years found that 25 to 30 percent continued to have height below the third percentile, and that most were significantly smaller than the controlled group of similar age and social class.[40] In addition, children with PSD have higher incidences of emotional and behavioral disorders and were significantly less socially mature. Moreover, they have significant delays in intellectual development. For example, Glaser et al. reviewed forty infants after an average of 3.75 years and found that 15 percent were either borderline or actually intellectually disabled and 30 percent of those who were by then of school age had significant difficulties in school.[41] In addition, Elmer et al. reported slow speech development and difficulty in conceptual thinking in children with PSD.[42] In a 12.5-year follow-up study, Oates found that these children scored significantly lower in verbal language and reading tests.[43]

The hypothesis that NFTT and PSD are the results of lack of love stems from the following observations. A study of the history of these children and their parents often showed that these infants had received little physical handling—their parents rarely held, cuddled, smiled at, played with, and/or communicated with, their children. Interviews with the mothers found that they often lacked positive feelings for their children. Observation of the mothers with their children found that the mothers were often insensitive to, and were unable to assess, the needs of their children, particularly with regard to hunger. Very significantly, when removed from their environment, many of these children experienced "catch-up" growth, which is a rapid recovery of weight and/or height in a short period of time. For example, Ellerstein found that most infants with NFTT less than six months of age began to gain weight in as little as two or three days.[44] According to many researchers, the speed of such recovery precludes an organic explanation for the disorders.

Furthermore, additional emotional stimulation encouraged growth in many of these children. Finally, in many cases, returning these children to their original environment without altering the environment, such as changing the attitudes of their carers toward their children, often resulted in an immediate slowdown of growth.

In short, the circumstances in which these children had these growth disorders and the fact that they experienced rapid growth when removed from their environment and when given emotional stimulation have led many researchers to conclude that lack of love is the cause of these disorders. If this is correct, since these disorders can adversely affect a child's various short- and long-term developments, these studies further contribute to the idea that lack of love can negatively affect a child's development.

3.3 Experiments on Monkeys in Laboratories

The motivation for using animals, in particular monkeys, to study the effects of lack of love on a child is that it is unethical to perform such deprivation experiments on human beings, although one should also ask whether it is ethical to perform these experiments on animals such as monkeys. In any case, in these experiments, infant monkeys were raised in varying degrees of maternal privation ranging from "total isolation," where the infant monkeys had no sensory contact with other monkeys or objects,[45] to "partial isolation," where the infant monkeys could see, hear, smell, but not touch other monkeys,[46] to "surrogate rearing," where infant monkeys were partially isolated, but had a cloth-covered inanimate surrogate mother,[47] to "peer rearing," where infant monkeys were reared with like-aged peers but did not have contact or experience with an adult mother,[48] to "variable foraging demand," where infant monkeys were raised by parents who were less available because they were required to forage for food in variable demanding situations.[49] Infant monkeys raised in these manners were then compared with those who were reared by monkey parents or foster parents who were more available.

The general finding is that infant monkeys raised in a manner other than by a real or foster monkey parent who had sufficient time to spend with them have hampered social, cognitive, and emotional development, which has serious consequences for their flourishing. For example, these studies found that infant monkeys raised in variable foraging demand (VFD) condition left their mothers less frequently to explore the room than infants raised in low foraging demand (LFD) or high foraging demand (HFD) conditions, owing to the fact that mothers undergoing variable foraging demand tend to exhibit inconsistent, erratic, and dismissive rearing behavior.[50] In a follow-up study 2.5 years later when the monkeys were in their adolescence, it was found that the VFD monkeys consistently exhibited a diminished capacity for affiliative social engagement when compared to LFD monkeys (e.g., they were less likely to initiate contact with unfamiliar monkeys and quicker to initiate aggression) and were consistently socially subordinate to the LFD monkeys when the two groups were placed together.[51] More recently, it was found that early life stress due to the variable foraging demand paradigm in bonnet macaques resulted in reduced corpus callosum size that correlated with fearful behavior when the animals were adults, and reduced volume in the hippocampus and middle and inferior temporal lobe gyri.[52] Or, an ongoing experiment of 231 rhesus monkeys that were randomly allocated at birth across three rearing conditions (mother rearing, peer rearing, and surrogate peer rearing[53]) found that lack of a secure attachment relationship in the early years engendered by adverse rearing conditions has detrimental long-term effects on health that are not compensated for by a normal social environment later in life.[54]

Such findings have bearings on the issue of whether children need to be loved, as they suggest that predictability in parental responsiveness can have significant behavioral and physiological consequences for the development of infant monkeys.

3.4 Neuroscientific Research in Animals and Humans

Psychobiologists, psychopharmacologists, and neuropsychologists have hypothesized that if adverse childhood experience such as lack of love can affect a child's development, then there should be a neurobiological basis for this. At least three kinds of research on animals and humans have found this to be so.

One type of study focuses on neurotransmitters such as serotonin (5HT), because serotonin is important for impulse control and because adverse childhood experience can result in the disregulation of the serotonin system. In the late 1970s, Asberg and Traskman-Bendz found that a group of depressed subjects with low cerebrospinal fluid (CSF) concentrations of 5-hydroxindoleacetic acid (5-HIAA), part of the serotonin system, had a history of serious suicide attempts.[55] Further research has found that low CSF 5-HIAA concentrations are also correlated with many other psychiatric disorders such as schizophrenia, alcoholism, Alzheimer's disease, anxiety disorders, personality disorders, bulimia; with men in the criminal justice system who have histories of violence and who are prone to recidivism; with adolescents who exhibit inappropriate or excessive aggression; and with men who exhibit unplanned violence of higher-than-average lifetime rates of aggression.[56]

At the same time, studies of rhesus monkeys found that adverse experience in childhood can result in the disregulation of the serotonin system, both in the short and the long term. In a number of studies using the peer-rearing paradigm, parentally neglected peer-reared monkeys exhibited lower CSF 5-HIAA concentrations than mother-reared monkeys.[57] In longitudinal studies, peer-reared subjects continued to exhibit lower CSF 5-HIAA concentrations than mother-reared subjects.[58] When the behavior of peer-reared monkeys was observed and compared to that of human beings and other monkeys with low CSF 5-HIAA, peer-reared monkeys exhibited similar deficits of impulse control. For example, during aggressive encounters, minor episodes of aggression were more likely to escalate to severe aggression with peer-reared monkeys. Or, peer-reared males and females were likely to exhibit aggression to infants, a behavior virtually never seen in mother-reared subjects. Finally, peer-reared females were more likely to give inadequate maternal care to their offspring.[59]

A second type of research focuses on the glucocorticoids (GC), the adrenal steroids secreted during stress. GCs, along with another hormone, catecholamines, are the frontline of defense for mammalian species under conditions that threaten homeostasis, conditions commonly referred to as stress. When a mammal is under stress, GCs and catecholamines serve to mobilize the production and distribution of energy substrates by increasing blood glucose level so that the mammal has additional energy to react to the stressors. Prolonged exposure of elevated levels of GC is dangerous to a mammal because the increased blood glucose level is achieved by inhibiting glucose transport in various peripheral tissues including certain locations in the hippocampus. When these areas do not receive glucose for a long time, they could atrophize and die. It is therefore in an organism's interest to limit such metabolically costly stress responses.[60]

Indeed, prolonged exposure to GC in human beings has been found to accelerate aging, cause memory loss, and result in susceptibility to other stressors.[61]

There is good evidence that the development of adrenal glucocorticoid responses to stress can be modified by early environmental events. For instance, rats that have been exposed to short periods of infantile stimulation or handling showed decreased pituitary-adrenal responsivity to stress, whereas rats that have been exposed to maternal separation, physical trauma, and endotoxin administration showed enhanced responsivity to stress.[62] Likewise, it has been found that infant monkeys reared by variable foraging demand (VFD) exhibited significantly elevated levels of CSF corticotropin-releasing-factor (CRF) concentrations compared to monkeys reared by mothers under consistently low or consistently high foraging demands.[63] In another study comparing mother-reared monkeys with nursery (or institution) reared monkeys, it was found that nursery infants had higher cortisol levels than did mother-reared infants.[64]

A third kind of research examines growth hormone (GH) secretion, because the loss of GH secretion had been observed by various researchers in the studies on psychosocial dwarfism discussed earlier, and because it has been found that certain interactions during childhood can affect this biochemical process. For example, Schanberg and colleagues restricted a group of preweanling rat pups from active tactile interaction with their mother by the separation procedure or by anesthetizing the mother.[65] Among other things, they found that there was a selective decrease in the GH levels, while the levels of other hormones that usually altered during stress, such as corticosterone, did not change. Studies on monkeys and premature newborn human infants found similar processes at work. For example, comparing nursery- (or institution-) reared monkeys with mother-reared monkeys, Champoux et al. found that nursery-reared infants had lower basal GH levels and that mother-reared infants exhibited higher GH levels in response to a pharmacological GH stimulation test.[66] Or, in their studies on premature newborn human infants, Scafidi et al. demonstrated that regular supplemental stroking and proprioceptive stimulation (flexion-extension of the limbs) increased the growth of preterm newborns by 20 percent, independent of caloric intake.[67]

Taken together, these research support and reinforce the idea that a child's psychological, social, cognitive, and even physical development can be seriously hampered if the child is not loved.

4. The Positive Effects of Love on a Child

There are two kinds of research that show the positive effects of love on a child: the correlation between secure attachment and positive development, and the correlation between warm parenting and positive development.

Drawing on Bowlby's and Ainsworth's work on attachment theory, researchers have assumed that secure attachment is a good proxy for love and they have investigated the longitudinal effects of secure attachment on a child's development. The general finding of this research is that children who were securely attached in infancy were later more sociable; more positive in their behavior toward others; less clinging and dependent on teachers; less aggressive and disruptive; more empathetic; more emotionally mature in their approach to school and other non-home settings; and showed greater persistence on problem solving. For example, in a number of studies, Sroufe et al. rated a group of children on the security of their attachments to their mothers at about age one, and then observed these children at preschool, school age, and early adolescence up to ages ten to eleven.[68] Sroufe et al. consistently found that securely attached infants were later more self-confident, had more favorable relationships with peers, engaged in more complex activities when playing in groups, expressed more positive emotions, and had a greater sense of their ability to accomplish things. Likewise, in a number of studies on teenagers' sense of well-being, it has been found that this is strongly correlated with the quality of their attachments to their parents (more so than with their peers).[69]

Other researchers take warmth and responsiveness to be a reliable indicator of parental love and they have investigated the long-term effects of warm and responsive parenting on a child. One finding is that children whose parents were warm and responsive performed better in cognitive tests.[70] For example, infants whose mothers gently directed their attention and encouraged them to manipulate the environment were more advanced in play, language, and problem-solving skills during the second year. Or, parents of children whose IQ showed a rising pattern with increasing age tended to respond warmly to the child's behavior, smiling when the child smiled, talking when the child spoke, and answering the child's questions.[71] Another finding is that children who were treated in a warm and responsive manner tended to be more altruistic and prosocial, and were more advanced in their moral understanding.[72] This is not true of children who were repeatedly scolded and punished.[73] Finally, a recent study shows that positive parental care can predict larger hippocampal volumes in children.[74] Ninety-two children between the ages of three and six and their parents were recruited and the parents' ability to nurture was rated by videoing and considering how the parents helped their children to cope with a mildly stressful task. Several years later, the children's hippocampus was measured using magnetic resonance imaging. It was found that children who were not depressed and who had nurturing, caring parents had a significantly larger hippocampus than children whose mothers were average or poor nurturers. This result is significant because the hippocampus is important for one's ability to cope with stress, for learning, and for memory, and because having a small hippocampus increases one's risk for depression, post-traumatic stress disorder, Alzheimer's disease, and other ailments. These two kinds of research therefore provide evidence that being loved can positively affect a child's development.

5. Conclusion

Being loved is a fundamental condition for children to pursue a good life, because children need to be loved in order to trust others, have positive conceptions of themselves, learn how to love others, and be motivated to obey commands; and they need to be able to do these things in order to develop adequately the fundamental capacities necessary for pursuing the basic activities. These theoretical explanations of why children need to be loved are supported and reinforced by a vast array of ongoing scientific research that shows the serious negative consequences if a person was not loved as a child and the positive consequences if a person was loved as a child. If all of this is right, we have good reasons to believe that being loved is a fundamental condition for children to pursue a good life. And if, as argued previously, human beings have human rights to the fundamental conditions for pursuing a good life, this provides us with a justification for why children have a right to be loved.

Here it is useful to consider whether adult human beings also have a right to be loved. This is a difficult question to answer because typically the kinds of love in which the adults are interested, namely romantic love and friendship, are different from parental love. Unlike parental love, part of the point of achieving romantic love and friendship is that one obtains these goods by one's own autonomous efforts. Given this, there may not be a right to be loved for adults.

The claim that children have a right to be loved presupposes that it is possible to have a duty to love. Before we can conclude that children have a right to be loved, we should show that such a duty is indeed possible. We should also answer questions such as who has this duty and how demanding this duty should be. I now turn toward these tasks.

4

The Possibility of a Duty to Love

1. The Commandability Objection

Children need to be loved in order to develop the fundamental capacities necessary for pursuing the basic activities. But can there be a duty to love? A well-known argument against the possibility of a duty to love is the commandability objection. It is generally accepted, after the Kantian point of "ought" implies "can," that to have a duty to do something, the action must be commandable, that is, one must be able to bring about the action with success or, as some would say, at will. Love, so this argument goes, is not commandable, because it is an emotion and emotions are not commandable. Therefore, there cannot be a duty to love. Kant, a proponent of this objection, says the following:

> Love is a matter of *feeling*, not of willing, and I cannot love because I *will* to, still less because I *ought* to (I cannot be constrained to love); so a *duty to love* is an absurdity.[1]

Similarly, Richard Taylor says,

> Love and compassion are passions, not actions, are therefore subject to no terms of duties or moral obligations. . . .

> Love, as a feeling, cannot be commanded, even by God,
> simply because it is not up to anyone at any given moment
> how he feels about his neighbor or anything else.[2]

If a duty to love were an absurdity, this would mean that there could not be a right of children to be loved, since this right requires that someone has a corresponding duty to love a child and therefore relies on a duty to love being a possibility.

Strictly speaking, feelings, emotions, and passions are different concepts. For example, emotions can include unfelt affects, whereas feelings by definition cannot.[3] Emotions can also include less passionate affections, whereas passions by definition cannot. There are other differences, but for our purposes, we can use the term emotion as an umbrella term for the other concepts.

Some philosophers have tried to respond to the commandability objection by arguing that love is not an emotion, but is instead an attitude. For example, Joseph Raz writes that some people

> believe that there cannot be a duty to love someone. The
> common reason for this supposed impossibility is that love
> is an emotion and the emotions cannot be commanded. This
> is a misguided view of both love and the emotions. Love is
> an attitude, not an emotion (though "being filled with love,"
> feeling "love swelling in one's bosom," and their like
> are—diverse—emotions).[4]

Love does involve having certain attitudes. As discussed previously, when we love someone, we should have the attitude of valuing the person we love for the person's sake. Other attitudes we should have when we love someone may include wanting to promote another person's well-being for the person's sake and wanting to be with the person.

However, love is not just having certain attitudes. Love also involves having certain emotions. The emotions associated with love, in particular, parental love, are wide ranging. They involve having, or the disposition to have, a strong sense of affection and warmth for the person we love, as well as a range of other emotions including grief, joy, anger, sadness, disappointment, and embarrassment. To simplify the discussion, let us take a strong sense of warmth and affection to be a crucial part of the emotional aspect of parental love at least sometimes during the course of loving another person. This strong sense of affection and warmth is stronger than a mere liking of the other person, and may cause one to be more excited in the presence of, and more sad in the absence of, the loved one. It is true that one can love someone without always feeling warmth and affection toward the loved one or always being excited in the loved one's presence. But there is typically a disposition toward having such emotions when one loves another. To see that love is not just having certain attitudes, but necessarily involves having these strong emotions, imagine a person, A, having all the attitudes typically associated with love for another person, B, such as valuing the other person and wanting to promote the other person's well-being for the other person's sake. Does it follow that A loves B? It does not seem so. A may just be a friendly colleague of B; or B may be someone whom A had loved but no longer loves, but with whom A still wishes to remain in touch. In both cases, A can have the attitudes associated with love for B such as valuing B for B's sake and wanting to promote B's well-being for B's sake, but not love B. If so, these cases show that love cannot be explained just in terms of attitudes. One way to distinguish these cases from a case in which one loves another is precisely the emotional aspect of love. In particular, when A loves B, A would also have a strong sense of affection and warmth toward B, which may make A want to be with B more often and make A sad when B is absent, whereas in the case where A is just a colleague of B or in the case where A is a former lover of B, A need not feel this strong sense of affection and warmth toward B. The emotional aspect of love therefore enables one to distinguish between love from the cases just discussed.

Given that love necessarily involves having certain emotions, the commandability objection cannot be refuted by arguing that love is an attitude. Nevertheless, the commandability objection can be met. The reason is that, contrary to the views of some, emotions generally, the emotional aspect of love in particular, and certainly the emotional aspect of parental love, are commandable. While I do not claim that emotions are always commandable, the claim that emotions are never commandable seems too strong. There are a number of ways by which human beings can bring about particular emotions, such as the emotional aspect of parental love, with success.

2. The Commandability of Emotions

It is often said that physical actions are voluntary and therefore commandable, but emotions are not voluntary and therefore not commandable. Indeed, it is often said that when we intend, for example, to raise our arm or to hold our breath, we can bring about such physical actions with success, while we cannot do this with emotions. For this reason, it is thought that love, because it is an emotion, is therefore also not commandable. The objection here is premised on the idea that emotions are never commandable. While emotions are not always commandable, there are at least three ways by which we can bring about particular emotions, including the emotional aspect of love, with success, when we intend to do so. Before outlining these three methods, let me make two preliminary points.

First, employing these methods will not bring us love proper, such as a loving relationship. However, by employing these methods we can bring about the emotional aspect of love, which is the aspect people have thought not to be commandable. Showing that this aspect is commandable only removes one objection against the commandability of love. There may be all sorts of reasons why love is not commandable in certain circumstances, such as when the other person is immoral. The point here is that the claim that emotions are never commandable is too strong.

Second, there are a number of competing theories of emotions. For example, there is the feeling theory of emotions proposed by William James, according to which an emotion is the feeling of certain bodily changes such as fluttering of the heart, epigastric activity, and shallow breathing, which are produced immediately by our perception of certain features of the world.[5] On this view, different types of emotions involve feelings of distinctive sets of bodily changes. For example, being angry is feeling certain bodily changes such as faster heart beats, and quicker breathing. An alternative to the feeling theory of emotions is the behavioral theory of emotions, according to which emotions are dispositions to act in a certain way.[6] On this view, a person who is angry would be predisposed to act in a certain manner such as pounding a table, picking a fight, or slamming a door. A third alternative, which many philosophers endorse, is the cognitive theory of emotions, according to which emotions are based on beliefs, or desires, or judgments. Robert Solomon says, for instance: "I cannot be angry if I do not believe that someone has wronged or offended me. Accordingly, we might say that anger involves a *moral* judgment . . . An emotion is an evaluative (or a 'normative') judgment, a judgment about my situation and about myself and/or about all other people."[7] There are also combined theories, such as Stuart Hampshire's view that emotions are a mix of feelings and cognitions. Hampshire writes: "Regret is a mode of unhappiness, or unpleasure, conjoined with a thought about the past."[8] Following writers such as Hampshire, I will assume that emotions are a complex of feelings, behavior, and cognitions.

A direct way by which we can bring about particular emotions with success, when we intend to do so, is through what we may call internal control, where we use reasons to motivate ourselves to have certain emotions. There are at least two methods of internal control. We can bring about a particular emotion with success by giving ourselves reasons to have particular emotions. For example, let us suppose that we are not in a good mood on a particular day and on the particular day, we by chance are also invited to attend a close friend's wedding. Knowing that our close friend would not want us to be in a bad mood and would instead want us to be joyful on her wedding day, we might tell ourselves that because it is a special occasion, we should not be in a bad mood and that we should instead be joyful. In giving ourselves a reason to be joyful and not to be in a bad mood, there is a good chance that we would not be in a bad mood, and would instead be joyful. Other examples might include a boxer telling himself to become angry in order to prepare for a fight, or Tolstoy telling himself that he should feel grief when attending his grandparent's funeral. By giving ourselves reasons to have particular emotions, we can bring about particular emotions with success, when we intend to do so.

Another method of internal control calls on us to reflect on the reasons why we tend to experience particular emotions in particular circumstances or toward particular persons. Through reflecting on these reasons, we might then decide to continue to have particular emotions, if the emotions are supported by good reasons; or to discontinue having particular emotions, if the emotions are not supported by good reasons. For example, in *The Sovereignty of Good*, Iris Murdoch gives an example where a mother-in-law feels contempt for her daughter-in-law even though the mother-in-law outwardly acts kindly toward the daughter-in-law. The mother-in-law then decides to reflect on the reasons why she feels contempt for the daughter-in-law, and realizes that the reason is because the mother-in-law is jealous that the daughter-in-law will threaten the mother-in-law's relationship with her son. After knowing the cause of her contempt for the daughter-in-law, the mother-in-law decides that her feelings of contempt for her daughter-in-law are not supported by good reasons. The mother-in-law then begins to view the daughter-in-law without her initial prejudice by perceiving the daughter-in-law as "not vulgar but refreshingly simple, not undignified but spontaneous, not noisy but gay, not tiresomely juvenile but delightfully youthful."[9] Through reflecting on the reasons why she feels a certain way toward the daughter-in-law and deciding that her emotions are not well-supported, the mother-in-law is able to develop affection for the daughter-in-law. To take another example, we might reflect on the reasons why we have friendly emotions toward a particular person and realize that some of the reasons are because the person appreciates us for who we are and because the person really cares about our well-being. Suppose we become engaged in an unpleasant dispute with the person. Having reflected on the reasons why we have friendly emotions toward the person, we might recall these reasons. In doing so, there is a good chance that we would be able to continue to have friendly emotions toward the person. In fact, there is evidence from neuroscience that we have the ability to focus on positive experiences and when we do so, this increases the chance of encoding these positive experiences into our long-term memories.[10]

A less direct, but nevertheless viable, way by which we can bring about particular emotions with success is deliberately to place ourselves in situations in which we know that we would probably experience particular emotions. We may call this the method of external control. For example, if we know that we tend to become angry when food is not available in the refrigerator or when we become trapped in traffic, then we know that we have a reasonable chance of becoming angry should we deliberately or inadvertently place ourselves in situations where food would not be available in the refrigerator, for instance, by not doing our shopping for the week; or where we would be trapped in traffic, such as by entering the traffic at a time when we know it is usually congested. Another example: if we know that we tend to feel pious when we attend church services, or if we know that we tend to feel compassion when we see homeless people, then we have a reasonable chance of feeling piety or compassion if we deliberately attend a church service or deliberately visit a homeless shelter. These examples demonstrate that one can bring about particular emotions with success by deliberately placing oneself in situations in which one knows that there is a reasonable chance one would experience particular emotions.

We have discussed ways of bringing about particular emotions in particular situations for particular persons. We can also cultivate our emotional capacities such that we would be more likely to have particular emotions in appropriate circumstances. As Aristotle says, cultivation involves habituation as well as reflection.[11] One strategy for cultivating certain emotions is to behave as if we have particular emotions. After some time and effort, it is likely that we would cultivate the capacities for these emotions. For example, if we wish to cultivate our capacity for joy, we might begin by behaving as if we are joyful. We might smile, whistle, sing, skip and hop, shout hurrah, and engage in various forms of behavior that are associated with joy. Through engaging in these forms of behavior repeatedly over time, it is likely that we would cultivate the capacity for joy. Indeed, Augustine observes that through enacting the behavior associated with religious rituals, we seem to increase our capacity for religious feelings:

> For when men pray they do with the members of their bodies what befits suppliants—when they bend their knees and stretch their hands, or even prostrate themselves, and whatever else they do visibly, although their invisible will and the intention of their heart is known to God. Nor does He need these signs for the human mind to be laid bare to Him. But in this way a man excites himself to pray more and to groan more humbly and more fervently . . . although these motions of the body cannot come to be without a motion of the mind preceding them, when they have been made, visibly and externally, that invisible inner motion which caused them is itself strengthened. And in this manner the disposition of the heart which preceded them in order that they might be made, grows stronger because they are made.[12]

Another strategy for cultivating our emotional capacities is by repeatedly using the method of external control, such as by repeatedly placing ourselves in situations in which we know that we would probably experience particular emotions. Using our previous examples, let us suppose that we know that attending church services and visiting homeless shelters often elicit emotions of piety and compassion in us. To cultivate our capacities for such emotions, we might repeatedly visit such places. In doing so, there is a good chance that we would cultivate these emotional capacities.

A third strategy for cultivating our emotional capacities is by repeatedly using the method of internal control described previously, such as by repeatedly using reasons to motivate us to have certain emotions. For example, let us suppose that we believe that life is more enjoyable when we have a joyful disposition, and we believe therefore that having an enjoyable life is a good reason why we should cultivate our capacity for joy. If we repeatedly remind ourselves of this reason, there is a good chance that we would cultivate the capacity for joy.

Finally, the method of cultivating emotional capacities involves not merely a repetition of internal and external control over time, but also deep reflection on the reasons why we tend to have particular emotions and whether we have good reasons for continuing or not continuing to have these emotions. For example, let us suppose that a person is easily angered and upon reflecting on why he is so easily angered realizes that the reason is because his anger allows him to intimidate others into submitting to his desires. He may decide that using anger to intimidate others is not a good way of getting things done. He may also decide that he does not want to be the kind of person who is so easily angered. If so, and if he repeatedly uses these reasons to motivate himself not to become so easily angered, there is a good chance that he would cultivate a disposition where he would not be so easily angered. This suggests that to cultivate our emotional capacities, we may be required to evaluate critically some of our fundamental values, and to alter some of our ingrained character traits, such as becoming more reflective than superficial, or becoming more altruistic than self-interested. Such cultivation can be difficult. However, the cultivation of physical abilities such as learning how to play the piano or to sail a boat is often equally difficult. Yet people acquire these capacities nevertheless. Moreover, in all these methods, the objective is not just to have the appearance of the emotions appropriate for the circumstance, but actually to have the genuine emotions appropriate for the circumstance.

I shall now argue that the three methods just discussed are also applicable to the emotional aspect of parental love.

3. The Commandability of the Emotional Aspect of Love

For instance, we can bring about the emotional aspect of parental love with success using the two methods of internal control. We can give ourselves reasons to feel warmth and affection for a child. Many reasons are possible, but a good reason is that children need this emotional aspect of love in order to develop certain fundamental capacities necessary to pursue the basic activities.[13] Or, we can reflect on the reasons why we tend to feel a certain way toward a particular child.[14] Perhaps we do not initially like a child, and, upon reflection, we realize that our antipathy toward the child is due to the fact that the child was unplanned and that the child was born at a time when we already had too many children.[15] We might then recognize that this is not the fault of the child and that therefore this is not a good reason for disliking the child. If we then begin to see the child without this initial prejudice, there is a chance that we would be able to bring about warmth and affection for the child.

Moreover, we can bring about the emotional aspect of love for a child with success through external control by deliberately placing ourselves in situations in which we would have a good chance to feel affection and warmth for the child. For example, if we know that getting enough sleep helps us to be more affectionate and warm toward the child, then we might make sure that we have enough sleep each night so that we would be more loving toward the child. Or suppose we know that being around other parents who are loving toward their children will help us to be more affectionate and warm toward the child; we may then try to arrange more play dates with these parents as a means to help us to be more loving toward the child.

Finally, we can cultivate our capacity to give affection and warmth for a child. We can do this, for example, through behavioral inducement. We might try to act affectionately and warmly toward a child, even if we do not initially feel these emotions for the child. By repeatedly doing so, there is a good chance that we would cultivate the capacity to feel affection and warmth for the child. Alternatively, we can try to cultivate this capacity through external control. If getting enough sleep and having play dates with parents who are loving toward their children help us to feel more affectionate and warm toward the child, then we might repeatedly do these things as a means to bring about affection and warmth for a child. Lastly, we might try to cultivate this emotional capacity through internal control. For example, we might repeatedly tell ourselves that this child needs to be loved as a means to get ourselves to love the child. Or, we might repeatedly reflect on the reasons why we do not feel love for the child, and determine whether our reasons are justified. In doing so repeatedly, there is a good chance that we would develop the emotional capacity to love the child.

The various methods are compatible with different theories of emotions. For example, the method of internal control can be used to achieve the commandability of our emotions if the cognitive theory of emotions were the correct theory of emotions. The method of external control is compatible with the behavioral theory of emotions as well as the feeling theory of emotions. For example, when we go to a homeless shelter to feel more compassion, we would be directly affecting the behavioral aspect of compassion in that the homeless shelter might predispose us to perform actions associated with compassion, such as being helpful. On the feeling theory, we would be placing ourselves in an environment that would indirectly influence the feeling component of our emotion in that our heart might flutter more being at a homeless shelter. As we have taken emotions to be a composite of feelings, attitudes, and behavior, all three methods are necessary for the commandability of emotions and the emotional aspect of parental love.

Again, we should not think that the entire aspect of parental love is commandable if we just employ the three methods. The dimensions of love are complex and love is not just an emotion, but involves having appropriate attitudes and behavior over a long period of time. Nevertheless, if these three methods can sometimes enable us to bring about the emotional aspect of parental love, then the claim that the emotional aspect of parental love is never commandable is too strong.

4. Reasonable Success and Guaranteed Success

Some people might draw a distinction between bringing about an action with reasonable success and bringing it about with guaranteed success. Supposing further that an action is commandable if and only if we can bring it about with guaranteed success, then emotions such as parental love would not be commandable, because it seems that they can at best be brought about only with reasonable, but not guaranteed, success. Indeed, visiting homeless shelters in order to feel compassion and telling ourselves to be joyful at our friend's wedding are all examples of bringing about particular emotions with reasonable, but not guaranteed, success, since we cannot guarantee that we will definitely experience particular emotions just by performing the activities suggested in these examples. Given this, some people might argue that at best there is a duty to *try* to love a child but not a duty to love the child.

First, even if there were just a duty to try to love a child, this would not undermine the idea of a right of children to be loved, if one accepts that rights are grounds of duties, that is, rights are reasons for the duties to which they give rise.[16] On this understanding of rights, a right to X can exist whether there is a duty to X or just a duty to try to X, since the right can be a reason for either duty. If so, there can be a right of children to be loved even if there were just a duty to try to love a child, since this right can be a reason for either a duty to love or a duty to try to love.

Second, guaranteed success is not necessary for an action to be deemed commandable. If it were, it would imply that many physical actions, which are paradigm examples of what is commandable, would not be commandable. For instance, more complex physical actions such as walking and speaking would not be commandable, because it is a fact that we occasionally fail to succeed in such actions. We might trip and fall and we might become tongue-tied. In fact, even more simple physical actions such as raising our arms or holding our breaths would not be commandable, because it is a fact that we sometimes fail to succeed in these actions. Our arms might be too tired and we might be too hyperventilated to be able to hold our breaths.

Some people might reply that guaranteed success can still be necessary for an action to be deemed commandable, if we add the clause "provided certain reasonable background conditions exist." For example, under ordinary circumstances, such as if our arm has not fallen asleep, if no one is holding our arm down, if our arm is not too tired, then because certain reasonable background conditions exist, we would be able to raise our arm with guaranteed success. Under ordinary circumstances, such as if we had not just run a hundred-meter sprint, we would be able to hold our breath with guaranteed success.

However, the clause "provided that certain reasonable background conditions exist" is too vague. On an ordinary understanding of it, even if reasonable background conditions were to obtain for a particular action, it seems that there is still a chance, however minute, that the action could fail. For example, in the case where we try to raise our arm, even if certain ordinary background conditions obtain, such as our arm has not fallen asleep, no one is holding our arm down, and our arm is not too tired, it remains possible that we can fail to raise our arm with guaranteed success.

Suppose instead we understand the clause "provided that certain reasonable background conditions exist" to mean that all possible factors that could defeat an action are rendered impotent so that an action really is guaranteed to succeed. On this understanding, someone would have to provide an argument as to why we could not speak about guaranteed success regarding emotions such as parental love. Indeed, if all possible factors that could prevent a parent from loving a child are rendered impotent, what reasons would be left for thinking that the parent could still fail to love the child?

In any case, it is not necessary that in order for one to have a duty to perform some action, V, V must be something that one can bring about with guaranteed success, supposing that certain reasonable background conditions obtain. Various examples illustrate this point. Professional basketball players have a duty to make free throws, and ordinarily, they can do so with ease. However, it is a fact that no basketball player can guarantee, even under ordinary circumstances, that they would make every basket they attempt. Sometimes they may just miss. Still, they have a duty to make free throws. Another example: professional chefs have a duty to make good dishes. Ordinarily, making good dishes is something that professional chefs can do with ease. Again, however, it is a fact that no chef can guarantee, even under ordinary circumstances, that the dishes they make will be good. Still, they have a duty to make good dishes. Given that there are these duties, it follows that it is not necessary that in order to have a duty to V, V must be something one can bring about with guaranteed success, supposing that certain reasonable background conditions obtain.

At this point, someone might accept that we can sometimes bring about emotions, including the emotional aspect of parental love, with success using the methods discussed. However, the notions of reasonable and guaranteed success are probability notions. Would a low probability of success mean that there could not be a duty to love?

It is difficult to offer a precise figure for the probability of being able to produce emotions such as the emotional aspect of parental love with success, since the probability will vary from person to person and from circumstance to circumstance. However, there is no reason to believe that, generally speaking, the probability of success would be low, because having emotions such as the emotional aspect of parental love is a common enough experience. As such, it seems that we have a fairly good chance of bringing it about if we put in the required efforts. We might take as a parallel that making free throws in basketball is a percentage shot. The probability of success will vary among persons and in various circumstances. However, because making such a shot is common enough, it seems that we have a fairly good chance of making it with some consistency if we practiced regularly. This said, let us suppose that the probability of our succeeding in producing emotions such as the emotional aspect of parental love remains low, even after employing the three methods. This still would not undermine the idea of a duty to love. Suppose that we find a drowning person who requires cardiopulmonary resuscitation and the probability of our success is low, for instance, because we get nervous and we are not very strong. Even so, it seems that we have a duty to provide cardiopulmonary resuscitation. Likewise, government agencies and aid workers in developing countries have a duty to reduce poverty and prevent deaths from diseases, even if the probability of their succeeding is low.

There will of course be cases where a person's emotional capacities are so damaged that there is no possibility of the person's acquiring the emotional aspect of parental love no matter what the person does.[17] In such cases, we should accept that the person will not have the duty directly to provide the kind of love that children need. However, this person would still have the duty to find someone who can provide this kind of love for a particular child. That is, it is important to distinguish between the source of the duty and the capacity of the dutybearer. Given that the duty stems from some fact in the world, namely, the fact that a child needs to be loved in order to develop properly, the duty would remain, even if certain people lack the capacity to fulfill the duty. The distinction between the source of the duty and the capacity of the dutybearer is particularly useful in the case of a parent who tries hard to love a child but, nevertheless, fails to have the appropriate emotions. One might say that the person fulfills the duty partially, and is not blameworthy, because the person tried his or her best. Nevertheless, if the child's need for love is not met, then one should conclude that the source of the duty remains. Consider an analogy: suppose I borrow a thousand dollars from you. I repay part of it, try my best to get a job, but through no fault of my own, I am simply unable to pay you back in full. From the perspective of the dutybearer, one may say that I have partially fulfilled my duty, and that given the circumstances, I am not blameworthy. However, from the perspective of the source of the duty, you are still owed the money.

5. Direct and Indirect Commandability

Other people may distinguish between direct and indirect commandability and may argue that emotions and love have not been shown to be directly commandable. It may be the case that the methods of internal and external control are more indirect ways of bringing about emotions such as love. However, a rationale of the third method of commandability, cultivation, is to help us bring about appropriate emotions and love directly or at will in appropriate circumstances. For example, suppose that we tried to cultivate the capacity for joy. A rationale for doing this would be so that we can bring about joy directly or at will in appropriate circumstances. As an analogy, we might consider a professional musician who practices playing a certain piece of music so that she can bring about this music directly or at will in appropriate circumstances.

Even if emotions such as love are only indirectly commandable, duties do not always require that an action be directly commandable. If Lester borrows five dollars from Mary, and therefore has a duty to repay Mary five dollars, a direct way of repaying Mary would be if he gives her five dollars. But lacking five dollars to repay Mary, he borrows five dollars from another person. In this case, he would be taking indirect steps to fulfill his duty to Mary. But doing so does not mean that he has not fulfilled his duty toward Mary. If this is correct, then duties do not always require that an action is commandable directly.

6. The Commandability of Attitudes

Parental love also involves having certain attitudes. In addition, some people believe that emotions have attitudinal components. Given this, it might be asked whether attitudes are commandable, since if they are not, then some aspect of parental love would not be commandable, and we would again face a version of the commandability objection. A reason for raising this question is that attitudes are based on beliefs, and it seems that beliefs are not commandable since they are based on facts, and we cannot just decide what facts to believe.[18] For example, we cannot just decide that $2 + 2 = 5$.

This issue need not concern us. Even if the factual aspect of an attitude is not commandable, the valuation aspect of an attitude is commandable. For our purpose, it is sufficient that the valuation aspect may be required as a matter of duty. Most, if not all, attitudes are made up of facts and values. For example, an attitude that animals that are as sentient as some human beings should be treated with equal consideration is made up of certain facts, such as that some animals are as sentient as some human beings—and certain values, such as that given equal sentience, such animals should be treated with equal consideration as some human beings. An implication of this fact-value distinction is that two people faced with the same facts may value the facts differently. For instance, a different person faced with the same facts may hold the attitude that while we should not be cruel to such animals, we should not treat them with equal consideration as some human beings.

The valuation aspect of an attitude is commandable in the same way emotions are. For example, we can bring about certain attitudes with success through internal control, such as by giving ourselves reasons to value a fact in a certain way, or through reflecting on the reasons why we tend to value a certain fact in a certain way. Let us suppose that we want to have a more positive attitude toward the environment. We might tell ourselves all the positive things that a better environment can bring us, such as better air, nicer landscape, and more habitable climates. In doing so, there is a good chance that we would have a more positive attitude toward the environment. In addition, we can also bring about certain attitudes with success through external control by deliberately placing ourselves in certain situations. If we want to have a more negative attitude toward the fact that adequate help is not being provided for some people in inner cities, we can deliberately place ourselves in such locations. In doing so, there is a good chance that we would develop a more negative attitude toward the fact that adequate help is not being provided for certain people. Finally, we can cultivate our capacity to have certain attitudes, for example, through behavioral inducement, where we would act as if we do have the attitude. This is a rationale behind positive thinking programs. We can also cultivate our capacity to have certain attitudes through repeatedly using the methods of internal and external control.

For our purpose, the valuation aspect of our attitude toward a child is what may be required as a matter of duty, because, as I argued previously, to feel loved, children need to be valued for their own sake. A child is born having certain temperament and genetic makeup and there is not much we can do to alter them. But we can still try to value the child positively. For example, faced with a child who is learning to eat, we can decide to regard the child as happy and persevering rather than as messy and annoying. Faced with a child who does not speak much, we can decide to regard the child as quiet and shy as opposed to unresponsive and uninterested. As with bringing about emotions, the objective is not just to have the appearance of attitudes appropriate for the circumstance or false valuations, but actually to have genuine and correct attitudes appropriate for the circumstance. In general, we can bring about positive attitudes for a child with success in the same way we can bring about general attitudes with success through internal and external control and through cultivation. Even though love involves having certain attitudes, love as an attitude is also commandable.

7. The Pretended Love Objection

The claim that parental love is commandable may raise the question of what would happen if someone pretends to love a child, that is, if someone behaves as if he loves a child when in fact he does not. For example, some nannies, nurses, or stepparents may behave as if they love a child even though they do not. Would their pretense fulfill the duty to love a child?

Such a case should be distinguished from the case discussed earlier, where someone is genuinely trying to love another person but fails to bring about the real emotions. As I noted, in that case, the person may have partially fulfilled his duty to love the child. In this case, there are several issues that are worth distinguishing. One issue is whether it is possible for anyone to pretend to love a child to such an extent that a child never finds out about this pretense. This seems highly unlikely, for at least three reasons.[19] First, as a child gets older, the child typically acquires the ability to distinguish between real and fake love. Indeed, there is evidence that infants as young as four months old prefer to listen to singing that is directed at them over singing that is not directed at them, and, importantly, this preference is correlated with the loving tone of the voice.[20] An explanation for why a child acquires such an ability is that a child needs this ability in order to distinguish between those who would really promote his well-being versus those who would not, and it seems reasonable to assume that those who would provide a child with real love are typically those who would actually promote his well-being, or at least, who would want to promote his well-being, whereas those who would provide a child only with fake love are probably those who would not promote his well-being, or at least, who are not really interested in promoting his well-being. Given that a child typically acquires this ability to distinguish between real and fake love, it would be more and more difficult to succeed in pretending to love a child as the child gets older. Second, unless the child lives in isolation, one would also have to convince those who come into contact with the child that one's love is real, even though it is in fact fake. Otherwise, the child may learn from them that the love he is receiving is not real love. Clearly, this is also difficult. Third, it seems a real possibility that while pretending to love a child, one develops real love for the child. This may occur because in order for pretended love to be convincing, one has to adopt the appropriate attitudes and emotions toward the child over a long period of time. However, doing so can affect one's character to the extent that one may actually adopt these attitudes and emotions toward the child. Obviously, if this occurs, then the child would be receiving real love, and pretended love would no longer be an issue. To prevent this from occurring, one would have continuously to make sure that one is just pretending, which can be difficult, since one must always stop oneself from really loving the child while still being able to convince the child and others that one's love is real, even though it is in fact fake. This seems an onerous task. For these reasons, then, it seems practically very difficult for one to pretend to love a child to the extent that no one would know that one's love is not real.

Another issue is, supposing that someone could pretend to love a child to this extent, would a child be able to develop adequately from such a pretense? This is an empirical question. I suggest that the answer is likely to be no. The reason is that an aspect of developing adequately is developing the capacity to differentiate between genuine and fake love, since people who pretend to love us are less likely to promote our well-being for our sake than people who genuinely love us. If someone could fool a child into believing that he loved the child when in fact he did not and the child was unable to figure out that this was a pretense, it seems that the child would have not acquired the capacity to differentiate between genuine and fake love. In other words, there appears to be a Catch 22 here.[21] If the pretense fails, the parent has violated his duty to love. But the parent has also violated his duty if the pretense succeeds, since the pretense could only succeed if the child failed to develop a capacity to distinguish real from fake love that is necessary to pursue a good life.

Finally, there is the normative issue of whether providing someone with pretended love would fulfill the duty to love, supposing that the person never found out that the love was fake. In my view, this would not fulfill the duty to love, just as giving someone fake money, when you owed the person money, and even if he (or anyone else) never found out that the money was fake, would not fulfill the duty you owe to him. Consider a different example: suppose that you borrowed a van Gogh from a wealthy friend. Suppose further that you know that your friend does not care very much for this piece of artwork; and that if you were to give her a fake van Gogh she would not notice and would just put it in a storage room and never look at it again. It seems that you would not have fulfilled your duty to her even if she never found out that you gave her a fake van Gogh.

8. The Motivation Objection

Some people might argue that really to love a person, we must be motivated to do so for the person's sake. To have a duty to love a person means, however, that we would not be motivated to love the person for the person's sake, but for the sake of duty. Therefore, to have a duty to love a person means that we do not really love the person. On this view, employing the three methods discussed earlier as a way to love someone means that we do not really love that individual. We may call this the motivation objection.

The motivation objection has its root in critiques of Kant's moral theory. Kant argues that an action has moral worth only if it is done for the sake of duty.[22] Critics of Kant argue that at least in personal relationships, we should act out of a direct concern for the others, but a Kantian agent cannot do this, because he is acting out of a concern for a moral principle, in particular, the duty. In recent years, this criticism has been extended to all impartial ethical theories. For example, Michael Stocker asks us to imagine that we are hospitalized and receive a visit from Smith, who alleges that he is our friend:

> You are very bored and restless and at loose ends when Smith comes in once again. You are now convinced more than ever that he is a fine fellow and a real friend—taking so much time to cheer you up, traveling all the way across town, and so on. You are so effusive with your praise and thanks that he protests that he always tries to do what he thinks is his duty, what he thinks will be best. You at first think he is engaging in a polite form of self-depreciation, relieving the moral burden. But the more you two speak, the more clear it becomes that he was telling the literal truth: that it is not essentially because of you that he came to see you, not because you are friends, but because he thought it his duty, perhaps as a fellow Christian or Communist or whatever, or simply because he knows of no one more in need of cheering up and no one easier to cheer up.[23]

Stocker argues that Smith is not really a friend, because Smith appears to be motivated to see you for the sake of some impartial rule but not for your sake. Smith, as it were, is doing the right thing but for the wrong reason. This, according to Stocker, shows that impartial ethical theories cannot adequately account for personal ethics.

Bernard Williams makes a similar point using a different anecdote. He asks us to suppose that two people are drowning, one of which is the rescuer's wife, and the rescuer can save only one of them. Williams points out that while most people would agree that the rescuer is permitted to save his wife, impartial ethical theories have the implication that this is justified because there is some impartial rule that says that whenever a person is in a situation of this kind, the person is permitted to save his wife. As Williams famously remarks, this is "one thought too many."[24] For Williams, someone who has an impartial thought in such a circumstance has failed to respect the personal-impersonal divide. The person who saves the wife, because of the impartial rule is not doing it only for his wife's sake, which Williams thinks he should. Since impartial ethics by definition require us to think impartially, Williams argues that they cannot explain why it is permissible to do something without any further impartial thoughts on the matter.

The rationale behind the motivation objection is based on three ideas, two of which are uncontroversial. The first uncontroversial idea is that we should do the right thing for the right reason or motive. A right action that is done for the wrong reason or motive has less moral worth than an action done for the right reason or motive. An illustration may be Kant's shopkeeper who should give correct change to his customers because it is the right thing to do, and not because it is good for him.

The second, also uncontroversial idea is that in personal relationships, we should be motivated to do things for the other person's sake. We would not be motivated to do something for the other person's sake if, for example, we were motivated to perform the action out of self-interest. If we were motivated to love another person because the relationship would benefit our career, then we would love someone for our own sake instead of for the other person's sake, and this would be loving someone for the wrong reason.

The third idea, which is controversial, is that in personal relationships, when we are motivated to do the right thing or when we are motivated to do our duty, this inevitably undermines the relationship, because as with being motivated to do things out of self-interest, we would not be motivated to do things for the other person's sake. We would be motivated instead to do it for the sake of an act's being a right thing to do or for the sake of duty. This is the point made by Stocker and Williams. The idea is controversial and false for the following reason. It presupposes that being motivated to do the right thing or for the sake of duty and being motivated to do something for the other person's sake are always distinct motivations. It is true that sometimes when we act for the sake of duty, we do not act for the sake of the other person. For example, a postman may deliver mail to us everyday just because it is his duty, and not because he is doing it for our sake. A father who is a teacher in his daughter's class may help his daughter with schoolwork in class because this is his duty as a teacher rather than because he is her father. But the two motives need not always be distinct. Sometimes, being motivated to do the right thing is being motivated to do it for the other person's sake. The content of the duty is just to be motivated for the other person's sake. For example, in the case of loving a child, being motivated to do the right thing is just being motivated to give the child love for the child's sake. In Stocker's example, being motivated to do the right thing is just being motivated to visit Smith for Smith's sake. In Williams's case, being motivated to do the right thing is just being motivated to save the wife's life for her sake. We could even claim that in these cases, there is a duty to be motivated for the other person's sake, and people who are not thus motivated would not have fulfilled their duty. If being motivated to do the right thing and being motivated to do things for another person's sake are just the same motivation in these cases, then the motive of duty and the motive of love would not conflict since they are one and the same. If so, the motivation objection would not undermine the idea of a duty to love.

However, some people might believe that being motivated to do the right thing and being motivated to do things for another person's sake are always distinct motivations. Even so, duty and love can still be compatible. For duty and love to be incompatible, we would have to assume that we cannot be motivated by both motives at the same time. For example, we would have to assume that a person who is motivated to love another person for the sake of duty cannot at the same time be motivated to love the other person for the other person's sake. But this assumption is false. We can be motivated to do something for the sake of duty, and, at the same time, for the person's sake. In Stocker's example, Smith could have been motivated to see you both for the sake of duty and because he wants to see you. To use another example, a professional cook who receives a visit from a friend while at work can be motivated to prepare delicious dishes for his friend both because he has a duty to do so, since he is hired to do so, and because he wants to do it for his friend.

Some people might respond that in personal relationships, a person should only have one motive for action, the motive to do things for the other person's sake. People who act out of additional motives, including a motive of duty, would, on this view, be violating a normative requirement, and the relationship would be undermined. This might be the rationale behind Williams's point that an additional impartial motive is one thought too many, because in personal relationships, we should just have one motive.

The claim here could be that in personal relationships there is a "duty" to have only one motive. Given this "duty," people who are motivated to act out of more than one motive in personal relationships would be violating a normative requirement. However, if this is the claim, then it is self-defeating. We are supposing that being motivated to do the right thing and being motivated to do things for the other person's sake are distinct motives. Suppose we do try to fulfill the "duty" to have only one motive, in particular, being motivated to do things for the other person's sake. In this case, we would be acting from two motives, the motive of the duty and the motive of doing things for the other person's sake. But acting out of two motives violates the "duty" to act out of only one motive. Hence, if the argument is that there is a "duty" to be motivated only for the other person's sake, then given the supposition that the motive of duty and the motive of doing things for the other person's sake are distinct, this argument would be self-defeating.

The claim could instead be that in personal relationships we should just not think impartially. We should do things for the other person just because it is the other person, and not because there is some impartial rule that tells us to do so. However, even in personal relationships, it is morally necessary to think impartially. We might consider a modified version of Williams's example where the wife is not drowning and is only slightly injured, while the other person is still drowning. It seems that the rescuer may be required to try to save the stranger instead of attending to his wife's minor wounds. If the rescuer chooses instead to attend to his wife's minor wounds, the rescuer may be blamed for having failed in his duty to try to save a drowning person. If this is correct, to reach such a conclusion, it seems that the rescuer would have had to have considered the situation impartially in order to recognize that his wife and the stranger are not in the same predicament. But if it is morally necessary in this case that the rescuer considered the situation impartially so that he would arrive at a correct moral decision, in the case where the wife and the stranger are both drowning, it seems also morally necessary that the rescuer considers that situation impartially. Indeed, it may be because, when viewed impartially, the stranger and the wife are in the same situation, except that the wife is in a special relationship with the rescuer, and because we think that this fact ought to be given some moral weight, that it seems morally permissible for the rescuer to save his wife. If this is correct, then even in personal relationships it is morally necessary to think impartially.

The claim that being motivated to do things for the other person's sake should be the only motive for action in personal relationships can be cogent if we drop the requirement that being motivated for the sake of duty and being motivated for the sake of the other person are distinct motivations. Once this requirement is dropped, then we can cogently say that there is a duty to act out of only one motivation in personal relationships, since we can view the motive to do our duty in this case as just the motive to do things for the sake of the other person. However, dropping this requirement means that duty and love are compatible. Hence, on the most plausible interpretation of this claim, it does not undermine the idea of a duty to love.

Given that being motivated to do what is right (that is, for the sake of duty) and being motivated to do things for the other person can be the same motivation, and given that even if they are distinct, one can be motivated by both motives at the same time, the motivation objection does not undermine the idea of a duty to love.

9. Conclusion

In this chapter, I considered and rejected several objections that tried to undermine the possibility of a duty to love. Supposing that my arguments are successful, they provide further support for the claim that children have a right to be loved.

There remain some unanswered questions regarding this right. In particular, who are the correlative dutybearers and what are the limits of their obligation? Previously, I argued that the right of children to be loved is a human right. A number of writers believe that human rights are typically rights against all other able persons in appropriate circumstances. This implies that every able person in appropriate circumstances has a duty to love every child. Some, however, may find this implication counterintuitive, especially because the common practice today is to assign child-caring duties primarily to biological parents. In addition, some may ask whether the duty to love is too demanding. I shall now address these questions.

The Duty to Love: Who Has It and to What Extent?

1. Biological Parents as Sole Dutybearers?

Suppose that children have a right to be loved. Who has the corresponding duty to love a child? A natural response might be that this duty belongs only to the biological parents. After all, the biological parents caused the child to come into existence. Since people are generally responsible for the consequences of their actions, one might think that the (mutually consenting and foreseeing) biological parents should be responsible for the consequences of bringing a child into existence. In fact, many do think that the fact that the biological parents caused their children to come into existence is a reason for assigning at least some child-caring duties to them. For example, Kant writes in the *Metaphysics of Morals*, "[T]he act of procreation [is] one by which we have brought a person into the world without his consent and on our own initiative, for which deed the parents incur an obligation to make the child content with his condition so far as they can."[1] Similarly, Frederick Olafson argues that parents are responsible for the predictable and avoidable consequences of their actions.[2] Hence, if two adults, recognizing the possibility that a child might be conceived, have sexual relations and such a child is indeed born nine months later, then, according to Olafson, they are responsible for its existence and have to care for it. Or, as Sidgwick states, "the parent, being the cause of the child's existing in a helpless condition, would be indirectly the cause of the suffering and death that would result to it if neglected."[3]

It seems correct that the biological parents should incur some responsibility as a result of causing a child to come into existence. I shall shortly explain the special role that biological parents should play in discharging the duty to love a child. Yet we should resist the thought that biological parents have the *sole* duty to love the child whom they have brought into existence. One reason is that this implies that if the biological parents of a given child were dead, no one else would have the duty to love the child. However, it seems that someone would have the duty to love a child if the child's biological parents became unavailable. Another reason is that while it may sometimes be the case that being responsible for one's own actions means having the sole duty to rectify the consequences caused by one's own actions, this is not always the case. Suppose that Jane pushes Kevin into a river, while Larry is just walking by, and Kevin starts to drown. Since people are responsible for their action, Jane is responsible for this action. It does not follow, however, that Jane has the sole duty to try to rescue Kevin. Suppose that Jane has also fallen into the river and has in fact drowned, so that Larry is the only person present. Even though Larry is not responsible for causing Kevin to be in the water, Larry typically has a duty to try to rescue Kevin, either by trying to bring Kevin out of the water, or at least calling for help, given that the harm to Kevin would be great if Larry did not act. This suggests that it is not true that being responsible for one's actions always means having the sole duty to rectify the consequences caused by one's own actions. There are good reasons to think the duty to love a child is like this case, since the harm to the child could also be great if someone did not take up this responsibility when the biological parents are unavailable. Given this, even though biological parents caused their children to come into existence and are responsible for the consequences of their action, this does not mean that the duty to love is solely theirs.

An alternative response might be that biological parents have the sole duty in the first instance; and when they are deceased or become unable to discharge their duty, then someone else would be required to take up this duty. For instance, with respect to general duties—duties toward all that everyone has—Robert Goodin has argued that

> our general duties toward people are sometimes more effectively discharged by assigning special responsibility for that matter to some particular agent . . . Suppose that someone has been left without a protector. Either he has never been assigned one, or else the one he was assigned has proven unwilling or unable to provide the sort of protection it was his job to provide. Then, far from being at the mercy of everyone, the person becomes the "residual responsibility" of all.[4]

Following this line of thought, one might think that the duty to love a child is a general duty that is more effectively discharged when we assign special responsibility to the biological parents in the first instance. Then, if and when the biological parents become unable to discharge their duty, someone else would be required to take up this duty. This proposal is better than the previous one in that it can explain how someone else would have a duty to love a child if the biological parents became unavailable. However, this proposal seems to imply that other people have this duty only when the biological parents are not available.

I believe that an even stronger conclusion can be reached. Not only do others have a duty to love a child if and when the biological parents become unavailable, every able person in appropriate circumstances has a duty to promote a child's being loved *even when the biological parents are available.*

2. Duty to Love as a Duty of All

How can every able person in appropriate circumstances have a duty to promote a child's being loved even when the biological parents are available? Earlier I argued that the right of children to be loved is a human right. A number of writers believe that human rights are rights against all able persons in appropriate circumstances. For example, Maurice Cranston says that

> To speak of a universal right is to speak of a universal duty . . . Indeed, if this universal duty were not imposed, what sense could be made of the concept of a universal human right?[5]

Or, Alan Gewirth says that

> The universality of a positive [human] right is . . . a matter of everyone's always having, as a matter of principle . . . the duty to act in accord with the right when the circumstances arise that require such action and when he then has the ability to do so, this ability including consideration of the cost to himself.[6]

If human rights are rights against all able persons in appropriate circumstances and if the right of children to be loved is a human right, this suggests that the right of children to be loved is a right against all able persons in appropriate circumstances. In other words, it suggests that every able person in appropriate circumstances has a duty to promote a child's being loved.

But exactly what does it mean for everyone to have the duty to promote a child's being loved? As we have seen from Chapter Three, loving a child is best done only if a few individuals are assigned to do so for each child. Given this, I suggest that we distinguish between primary and associate dutybearers and have the following division of labor with respect to this duty: Under normal circumstances, biological parents would have the primary duty directly to love their children, while all other able persons would have associate duties to help the primary dutybearers successfully discharge their duties.

Biological parents should typically be the primary dutybearers for the following reason: Usually, when there is a general duty that everyone has but where it would be impractical if everyone tried to fulfill that duty at the same time, a primary dutybearer might be assigned using such criteria as responsibility, proximity, ability, and motivation. For example, consider the general duty to help someone who is drowning. In theory, every able person has this duty, although in practice, it would be impractical if everyone tried to fulfill this duty. In this case, the primary responsibility to discharge this duty could be assigned to someone using the criteria mentioned above. For instance, suppose that I caused a person to fall into a river. The fact that I am responsible for this act makes me a good candidate to be assigned the primary duty to help this person. Suppose instead that someone is drowning and I am the nearest person around. The fact that I am the nearest person also makes me a good candidate to be assigned the primary duty to help this person given that I am more likely to succeed. But ability is also important. Suppose that this drowning person is being carried by the waves toward the ocean and I am not a good swimmer. Nearby there is someone else, Y, who is a much better swimmer. The fact that Y has this ability would make him a good candidate to be assigned the primary duty to rescue the drowning person. Finally, motivation is also important. Suppose X is drowning, and Y and Z are equal distance from X. Suppose that Y and Z are fairly good swimmers, but suppose that Y cares very little whether X drowns or not, while Z cares a lot. In such a case, it seems that one would want to assign the primary duty to Z, because given Z's motivation Z would be more likely to do a better job than Y. Of course, if Y were the only person present, then Y would have this duty despite his motivation. Other things being equal, it seems that one would want to assign the primary duty to people who have the stronger motivation.

In the case of a duty to love children, biological parents seem good candidates for being primary dutybearers because they normally meet at least three of the four criteria mentioned. They typically caused their children to come into existence, and therefore bear some responsibility for their action. In addition, they typically are physically most proximate to their children. Moreover, they typically are motivated to love their children. In fact, a number of writers seem to think that the fact that biological parents are typically motivated to love their children is a sufficient reason for assigning them the primary childcare duties. Hence, Jeffrey Blustein writes, "It is in large measure because biological parents are believed to have special natural affections for their offspring that they are regarded as especially well-qualified to be parents in the non-biological sense of the term and to have primary responsibility for their child's care and development, however attenuated this responsibility may be."[7] Or, Peter Hobson writes, "parents should be the prime agents in their children's upbringing, other things being equal, because they are the ones most likely to best promote the welfare of their children. It is the parents who have the most direct interest in their children's welfare and the parent-child bonds of affection are more likely to ensure the continuous care and attention needed, even under the most difficult circumstances."[8] Or, as Rousseau writes, "He [the child] will be better educated by a sensible though ignorant father than by the cleverest master in the world. For zeal will atone for lack of knowledge, rather than knowledge for lack of zeal."[9]

One cannot say, as a general rule, that biological parents also have the ability, since adequate parenting involves, among other things, knowledge about prenatal development, the role of proper nutrition during pregnancy, an infant's perceptual, motor, learning, and social skills, sleeping patterns, eating habits, and temperament, the varying needs of children from birth to adolescence, and so on; and there are (all too) many examples where biological parents seem to lack the ability. But parents can certainly acquire this ability through some sort of formal or informal parental education, as we shall later discuss.

Here it is worth pointing out that some people may think that besides the kind of coordination reasons I have been considering, biological parents should be assigned the primary duty just because they have the right to be parents to their own biological children. I am open to the idea that this could be a different, sufficient condition for assigning the primary duty to biological parents. In fact, in the next chapter, I shall argue that biological parents have the right to parent their biological children. However, as explained earlier, being a biological parent should not be a necessary condition for assigning the primary duty, as it would imply that if the biological parents were dead, no one else would have the duty to love the child.

To see how everyone else has an "associate" duty to see to it that primary dutybearers can successfully discharge their duty to love their children, consider again the drowning analogy. Suppose there is a general duty to rescue someone when the cost to the agent is minimal. Suppose further that X is drowning, and you and another person, Y, who is a lifeguard, are present. Since Y is a lifeguard, he may have the primary duty to save this person and may try to fulfill this duty by swimming toward X and trying to bring X out of the water. Although you are not the primary dutybearer, you have the associate duty to try to assist the primary dutybearer in whatever way you can, because of the general duty to rescue. For example, you may have to call for additional help or you may just have to be around to see if further help is needed. Or, suppose that you are not near the scene. Since there is a general duty to rescue, you may have to support certain tax policies that would allow States to pay for well-trained lifeguards or support governmental policies that require lifeguards to be stationed at every public beach.

One can apply this line of thinking to the case of a duty to love a child. A successful discharge of this duty involves a substantial amount of time and resources. It may be the case that some biological parents can successfully discharge this duty using their own resources. However, for many others, this can be quite difficult, perhaps owing to the demands of employment and the demands of other family members. The fact that other able persons have associate duties toward the child means that they can help to alleviate the burdens on the primary dutybearers. For instance, the associate dutybearers can support better childcare programs and more flexible workplace policies that make it easier for primary dutybearers to discharge their duty. Or, as citizens of a State, they may try to fulfill this duty by paying taxes and voting for governmental policies that help parents discharge their duties. The general idea here is that the duty to promote a child's being loved gives us further reasons to promote the primary dutybearers' welfare, health, psychological well-being, and so on, through generous welfare policies. These policies could be defended on other grounds, but the duty to love a child further underwrites their normativity. In subsequent chapters, I shall say more about what kind of policies we should implement to promote the duty to love a child.

3. Same Duty, Different Responsibility

Some people would agree that it is not only the biological parents who have duties with respect to children; others, such as States, social agencies, and other institutions can and should support conditions for loving relationships between parents and their children. However, they might think it odd to make the point by saying that every able person in appropriate circumstances has a duty to promote a child's being loved.

For those who really do agree that all able persons in appropriate circumstances, including people other than the biological parents, the States, and the international community, have a duty to promote and support conditions that are conducive to a child's being loved, this may just be a semantic dispute. But there are good reasons to describe the duty to love a child this way. For one thing, some people seem to think that if two people have the same duty, then they must do the same thing to fulfill the duty. As an example, in his discussion of the right to have one's life sustained, Carl Wellman appears to hold such a view, as he argues that the right to have one's life sustained cannot be a right against everyone because it would lead to a tremendous duplication of effort. As Wellman says,

If each individual's human right to have his or her life sustained really does hold against the world, then it imposes on each other individual, private organization, and state government a correlative duty to sustain the life of the individual right-holder. But if all second parties perform their duty to the right-holder, presumably a morally desirable thing, there would be tremendous duplication of effort to no practical advantage or moral purpose. Thus, not all potential second parties can have an actual duty to sustain the life of any given individual human whose life is threatened. And if not all correlative duties are real, then not all the ethical claims against the potential second parties are genuine either. In the end, then, it seems that this alleged human right cannot hold against the world.[10]

The problem of a tremendous duplication of effort arises because Wellman assumes that everyone would do the same thing as a result of having the same duty. Similarly, in the case of a duty to love a child, it is tempting to think that if two people both have this duty, then they must do the same thing, which is to love the child directly. However, it is a mistake to think that two people's having the same duty means that they have to do the same thing. Using the drowning analogy again, suppose that someone, X, is drowning, and you and another person, Y, are present and have a duty to try to save X. The fact that both you and Y have the same duty does not mean that both you and Y have to do the same thing, that is, to jump into the water and try to get X out. For example, as noted earlier, suppose that Y is a lifeguard. He may indeed try to fulfill this duty by swimming toward X and trying to bring X out of the water. You, on the other hand, are a bystander. You may try to fulfill this duty by calling for additional help or just by being around to see if further help is needed. If so, then even though both of you have the same duty, that is, the duty to save X, you would fulfill the duty in different ways. Or, to use a non-moral example, in baseball, the team on the field has a duty to "get out" players from the team that is batting through its pitching, or failing that, through its nine players. Suppose that the Cincinnati Reds are on the field and the New York Yankees are batting. All nine players on the Reds team would have the duty to "get out" the players from the Yankees team who are batting. However, though everyone on the Reds team has the same duty, it does not follow that the players would be doing the same thing. To fulfill his duty, the Reds' pitcher would have to try to fool the Yankees' batter to swing and miss the ball. The Reds' catcher would have to try to give signals to the pitcher regarding what kind of a ball to pitch. All nine players on the Reds team would have to be ready to intercept any ball that comes in their way should the pitcher and the catcher fail to fool the batter. All nine Reds players therefore have the same duty to "get out" players from the Yankees team who are batting, but all nine players would fulfill this duty in different ways.

Once one recognizes that two people's having the same duty does not mean that they have to do the same thing, as far as I can see, Wellman's concern with duplication of effort would disappear and it seems unproblematic to say that every able person in appropriate circumstances has a duty to promote a child's being loved. As explained earlier, what this means is that biological parents would try to fulfill this duty by directly trying to love the child, while other people would try to fulfill this duty by, for example, supporting programs that would assist biological parents in discharging their duties.

Moreover, if one did not describe the duty to love a child in this way, it might be unclear where the associate duties come from. For instance, suppose that we think that there are duties to support better childcare programs and more flexible workplace policies. Where do these duties come from? That is, what justifies these duties? Stating that every able person in appropriate circumstances has a duty to promote a child's being loved allows us to see more clearly that the associate duties are derived from this ultimate duty. Likewise, suppose that we think that someone else has a duty to love a child directly if the biological parents become unavailable. Where does this duty come from? Again stating that every able person in appropriate circumstances has a duty to promote a child's being loved makes clear that the duty to love a child is always present for everyone, but in part for coordination reasons, biological parents are assigned the primary duty in the first instance. I see it as a virtue of this proposal that it implies that other able persons now have associate duties to help primary dutybearers discharge their duty to love a child even when the primary dutybearers are available; and that it provides a straightforward explanation of why someone else would have to assume the primary duty of loving a child directly should the biological parents become unavailable.

4. How Demanding Is the Duty to Love?

If the duty to love a child belongs to everyone, to what extent do we have this duty? That is, how demanding should this duty be? To answer this question, we need a theory of how demanding morality should be. As readers will know, there is a large literature on this topic. Hence, rather than trying to be comprehensive, I shall instead focus on identifying some of the issues in this debate and presenting points that bear on how demanding the duty to love a child should be.

According to common sense morality, morality should not be too demanding. In particular, the general view is that an act would be too demanding if it required one to sacrifice something of "substantial significance." For instance, as Judith Jarvis

Thomson writes regarding the duty to rescue, "nobody is morally *required* to make large sacrifices, of health, of all other interests and concerns, of all other duties and commitments . . . in order to keep another person alive."[11] At the same time, according to common sense morality, one can be obliged to do something if the benefit to others is great while the cost to one is negligible. For instance, commenting on one's obligation to prevent death, John Arthur says that "If it is in our power to prevent death of an innocent without sacrificing anything of *substantial* significance then we ought morally to do it."[12]

Other people believe, however, that morality should be quite demanding. For instance, Peter Singer believes that "[W]e ought to give until we reach the level of marginal utility—that is, the level at which, by giving more, I would cause as much suffering to myself or my dependents as I would relieve by my gift."[13] As Singer elaborates, this means that one can be required to "reduce oneself to very near the material circumstances of a Bengali refugee."[14]

Singer's view has received a lot of criticisms. An important point is that acting on such a view would prevent people from being "deeply partial," that is, from being able to be deeply committed to one's personal relationships, goals, and projects.[15] Indeed, as long as one is required to give until the level of marginal utility, one must constantly seek opportunities to do so. However, especially in our non-ideal world where there are ample opportunities to relieve suffering, constantly seeking to give until the level of marginal utility would seem to leave one with very little time and resources to be able to be deeply committed to one's personal relationships and projects. Of course, in theory, Singer's view could be compatible with "deep partiality," if people made relieving suffering their personal project. However, most people do not strive to be Mother Theresa. Given this, in practice, Singer's view appears to be in deep tension with deep partiality.

I shall make three points regarding how demanding morality should be that should also have bearing on how demanding the duty to love a child should be. First, as we have seen, it is generally thought that morality does not require us to sacrifice something of "substantial significance." To advance this debate, it would be helpful to have a clearer idea of what counts as of "substantial significance." I propose that we can give content and theoretical unity to the notion of "substantial significance" by drawing on the account of human rights I have given in Chapter Two. In particular, I propose that what are of "substantial significance" are the fundamental conditions for pursuing a good life—the fundamental goods, capacities, and options necessary for pursuing the basic activities. Since these are conditions that human beings qua human beings need whatever else they qua individuals might need in order to pursue the basic activities, and since human beings have human rights to these fundamental conditions, we should not be required to sacrifice these fundamental conditions for the sake of others, at least in normal circumstances.

To illustrate, consider life, which is a fundamental condition for pursuing a good life. Under normal circumstances, it would be too demanding to require one to sacrifice one's life for the sake of others. As Locke writes, "Every one as he is bound to preserve himself, and not to quit his Station willfully; so by the like reason *when his own Preservation comes not in competition*, ought he, as much as he can, to preserve the rest of Mankind" (my italics added).[16] There may of course be times when one may be required to sacrifice one's life. For example, in times of war when an entire system of justice is under threat, or when the world is on the brink of a nuclear disaster that can only be prevented if one throws one's body against a de-activation button that will also kill one, one may have the duty even to sacrifice one's life in these circumstances. However, under normal circumstances, sacrificing one's life does not seem to be a moral requirement. Some may of course choose to do so, but their doing so would be heroic and supererogatory.

Understanding "substantial significance" this way provides us with a theoretical framework for explaining, *pace* Singer, why being required to reduce oneself to very near the material circumstances of a Bengali refugee would be too demanding—namely, because this would require one to sacrifice much of one's fundamental goods, capacities, and options. Likewise, it can also support the common sense view that being required to sacrifice deep partiality would also be too demanding, since being able to pursue deep personal relationships and being able to determine one's life course are also fundamental conditions for pursuing a good life.

Second, it seems acceptable to require us to sacrifice what might be called "surplus conditions,"—goods, capacities, and resources that are not necessary for pursuing the basic activities. To be as uncontroversial as possible, let us be generous with respect to our assumption about how one determines what are necessary for a human being (qua an individual) to pursue the basic activities; in particular, let us allow a significant amount of subjectivity in determining what an individual would need in order to pursue the basic activities. For instance, suppose that Bill Gates has eighty billion dollars. Suppose that he needs (or that he judges that he needs) fifty billion dollars in order to pursue the basic activities. It seems acceptable to require him to sacrifice his surplus conditions, that is, thirty billion dollars. Or, suppose that Bill Gates needs (or that he judges that he needs) only ten billion dollars in order to pursue the basic activities. It seems acceptable to require him to sacrifice his surplus conditions, that is, seventy billion dollars. While thirty or even seventy billion dollars may seem like a lot of money, since surplus conditions are by definition conditions that one does not need in order to pursue the basic activities, even if one were required to sacrifice all of one's surplus conditions, this seems acceptable and not too demanding as it would not affect one's pursuit of the basic activities.

Third, in a non-ideal world, morality is more demanding than what common sense morality supposes, even if it is not as demanding as what Singer thinks. In particular, we may be required to sacrifice some of what we qua individuals need for pursuing a good life (but not the fundamental conditions, which are what we qua human beings need whatever else we qua individuals might need for pursuing a good life). An example involving the duty to love a child can bring this point out. Consider the following case:

> **Hermit:** Suppose that you are a hermit living in a very remote region of the world, 500 miles away from civilization. You became a hermit because you wanted to leave the troubles of the world behind and lead a quiet, ascetic life. You have enough supplies for you and another person. One day you hear a crying sound outside your door. You open your door and you find a newborn baby. You can (a) keep the child and raise the child; (b) travel five hundred miles to the next town and find someone else to take care of the child; or (c) let the child die.

What does morality require of you? It seems that it requires that you not let the child die. That is, morality requires that you choose option (a) or (b). This is so, even if option (a) or (b) requires that you sacrifice some of what you qua an individual need for pursuing a good life. For instance, if you were to keep the child, given what we have said about what a child needs in order to develop into an adequately functioning individual, you would be required not just to provide for the child but also to love the child. This would require that you give up the quiet, ascetic life that you had sought, and it would require that you cultivate and adopt a new narrative identity, namely, that of a loving parent. Or, suppose that being a loving parent is not for you. Suppose that to travel five hundred miles to the next town, you would be required to use your prized wagon, which took you several years to make. The wagon would be destroyed upon the completion of the trip. You would be required to do so even if you would lose your prized wagon in the process. Note that in either case, you would still not be required to sacrifice the fundamental conditions necessary for pursuing the basic activities. For example, suppose that you only have just enough food for yourself and suppose that there is no way of getting to the next town without jeopardizing your life. In such a case, it may be permissible for you to let the child die. If all of this is right, the Hermit case suggests that in a non-ideal world, morality is more demanding than what common sense morality supposes.

These points bear on how demanding the duty to love a child should be. For one thing, the duty to love a child should not be so demanding that it requires one to sacrifice one's fundamental conditions for pursuing a good life. Hence, if one would fall into destitution if one had to raise a child, morality would permit one to give up the child. In addition, it is acceptable to require one to sacrifice one's surplus conditions in order to see to it that the duty to love a child is fulfilled. Finally, in our non-ideal world, we are required to sacrifice more than what common sense morality supposes in order to fulfill the duty to love a child. In particular, we may be required to sacrifice some of what we qua individuals need for pursuing a good life in order to see to it that a child is adequately loved. Exactly how much each person is required to sacrifice will depend on a host of other factors, such as how much priority we should give to this duty as opposed to other duties that we have—for instance, the duty to promote a child's education, the duty to help the needy in general, and the rights that other people have to pursue their own goals and projects. I shall examine these issues in a subsequent chapter.

At this point, some may ask, what if someone does not have enough resources fully to discharge this duty? Or what if the society does not have enough resources to see to it that every child is loved? Can an individual and/or the society still have this duty? In his discussion of a human right to sustain lives, Wellman refers to this as the "problem of scarce resources," and argues that it undermines the duty at issue:

> If the claim-right [to sustain life] is really a universal human right, then each potential duty-bearer finds himself or herself confronted with vast numbers of claimants, all of whose lives require sustenance. This raises the problem ... of scarce resources. If the individual, organization or state lacks sufficient resources to sustain the lives of all the claimants, then the addressee of so many claims can have no duty to do the impossible. And since claim and duty are logical correlatives, there can be no genuine claims where there are no actual duties (p. 159).

In my view, the problem of scarce resources does not undermine the duty at issue because one can have "partial duties." By a partial duty, I mean that even if a person cannot fulfill all that is required of a duty, as long as he is able to fulfill part of what is required, then he has a duty to do as much as he can. For example, suppose that X owes Y five dollars, X has five dollars, but X needs three dollars to survive. Because X is able to pay Y two dollars, it seems reasonable to expect X to pay Y two dollars, that is, X still has a partial duty to pay Y. The idea of partial duties is applicable both to Wellman's case of the human right to sustain lives and to our case of the duty to love a child. Although individuals, institutions, and States may not have enough resources to sustain all lives, they may have some surplus resources that can be used to sustain some lives. If so, then they can be obliged to use these resources to help as many as possible, even if they are not able to help all. Similarly, in the case of the duty to love children, even if individuals, institutions, and States do not have enough resources to make sure that this duty is fulfilled in all cases, they may have some surplus resources that they can use partially to fulfill part of what is required of the duty. If so, they can also be obliged to do so, even if they do not have enough resources to fulfill all that is required of the duty.

5. Conclusion

In this chapter, I challenged the common notion that the duty to love a child belongs only to the biological parents and I argued that every able person has a duty to promote a child's being loved. I proposed that in practice, this means that in the first instance, biological parents should be assigned the status of primary dutybearers and try to love the child directly, while everyone else should be given the status of associate dutybearers and support programs and policies that would facilitate a child's being loved. As I explained, the virtue of this proposal is that it implies that other able persons now have associate duties to help primary dutybearers discharge their duty to love a child even when the primary dutybearers are available; and it provides a straightforward explanation of why someone else would have to assume the primary duty of loving a child directly should the biological parents become unavailable.

In addition, I considered how demanding the duty to love a child should be and I argued that while we may not be required to sacrifice the fundamental conditions necessary for pursuing the basic activities in order to fulfill this duty, we may be required to sacrifice more than what common sense morality supposes and certainly we are required to sacrifice any surplus conditions that we may have. Moreover, even if we do not have enough resources fully to discharge this duty, I argued that we may have partial duties as long as we have some resources that we can use toward the fulfillment of this duty.

Suppose that everyone has the duty to promote a child's being loved and suppose that this duty can be fairly demanding. Does this mean that biological parents have the right to parent their biological children only insofar as doing so would be in a child's best interest? Does it mean that if someone else can provide a child with even more love, then we should assign that individual the primary duty instead of the biological parents? I now turn toward these questions.

Regulating Biological Parenting: The Problem of Possibly Inadequate Parents

1. Should We License Parenting?

There is ample evidence that some biological parents are grossly inadequate parents. Each year, child protective services in the United States alone receive an estimated 3.4 million reports of abuse and neglect concerning approximately six million children.[1] About one-fifth of these children (680,000) were found to be victims of maltreatment.[2] More than 75 percent suffered neglect; more than 15 percent suffered physical abuse; and close to 10 percent suffered sexual abuse.[3] An estimated 1,500 children die each year as a result of abuse and neglect.[4] Many more suffer long-term physical and psychological damages.[5] Children who were abused and neglected are more likely to become criminals.[6] About 30 percent of abused and neglected children will later abuse their own children.[7] For our purpose, 80 percent of the perpetrators were parents; and of these perpetrators, close to 90 percent were biological parents.[8] These are cases that were reported to the child protective services. The total number of abuse and neglect is likely to be much higher once unreported cases are also included. The estimated annual cost of child abuse and neglect for victims and society in the United States in 2012 was \$80 billion.[9]

In light of such staggering statistics, it is tempting to think that a potential way to reduce these incidences of abuse and neglect is to license biological parenting, that is, to require biological parents to demonstrate certain competence and character before they are permitted to parent their biological children. Note that the focus here is on *possible* parents since there are already laws and procedures for dealing with parents who abuse and/or neglect their children or who have such a history (whether these laws and procedures are adequate is a separate matter, which I will set aside here).[10] Focusing on possible parents has the potential of preventing abuse and/or neglect from occurring in the first place. We can call this the problem of possibly inadequate parents.

To address this problem, a number of people, including John Stuart Mill, Hugh LaFollette, Jack Westman, and Robert Taylor, have advocated a parental licensing scheme.[11] The basic arguments for such a scheme can be found in LaFollette's seminal work.[12] According to LaFollette, licensing is required if and when

1. an activity is potentially harmful to others;
2. the activity requires a certain level of competence for its safe performance; and
3. there exists a reliable procedure for determining whether an individual is competent to perform the activity safely.[13]

For instance, LaFollette argues that individuals are required to have driver's licenses because the three criteria are satisfied: driving is potentially harmful to others; it requires a certain level of competence for its safe performance; and there is a reliable procedure for determining driving competence. Dentists, pharmacists, chiropractors, lawyers, counselors, and physical therapists are also licensed for similar reasons. Likewise, or so LaFollette argues, parenting also meets these three criteria. Parenting is potentially harmful to children. As we have seen from the statistics above, parents can abuse or neglect their children or provide inadequate care to their children. Also, parenting requires a certain level of competence for its safe performance. As LaFollette points out, adequate parenting requires, among other things, certain knowledge, abilities, judgment, and disposition. Finally, LaFollette argues that there can be reliable ways of determining parenting competence, such as using the Child Abuse Potential Inventory.[14]

Moreover, as LaFollette observes, those who wish to adopt a child are currently expected to submit to an extensive screening, akin to licensing, to determine their suitability to be parents to a child. Given this, according to LaFollette, consistency requires that we also license biological parents. LaFollette speculates that our reluctance to license parents is due to a deeply ingrained attitude that biological parents in some sense own their children—in other words, children are their biological parents' properties.[15] In LaFollette's view, once we give up the idea that children are their biological parents' properties, those who are against a parental licensing scheme will have no real theoretical reasons against such a scheme. Other advocates of a parental licensing scheme typically accept some version of LaFollette's basic arguments.[16]

Despite these powerful arguments, many people have objected to the idea of a parental licensing scheme.[17] Some question whether there can really be a reliable way of determining who will be a competent parent. For instance, Sandmire and Wald argue that these predictive tests would overestimate the number of parents who are likely to abuse and neglect their children, that is, there would be too many false positives.[18] Others are concerned that the solution would be worse than the problem.[19]

To ensure compliance with a parental licensing scheme, advocates of such a scheme have suggested measures such as imposing fines on unlicensed parents, placing non-compliant parents under supervision, or, as a last resort, removing children from the homes of unlicensed parents and putting them up for adoption.[20] Among other things, these measures assume that children who are taken away from their biological parents will swiftly be adopted. However, there are good reasons to doubt that this will be the case in light of current rates of adoption.[21] Hence, if a large number of children will have to spend a significant amount of time in the care of child protection services, arguably, this is likely to be worse for these children than suboptimal parenting. Still others have argued that a parental licensing scheme would place unequal burden on women.[22] For instance, if a pregnant woman or her partner were found to be unfit for parenting prior to the birth of a child, it seems that the burden would fall on the woman either to have an abortion or to carry the pregnancy to term in full knowledge that she would not be able to raise the child.[23]

Concerns such as whether there can be a reliable test to determine who is a competent parent and whether the parental licensing scheme can be enforced are *practical concerns*. While these practical concerns seem vaild, they leave open the possibility that licensing parents is in principle correct. In fact, Engster, an opponent of the parental licensing scheme, says that, "If it were possible to implement a parental licensing plan without generating significant negative consequences, it might be desirable to do so."[24]

In this chapter, I shall offer a theoretical case against parental licensing. In a nutshell, I shall argue that biological parenting is a fundamental (human) right, and fundamental rights should not be licensed; therefore, biological parenting should not be licensed. I begin by explaining why biological parenting is a fundamental right.

2. Biological Parenting as a Fundamental Right

In Chapter Two, I argued that we have human rights to the fundamental conditions for pursuing the basic activities. Here I shall explain why biological parenting is (an instance of) a basic activity. If I am right, this explains why we have fundamental (human) rights to the fundamental conditions for pursuing biological parenting.

Recall that basic activities are ones that are important to human beings qua human beings' life as a whole. That is, they are ones that if a human life did not have any of them, then that life could not be a good life. Some of the basic activities are deep personal relationships with, for instance, one's partner, friends, parents, children; knowledge of, for example, the workings of the world, of oneself, of others; active pleasures such as creative work and play; and passive pleasures such as appreciating beauty.

Biological parenting is one of those activities that are important to human beings qua human beings' life as a whole. How so? Here are some of the factors that *jointly* make (consensual) biological parenting such a valuable, basic activity.[25] First, in becoming a biological parent, one is creating a new being, a new individual. It seems clear that there is value in creating a new individual, other things being equal, given that one is exercising one's agency and autonomy and there is value in exercising one's agency and autonomy. Compare: there is value in creating a beautiful piece of artwork, other things being equal, as one is exercising one's agency and autonomy.

Second, this new being would not just be any being. On the view of rightholding I defended in Chapter One, this new being would typically be a rightholder, as it would have the genetic basis for moral agency. Or, if one does not accept my view of rightholding, arguably, this being would typically still be a being with the potential to be a rightholder. In either case, this being would typically have a very weighty moral status. This further contributes to the value of creating a new individual, other things being equal. It is true that creating a new individual has, among other things, potentially negative implications for scarce global resources, greenhouse gas emissions, and the like, such that all things considered, it may be better not to create a new individual. I take it, though, that these considerations do not affect the claim that there is some value to creating a new individual, other things being equal.

Third, this new individual would be created in part using one's own genetic material. Since one's genetic material determines in part the genetic identity of this individual and since the genetic identity of an individual does not change much if at all and plays an important role in shaping the phenotypic identity of an individual, one's own genetic material is also playing a significant role in shaping the phenotypic identity of an individual. Irrespective of one's views about genetic determinism, and accepting that epigenetic factors can play a significant role in affecting gene expression, it seems uncontroversial that one's genetic material forms a core aspect of one's identity. Given this, when a new individual is created in part using one's own genetic material, this new individual is created using some core aspect of one's identity. The value here is akin to one's brain coming up with an interesting idea. On one level, one's brain coming up with an interesting idea involves just a series of chemical reactions. Nevertheless, it seems that there is value in such a biological process because such a biological process involves some core aspect of one's self. This makes the activity of one's brain coming up with an interesting idea valuable, even if a similar idea could be generated using other means, such as a computer. Likewise, on one level, a new individual's being created using one's genetic material also involves just a series of chemical reactions. Nevertheless, it seems that there is also value in this biological process because this biological process, too, involves some core aspect of one's self—some core aspect of one's identity.

Fourth, in being a biological parent, one has the opportunity to see how this new individual partly created using one's genetic material grows and develops. Moreover, one has the opportunity to shape and nurture the growth of this new individual. To see why these activities are valuable, consider again the analogy between a new individual's being created using one's genetic material and one's brain coming up with an interesting idea. Suppose that this analogy is apt. The value of shaping and nurturing the growth of this individual is akin to having the opportunity to see and shape the growth of one's idea.

In short, these four factors—that one is (a) creating a new life; (b) a rightholder; (c) with one's genetic material which in part determines the genetic identity of this new individual; (d) and one has the opportunity to see and shape the growth of this new individual—jointly explain why biological parenting is one of those activities that are important to human beings qua human beings' life as a whole—in other words, why biological parenting is a basic activity. I say "jointly" because I do not think that just creating a rightholder with one's genetic material, that is, merely procreating, is itself a basic activity. More controversially, I also do not think that shaping and nurturing the growth of a new individual is in itself a *basic* activity. As I shall shortly explain, there is no doubt that shaping and nurturing the growth of a new individual is a very important and worthwhile activity. But, as noted previously, not every important and worthwhile activity is a basic activity, understood as an activity that is important to human beings qua human beings' life as a whole.

This account of the value of biological parenting can make sense of many common platitudes about biological parenting. For example, people often say that biological parenting gives meaning to a human being's life. This makes sense since biological parenting is a basic activity—an activity that is important to human beings qua human beings' life as a whole. Or, some people say that biological parenting is the most challenging yet rewarding job one can do. This sentiment is understandable given the power and the responsibility involved in creating and shaping the life of a new individual. Others say that biological parenting is a way of expressing one's love for one's partner. This attitude is comprehensible because in becoming biological parents, among other things, one and one's partner are *together* creating a new life that shares both one's and one's partner's genetic material and *together* making an implicit if not explicit long-term commitment to shape and nurture the growth of that new life. Still others say that biological parenting is a way to continue one's legacy in the world. There are, of course, many other ways of leaving a legacy in the world, such as producing great works as did Plato or Aristotle. Nevertheless, since the new being is created in part using one's genetic material, and supposing that one does also participate in shaping the life of this new individual, there may be some grain of truth to this claim.

Given that we have fundamental rights to the fundamental conditions for pursuing the basic activities, and given that biological parenting is a basic activity, it follows that we have fundamental rights to the fundamental conditions for pursuing biological parenting. Indeed, Article 16 of the Universal Declaration of Human Rights recognizes that "Men and women of full age, without any limitation due to race, nationality or religion, have the right to marry and *to found a family*" (my italics).

What are the fundamental conditions for pursuing biological parenting? Recall that the fundamental conditions are various *fundamental goods, capacities, and options* that human beings qua human beings need whatever else they qua individuals might need in order to pursue the basic activities. One thing we need to pursue biological parenting is control over our body and our body parts (such as our gametes), that is, we need bodily integrity. Another thing we need is some liberty and autonomy to plan and pursue biological parenting. Without control over our body and without some liberty and autonomy to plan and pursue biological parenting, we would not be free to decide whether and when we want to be biological parents. Moreover, we also need the power to exclude others from trying to be the primary providers for our biological child. Without such power, we would not be free to determine the shape of our relationship with our child. For instance, if we did not have this power, it would be permissible for someone else to take our child home after school to look after her. We may also need to have the autonomy to teach or to decide who will teach our child how to be an adequately functioning individual in a given society. I set aside this point, as some people would dispute this, and the argument below does not depend on it.

If we have fundamental rights to the fundamental conditions for pursuing biological parenting, and if, among other things, having bodily integrity, the liberty and autonomy to plan and pursue biological parenting, and the power to exclude others from trying to be the primary providers for one's biological child are such fundamental conditions, then this implies that, among other things, we have fundamental rights to bodily integrity, the liberty and autonomy to plan and pursue biological parenting, and to exclude others from trying to be the primary providers for one's biological child.

Here it is worth mentioning that as with all human rights, these rights are not absolute, that is, these rights are defeasible. For instance, these rights can be restricted in cases of parents who abused and/or neglected their children. These rights may also be defeasible if there is a supreme emergency. For instance, if human beings would become extinct if everyone continued to reproduce, this might be a reason to curb our right to pursue biological parenting. The claim here is that under ordinary circumstances, and subject to certain conditions such as the parents not abuse and/or neglect their children, everyone has these rights.

3. Compare and Contrast with Other Accounts of Parental Rights

The idea that biological parenting is a fundamental human right provides an explanation of why biological parents have the right to parent their own biological children and gives us an account of parental rights. We can call this the human rights account of parental rights. To develop this account further, I shall now compare and contrast it with some of the latest and more promising accounts of parental rights. Owing to space, I shall not attempt to be exhaustive.[26]

One alternative account of parental rights is what might be called the property account. On the property account, biological parents have the right to parent their own biological children because they own their children. One reason for thinking that biological parents own their children presumably stems from the thought that biological parents created their children and therefore they should own them. Another reason may be that if parents did own their children, this would give us a quick argument for why biological parents have the right to exclude others from trying to be parents to their own biological children.[27]

The property account might seem like an anathema to us, but in Roman, and later in English, common law, children were viewed as the property of the father, who had the right to sell their children and to enter them into enforced labor.[28] As we have seen, LaFollette speculates that people resist the idea of a parental licensing scheme in part because they implicitly, if not explicitly, believe that biological parents own their children; and LaFollette believes that once this is pointed out, we would be more ready to accept a parental licensing scheme.[29]

I agree that the property account is mistaken and I shall explain how the human rights account is different from it. For one thing, rightholders cannot be owned by others. Among other things, rightholders are ends in themselves. This means that a rightholder cannot be owned by others, since being owned by others implies that others would have the right to use one as a mere means. As I have argued in Chapter One, children are rightholders. It follows that they cannot be owned by others. This is a reason to reject the property account.

In addition, being able to own one's biological children is not a fundamental condition for pursuing biological parenting. As far as I can see, human beings can pursue biological parenting without having ownership over their biological children. On the human rights account, the fact that biological parents created their biological children partly explains the value of biological parenting. This gives biological parents the rights to bodily integrity, the liberty and autonomy to plan and pursue biological parenting, and, relevantly, to exclude others from trying to be parents to their biological children. But this does not give biological parents a property right over their biological children. If so, this is a further reason to reject the property account. Indeed, on the human rights account, biological parents may not do whatever they want with their biological children. If, for example, one abused and/or neglected one's child, one's right to continue to be a parent to the child may be curtailed. This suggests that the human rights account is different from some construal of the property account.

Next let us consider the idea that parental rights are derived from the interest that parents have in a certain kind of intimate relationship with their children.[30] Harry Brighouse and Adam Swift, who have put forward such a view, begin by noting that the kind of intimate relationship that parents have with their children is uniquely different from other kinds of intimate relationships, such as adult friendships, in at least four ways. First, children are intrinsically vulnerable and depend on their parents to secure their basic needs. Second, unlike adults, children typically do not have the power to exit the relationship. Third, children love their parents in a spontaneous and unconditional way. Finally, parents are charged with the responsibility to care for the child. Brighouse and Swift argue that people have an interest in this kind of relationship precisely because this relationship is "for many, not substitutable by relationships of other kinds."[31] Brighouse and Swift then argue that this interest gives people a right to become and be parents.[32]

One issue with Brighouse and Swift's account of parental rights is that it is not clear that the parent-child relationship is really non-substitutable. Consider the relationship between, say, a dog owner and her dog. At least based on the four criteria Brighouse and Swift have identified, this relationship would also seem to meet these four criteria: the dog is intrinsically vulnerable and depends on the dog owner to secure his basic needs; the dog typically does not have the power to exit the relationship; the dog loves the owner in a spontaneous and unconditional way; and the dog owner is charged with the responsibility to care for the dog. If so, either Brighouse and Swift have not fully identified what makes the parent-child relationship non-substitutable, or else, the parent-child relationship is not as non-substitutable as they have claimed.

But suppose that the parent-child relationship is non-substitutable. There are many other valuable activities that arguably also do not have close substitutes. At the same time, it seems that one would not want to claim that one has a fundamental interest and therefore a fundamental right to pursue these activities. For example, being an astronaut does not seem to have a close substitute. At the same time, it seems that one would not want to claim that there is a fundamental interest and therefore a fundamental right to be an astronaut.

Most importantly, as Brighouse and Swift have also acknowledged, their account of parental rights does not explain why one has the right to be a parent *to one's own biological child*.[33] Their account offers an explanation of why being a parent is valuable. But the value of parenthood they have identified—the fact that this relationship is non-substitutable—applies to everyone who has an interest in being a parent. Their account therefore implies that everyone who has an interest in being a parent has a right to be a parent. But it does not explain why one has a right to be a parent to one's own biological child.

As we have seen, the human rights account explains the value of biological parenting in terms of the power to create and shape a new life, the life of a rightholder, using one's own genetic material. This distinguishes biological parenting from other kinds of activities that do not create and shape a new life. Also, the power to exclude others from trying to parent one's own biological child is a fundamental condition for pursuing biological parenting. Given this, unlike Brighouse and Swift's account, the human rights account has the resources to explain why one has the right to parent one's own biological child.

Consider also Norvin Richards's account of parental rights.[34] According to Richards, people have a right to be parents to their own biological children, because they have the right to continue with a project that they have started as long as they did not violate anyone else's rights when starting the project. He writes,

> There is a principle of broad appeal, usually traced to John Stuart Mill, according to which we have a right to act as we

choose if our actions are suitably innocent with regard to others . . . I am going to suggest that we take the rights of parenthood as an instance of this more general right to continue with whatever we have underway.[35]

As an analogy, Richards points out that a pianist has a right to continue with her performance even if a superior pianist is in the audience.

One issue with Richards's account is that he simply assumes that becoming biological parents is "suitably innocent." From this, Richards then claims that people have the right to continue with biological parenting, that is, to be biological parents. But part of the issue here is precisely why people are entitled to become biological parents—why people have a right to become biological parents. Given this, it seems that Richards needs to explain why becoming biological parents is "suitably innocent" rather than simply assuming this. As we have seen, on the human rights account, there is a right to become biological parents because biological parenting is a basic activity.

In addition, by a "right to continue with a project that they have started," Richards has in mind a *liberty* right, that is, a right to ϕ and where others have no right that one not ϕ.[36] Indeed, Richards writes on a number of occasions "the right to be at liberty" and the "right to act as one chooses," which makes clear that he has in mind a liberty right.[37] If this interpretation is correct, the problem is that a liberty right to ϕ does not, by itself, give one the power to exclude others from also having a right to ϕ. For instance, suppose that I have a liberty right to walk down the street. My having this liberty right does not, by itself, give me the power to prevent others from also having a liberty right to walk down the street. Or, to continue with Richards's musical analogy, the pianist's liberty right to continue with his performance does not, by itself, give the pianist the power to prevent the superior pianist from hauling out her Steinway to play while the pianist onstage is midway through a piece. Given this, if the right to be a parent to one's own biological child were just a liberty right, this would not give one the power to exclude others from also trying to be a parent to one's child. A consequence of this is that if someone were to get up in the morning before one does so that she can take one's child to school, on Richards's account, that person would have the liberty right to do so. Unlike Richards's account, the human rights account, as we have seen, can explain why one has the power to exclude others from trying to be a parent to one's biological child, namely, because this is a fundamental condition for pursuing biological parenting.

A number of people have defended what might be called a gestational account of parental rights.[38] For instance, Anca Gheaus argues that there are two features of pregnancy that give biological parents the right to be parents to their biological children. First, pregnancies involve a variety of physical, psychological, social, and financial cost that can in most cases "only be shouldered by pregnant women and, to some extent, their supportive partner."[39] For instance, pregnant women experience fatigue, high blood pressure, excessive water retention in their hands and feet, nausea and vomiting, an inability to carry heavy objects, and "a distinctive sense of losing control over one's life and a diminished ability to pursue other projects and interests during pregnancy as well as during recovery from childbirth."[40] Also, many pregnant women become limited in what they can eat and drink, the recreational drugs they can take, and the sports and other physical activities that they can pursue. Finally, women also shoulder specific emotional burdens such as fear of miscarriage and the anxiety of deciding whether to continue a pregnancy with significant health risks.

Gheaus argues that this feature of pregnancy is shared by everyone who has experienced pregnancy and therefore, it gives one the right to be a parent to a child, but not necessarily the right to be a parent to one's own biological child.[41] To explain why biological parents have the right to be parents to their biological children, Gheaus then points to a second feature of pregnancy, namely, the fact that pregnancy facilitates the creation of an intimate relationship between the bearing parents and the future baby. As Gheaus explains,

> Through their bodily connection with the baby and their various psychological investments, expecting parents normally build a relationship with their future baby, which is sometimes highly emotional and already quite developed at birth. Bearing parents and their newborns already share a common history including numerous embodied common experiences ('you kicked me on the 1st of March,' 'you made me worry,' 'you made me so happy'). The fact that the body plays such a central part in pregnancy makes pregnancy a uniquely privileged context for developing a bond that is both physical and imaginative with the future child.[42]

According to Gheaus, this second feature of pregnancy provides the missing step in explaining why biological parents have the right to be parents to their biological child.

The burden of pregnancy and the intimacy developed during pregnancy do not seem to be the right place to develop an account of parental rights. For one thing, they imply that men have lesser right than women to be parents to their biological children. To be sure, Gheaus is keen to point out that men can share some of the cost of pregnancy, such as accompanying the pregnant woman to medical visits, supporting her during childbirth, sharing in and trying to soothe her worries, and so on.[43] But it remains the case, as Gheaus herself recognizes, that men cannot directly experience pregnancy, labor, childbirth, and postpartum recovery.[44] Given this, if the burden of pregnancy and the intimacy developed during pregnancy were the basis for assessing whether one has a right to parent one's biological child, then it seems that on this basis, men would not have equal rights as women to be parents to their biological children, which seems unfair.

In addition, the gestational account has other counterintuitive implications. To illustrate, consider surrogacy. Let us set aside the myriad complicated ethical issues surrounding surrogacy, such as the exploitation of women. Suppose that a couple asked a surrogate mother to bring their (the couple's) fertilized eggs to term using in vitro fertilization. The gestational account implies that the surrogate mother would have more right to be a parent to the child, owing to the burden of pregnancy and the intimacy developed during pregnancy. We can agree that while the fetus is inside the surrogate mother's womb, the surrogate mother has the right to determine what happens to the fetus because she has the right to bodily integrity. However, once the fetus is delivered, it seems that the couple would have the right to be parents to their biological child.

To make this point in a different way, consider the following case: Two different couples are receiving in vitro fertilization treatment at a fertility clinic. Unfortunately, the fertilized eggs of the two different couples were switched. Consequently, the women brought to term fetuses who were not their own biological children. Immediately after the women had given birth, the error was discovered. Do the different couples/women have the right to be parents to their own biological children or to the fetuses whom they had brought to term? The gestational account implies that the women have the right to be parents to the fetuses they had brought to term, but not the right to be parents to their own biological children. Again, this seems counterintuitive.

Consider one other account of parental rights, namely, Joseph Millum's "investment" account.[45] According to Millum, this account of parental rights is based on

The investment principle: Ceteris paribus, the extent of an agent's stake in an object is proportional to the amount of appropriate work he or she has put into that object.[46]

In the case of parenting, the investment principle says that those who have invested substantial parenting work into a child, such as biological parents and adoptive parents, are the ones with the right to be parent to the child. For instance, consider a case in which biological fathers, sperm and egg donors, and the physicians performing IVF are all involved in doing something to bring a particular fetus to term. According to Millum, on the investment account, they would all have some parental stake in the resulting child. Millum argues that "absent a persuasive account of parental work that excludes [such a case,] we should err on the side of caution and allow any work that positively contributes to the child's development to count."[47]

The problem with the investment account is that it seems too inclusive; it does not seem to have a principled way of excluding others from becoming a parent to one's child. For example, suppose that I start to pay for your child's education or I start to pick up your child from school or I start to buy your child books. On the investment account, I would begin to acquire a parental stake in your child. This is also counterintuitive.

In this section, I have compared and contrasted the human rights account with several other accounts of parental rights, and I have argued that there are problems with these other accounts of parental rights, while the human rights account does not share these problems. If I am right, we have further reasons to accept the human rights account of parental rights.

4. Fundamental Rights Should Not Be Licensed

Let me now explain why fundamental rights should not be licensed, or more specifically, why fundamental rights to the fundamental conditions for pursuing the basic activities should not be licensed.

Having fundamental rights to the fundamental conditions for pursuing the basic activities means, among other things, having the right against others that they not interfere with one's pursuit of the basic activities. We have this right because having the liberty and the autonomy to pursue the basic activities are fundamental conditions for pursuing the basic activities, and having the liberty and the autonomy to pursue the basic activities means that we have the right against others that they not interfere with our pursuit of the basic activities.

Whatever else one qua an individual might need to pursue the basic activities, one qua a human being needs to have the liberty to pursue the basic activities and the autonomy to determine whether and when one would like to pursue the basic activities in order to be effective at pursuing the basic activities. Hence, the liberty and the autonomy to pursue the basic activities are fundamental conditions for pursuing the basic activities.

Having the liberty and the autonomy to pursue the basic activities means that we have the right against others that they not interfere with our pursuit of the basic activities, because having the liberty and the autonomy means, among other things, that we have the immunity against others from trying to prevent our exercise of our liberty and autonomy, and having this immunity means that we have the right against others that they not interfere with our pursuit of the basic activities. For instance, as we have said, the pursuit of deep personal relationship is a basic activity. Given this, we have the fundamental right to pursue deep personal relationships, and, in particular, we have the right against others that they not interfere with our pursuit of deep personal relationships. We have this right because we have the liberty and the autonomy to pursue deep personal relationships, and having the liberty and the autonomy to pursue deep personal relationships means, among other things, that we have the immunity against others from trying to prevent our exercise of our liberty and autonomy to pursue deep personal relationships.

Licensing interferes with one's pursuit of an activity. As we have seen, licensing requires that one prove one's competence and character with respect to an activity before one can pursue that activity. If one has to prove one's competence and character with respect to an activity before one can pursue that activity, then one is not really at liberty to pursue that activity. One is effectively prevented from pursuing that activity until one can prove one's competence and character with respect to that activity. Placing a hold on one's liberty to pursue an activity and effectively preventing one from pursuing an activity until one can prove one's competence and character interfere with one's pursuit of that activity. Hence, licensing interferes with one's pursuit of an activity.

Since having fundamental rights to the fundamental conditions for pursuing basic activities means having the right against others that they not interfere with one's pursuit of the basic activities, and since licensing an activity interferes with one's pursuit of that activity, having fundamental rights to the fundamental conditions for pursuing basic activities means that one has a right against others that they not license the basic activities. In other words, fundamental rights to the fundamental conditions for pursuing the basic activities should not be licensed.

We are now in the position to explain why biological parenting should not be licensed. As argued previously, biological parenting is a basic activity. Given this, we have the fundamental rights to pursue biological parenting. Among other things, we have the right against others that they not interfere with our pursuit of biological parenting. We have this right because we have the liberty and the autonomy to pursue biological parenting, and having this liberty and autonomy means, among other things, that we have the immunity against others from trying to prevent our exercise of our liberty and autonomy to pursue biological parenting. Licensing biological parenting interferes with our pursuit of biological parenting, because it requires that one prove one's competence and character with respect to biological parenting before one can pursue biological parenting, and doing so places a hold on one's liberty to pursue biological parenting and effectively prevents one from pursuing biological parenting until one can prove one's competence and character. Since we have the right against others that they not interfere with our pursuit of biological parenting and since licensing interferes with our pursuit of biological parenting, it follows that we have a right against others that they not license biological parenting. In other words, biological parenting should not be licensed.

To be clear, that we have a right against others that they not license biological parenting does not mean that this right is absolute. As with other rights, there may be circumstances in which this right can be overridden. As with other rights, the claim here is that in ordinary circumstances, one has this right and therefore there is a presumption in favor of one's not having to prove one's competence and/or character before one can pursue biological parenting.

We are now also in the position to explain why driving, practicing medicine and law, and the like can be licensed. Unlike biological parenting, driving, practicing medicine and law, and the like are not basic activities. These activities may be important to certain individuals' life as a whole, but they are not activities that are important to human beings qua human beings' life as a whole. As such, we do not have fundamental rights to the fundamental conditions for pursuing driving, practicing medicine and law, and the like, which means that we do not have the right against others that they not interfere with our pursuit of driving, practicing medicine and law, and the like. As such, licensing can be appropriate with respect to these activities. The mistake of advocates of a parental licensing scheme is in their failure to realize that biological parenting, unlike driving and practicing medicine and law, is a basic activity.

Recall that advocates of a parental licensing scheme such as LaFollette have argued that since we currently license adoptive parents, consistency requires that we also license biological parents. Suppose that licensing is appropriate with respect to adoptive parenting. What justifies this asymmetry? There are at least two reasons. First, there is no doubt that adoptive parenting is a very valuable activity, for both the children involved and the adoptive parents. In fact, in the next chapter, I shall argue that there is a duty to adopt and I shall propose a way of encouraging more adoptions. However, adoptive parenting is also different from biological parenting in important ways. In particular, adoptive parenting is not a basic activity, that is, it is not an activity that is important to human beings qua human beings' life as whole. To be sure, some of the values inherent in adoptive parenting are similar to the values inherent in biological parenting. For instance, in adoptive parenting one also has the opportunity to see and shape the growth of a new individual. Also, there are other important moral values in adoptive parenting that may not be present in biological parenting, such as rescuing a child from an unloving or incapable family or institution.[48] However, unlike biological parenting, adoptive parents are not (a) creating a new life; (b) a rightholder; (c) with their genetic material which in part determines the genetic identity of this new individual. As I have argued earlier, these factors are necessary components in explaining why biological parenting is a basic activity. It might be asked, why not think that parenting, understood as having the opportunity to see and shape the growth of a new individual, is in and of itself a basic activity? The reason is that this is just not the case. Basic activities are activities that are important to human beings qua human beings' life as a whole rather than activities that are important to human beings qua individuals' life as a whole. Doing philosophy and helping people who are in poverty are very important activities, but they are not basic activities. Similarly, many people would not pursue parenting at all if they could not be biological parents. The fact that so many couples seek IVF treatments despite significant financial, physical, and emotional costs to themselves and despite the fact that there are millions of children in the world without adequate parents and in need of adoption lends support to this claim.[49]

Second, in the case of adoptive parenting, at least initially, either someone else still has the right to be parent to the child to be adopted, or no one else has this right, for example, because the biological parents are deceased or have lost their right to be parents to the child. In either case, the prospective adoptive parent does not (yet) have the right to be a parent to this child. Since the prospective adoptive parent does not (yet) have a right to be a parent to this child, the prospective adoptive parent does not have the right against others that they not assess her competence and character to determine if she should be given the right to be a parent to this child. Given this, licensing would not interfere with the prospective adoptive parent's rights. Consider an analogy. Suppose a famous writer has produced a draft of a highly anticipated novel, but the writer dies before she is able to complete the novel. Suppose the writer's spouse is now looking for someone to complete the novel. In this case, it seems permissible for the spouse to require those who wish to take on this task to take some kind of competency/character test before being granted the right to complete the novel. The reason is that at least initially a prospective writer does not (yet) have the right to complete this novel. Given this, a prospective writer does not have the right against the spouse that the spouse not assess her competence and character to determine if she should be granted the right to complete the novel. This is so even if requiring writers to take some kind of competency/character test before they can begin to write and publish the kind of novels that they wish to write would generally be a violation of their right to free expression—much like licensing a biological parent would interfere with the biological parent's rights to become and be parent to her biological child. If all of this is right, there are principled reasons why we can license adoptive parenting but not biological parenting.

5. A Case for Mandatory Parenting Education

If biological parents have fundamental rights to pursue biological parenting, how should we address the problem of possibly inadequate parents? How can we reduce the number of such parents?

To start, it is worth reminding ourselves that the human rights account of parental rights is fully compatible with children's having real and robust rights. In Chapter Two, I argued that human beings have human rights to the fundamental conditions for pursuing a good life. This claim applies to children as well as adult human beings. This means that, among other things, children have a right to be fed, nurtured, educated, and loved. As far as I can see, there is no reason why one's having fundamental rights to the fundamental conditions for pursuing biological parenting would require denying that children have these rights. Of course, rights can conflict in practice, which means that parental rights and children's rights can conflict. But acknowledging this does not require the denial of the existence of either parental rights or children's rights. Compare: one person's right to free expression can sometimes conflict with another person's right to privacy. Acknowledging this does not require the denial of the existence of either the right to free expression or the right to privacy.

With respect to the problem of the possibly inadequate parents, I propose that we should consider introducing *mandatory basic parenting education* for all children during middle- and high school years.[50] Basic parenting education, as I envision it, would focus on teaching to middle- to high schoolers basic scientific knowledge about childhood development; the nature of parenting; and how society can influence the parent/child relationship. Such an education would seek to inform middle- to high schoolers about the latest scientific research and theories on prenatal development; the role of proper nutrition during pregnancy; an infant's perceptual, motor, learning, and social skills, sleeping patterns, eating habits, and temperament; the varying needs of children from birth to adolescence; and how to create a safe, healthy, stimulating, and loving environment for children generally.

A rationale for mandating basic parenting education in schools is that one of the aims of basic education is to help one acquire the knowledge necessary for developing into an adequately functioning individual, that is, an individual who has enough goods and capacities to pursue the basic activities. Since for many people biological parenting is a basic activity, having the knowledge necessary to become and be good parents will be important for many people. In fact, for many, having basic parenting education will be as important as learning math and science. Some might be concerned that middle schoolers are too young and immature to absorb the kind of education I have proposed. However, middle schoolers do engage in sexual activities, and sex education is already offered at this age. As I envisage it, mandatory basic parenting education would complement sex education as it can inform middle- to high schoolers of the duties involved in parenting, thereby giving them fuller information regarding the potential consequences of sex—a goal that both "abstinence only" and "abstinence-plus" advocates can share.[51] Logistically speaking, basic parenting education could be taught in conjunction with sex education or other existing courses such as general science, biology, home economics, or psychology, to avoid overcrowding the existing curriculum. Though basic parenting education would be mandated, students are not required to pass the course in order to be permitted to marry or procreate, as such a requirement would be a form of licensing.[52]

Another rationale for providing basic parenting education in schools is that it ensures that everyone will receive some basic knowledge about the important task of parenting, irrespective of socioeconomic background and culture.[53] A national survey of more than ten thousand parents showed that nearly a third of the parents in the United States knew little about normal infant development.[54] At the same time, because basic parenting education would restrict itself to teaching about the scientific facts regarding childhood development and the like, basic parenting education would not involve teaching "morals" to children—an objection some have leveled against what might be called "comprehensive parenting education," which seeks to teach not just basic scientific facts about child development but also more value-laden types of parenting skills, such as empathy and caring.[55] For example, the former governor of California, Gray Davis, vetoed two bills, Senate Bill No. 305 and 1348, on the ground that comprehensive parenting education should be left to parents in their own homes. While I am skeptical that any teaching can be completely value-neutral (even neutrality is arguably not a "neutral" value), basic parenting education that focuses only on scientific facts of childhood development should be able to avoid this particular problem.

Indeed, court judges, social workers, and educators who are part of the prison system already rely on some kind of parenting education as a remedial response to families who abuse or neglect their children.[56] Mandating parenting education in schools would provide basic knowledge about parenting before abuse and neglect can occur. No doubt, instituting mandatory basic parenting education will not guarantee that there won't be abuse and/or neglectful parents. However, there are good reasons to believe that as everyone acquires such knowledge, those who then decide to become parents will better understand the various stages of their children's physical, verbal, cognitive, emotional, and social development, as well as their nutritional and health needs, and will therefore have better interactions with their children; be less frustrated with their children; and be less likely to abuse or neglect them. In fact, there are studies of the effectiveness of parenting education in schools in the United Kingdom and elsewhere and the results are generally very positive.[57]

6. Conclusion

It is inexcusable that there are some biological parents who are grossly inadequate parents and who abuse and/or neglect their children. Nevertheless, we should not license *possible* biological parents, because biological parenting is a fundamental right, and fundamental rights should not be licensed. Biological parenting is a fundamental right because, among other things, one has fundamental rights to the fundamental conditions for pursuing the basic activities, and biological parenting is a basic activity. I called this the human rights account of parental rights. Among other things, I have explained why this account does not require thinking that biological parents own their biological children. Fundamental rights should not be licensed because having fundamental rights to the fundamental conditions for pursuing a basic activity means, among other things, having the right against others that they not interfere with one's pursuit of the basic activity, and licensing an activity is interfering with one's pursuit of that activity.

Unlike biological parenting, driving, practicing medicine and law, and the like are not basic activities. These activities may be important to certain individuals' life as a whole, but they are not activities that are important to human beings qua human beings' life as a whole. This explains why these activities may be licensed.

Likewise, the fact that biological parenting is a basic activity while adoptive parenting is not also explains why adoptive parenting can be licensed. Another reason why adoptive parenting can be licensed is that in adoptive parenting, the prospective adoptive parents do not (yet) have a right to be a parent to a particular child. Given this, licensing would not interfere with their rights.

If biological parents have the right to parent their biological children, what should we do about the problem of possibly inadequate parents? I first pointed out that biological parents' having this right is compatible with children's having real and robust rights. I then proposed that we should institute mandatory basic parenting education in middle- and high schools so that everyone would have basic scientific knowledge about childhood development and the importance of good parenting. This will not eliminate abusive and neglectful parents, but there are good reasons to believe that it will reduce their incidence.

Children without Adequate Parents and the Duty to Adopt

1. Children without Adequate Parents

According to UNICEF, there are over 150 million orphans in the world, where an orphan is defined as a child who has lost one or both parents.[1] There are at least 17 million orphans who have lost both parents and who are living in orphanages or on the streets.[2] More than 2 million children are in institutional care.[3] This estimate is likely to be low, as many institutions are unregistered and many countries do not regularly collect and report data on children in institutional care.[4] In the United States, there are over four hundred thousand children without permanent families in foster care.[5] If children have a right to be loved, what should we do about these children?

One might think that the solution is for as many of these children to be adopted as early and as quickly as possible.[6] In Chapter Three, we have seen that children who are not adequately loved are at risk for serious delays in their physical, cognitive, emotional, and social development. Indeed, in a meta-analysis of seventy-five studies on more than 3,888 children in nineteen different countries, it was found that children raised in institutional care have an IQ twenty points lower than children in foster care.[7] Also, each year in the United States, over twenty thousand children "age out" of foster care.[8] The outcome for these children is grim. Twenty-five percent will be incarcerated within the first two years after they leave the system.[9] Over 20 percent will become homeless at some time after age eighteen. Many will fail to maintain regular employment and many will experience early pregnancies.[10]

However, adoption may not be the correct thing to do with respect to all these children. Suppose that the estimates provided by UNICEF are correct. More than 80 percent of the 150 million children have at least one parent.[11] Arguably, at least some of these parents love their children. If so, what these parents may need is welfare assistance of some kind rather than someone else adopting their children. This is equally true in the United States with respect, for instance, to some cases of teenage pregnancy. Arguably, what needs to be done in some of these cases is not for someone else to try to adopt the teenager's child. If a teenager loves the child and wants to keep the child, sometimes what should be done is to support the teenager in other ways, such as by providing free daycare so that the teenager can finish school, stay employed, and so on.

For similar reasons, the fact that there are over seventeen million children who have lost both parents does not mean that these children should be adopted by non-relatives. Some of these children may have relatives such as grandparents, aunts, and uncles who love them. If so, again, what we should do in these cases may be to provide welfare assistance of some kind to these relatives rather than trying to adopt these children.

At the same time, the estimates provided by UNICEF leave out certain children who should be adopted. For instance, the fact that a child has two parents does not mean that the child is receiving the kind of love and care that she needs. As we have seen from Chapter Six, some parents neglect and abuse their children. Other parents may unfortunately be unable to provide the kind of love and care that a child needs, even if they do love their children, perhaps because they have too many children. It is also a fact of life that some parents may just not love, or care about, their children. In these cases, these children may need to be adopted (either by relatives or non-relatives), even if these children still have both parents.

Our focus should therefore not be on children who are orphaned per se, but rather on children who do not have adequate parents. While there are no estimates on the number of children without adequate parents, there are reasons to believe that the number is still in the millions. We know, for example, that there are at least two million children in institutional care. It is true that some of these children still have parents, but it seems reasonable to assume that many of these children are in these institutions because they do not have parents who can provide the kind of love and care that they need—in other words, they do not have adequate parents. So what should we do about children without adequate parents?

In this chapter, I shall argue that there is a duty to adopt these children and that we can derive this duty straightforwardly from the right of children to be loved. The United Nations Department of Economic and Social Affairs/Population Division estimates that about 260,000 children are adopted each year worldwide.[12] This is far short of the millions of children without adequate parents who need to be adopted. In the United States, over a hundred thousand children in foster care are eligible for adoption, but nearly 40 percent of these children will wait over three years in foster care before being adopted.[13] Hence, if there is a duty to adopt, this will have significant implications for our public policies.

Here it is useful to point out that some people have advanced a similar claim of a duty to adopt. Drawing on Peter Singer's idea of a duty of easy rescue, some people have argued that those who want to have children have a duty to adopt rather than have biological children.[14] The reason is as follows: There are millions of children who will suffer great harm if not adopted. If one can prevent a great harm to another by doing, X, without sacrificing anything of substantial significance, then one has a duty to X. Those who want to have children can prevent a great harm by adopting rather than having biological children without sacrificing anything of substantial significance. Therefore, those who want to have children have a duty to adopt rather than to have biological children. We can call this the Easy Rescue view. As Daniel Friedrich, one of the advocates of this view, puts it: "If we can protect others from serious harm at little cost to ourselves we morally ought to do it. Moreover, we can protect parentless children from serious harm at little cost to ourselves by adopting them. . . . [therefore] all of us who are thinking about having a family ought to consider very seriously adopting a child rather than having a biological child."[15]

The Easy Rescue view may seem plausible, and indeed, attractive. Given this, I shall begin by assessing this view. I shall first explain how someone might think that adoption can be a case of easy rescue. Next I shall argue that there are problems with deriving the duty to adopt from the Easy Rescue view. I then show how the duty to adopt can instead be derived from the right of children to be loved, and I argue that this view, what I call the Human Right view, is a better way to justify a duty to adopt than the Easy Rescue view. Finally, I shall propose a potential way of encouraging more people who are motivated to adopt actually to adopt.

2. Adoption as Easy Rescue?

That there is a duty of easy rescue stems from the idea that if one can prevent a great harm to another by doing, X, without sacrificing anything of substantial significance, then one has a duty to do X. Indeed, if a child were drowning in a shallow pond and you could easily save the child but doing so would get your expensive clothes wet, it is generally agreed that you would have a duty to rescue the child because you would be preventing a great harm without sacrificing anything of substantial significance. While saving a child from a shallow pond is a paradigm case of easy rescue, it might be asked, how can adopting a child be a case of easy rescue? That is, how can adopting a child not involve sacrificing anything of substantial significance? For instance, adopting a child means that one would be committing to being a parent for the next eighteen years. The United States Department of Agriculture estimates that parents in a middle-income household will spend an average of $241,000 to raise a child born in 2012 to the age of seventeen, which does not seem to be an insignificant amount.[16] Also, children adopted at an older age tend to have special needs. In particular, they tend to have a higher rate of physical and mental health issues, including learning disability, Attention Deficit Disorder, and behavior problems.[17] Given this, adopting these children would not be an easy task by any means. Moreover, people have a strong preference to have children who are genetically related to them, that is, biological children. Given this strong preference, wouldn't imposing a duty to adopt on those who want to have biological children be too demanding for them?

In response to these points, advocates of the Easy Rescue view may agree that imposing a duty to adopt on those who do not want to have children at all would be too demanding, precisely because adopting a child would mean committing to being a parent for eighteen years. However, advocates of the Easy Rescue view would point out that those who want to have children are already committed to meeting the cost of biological parenting such as being a parent for eighteen years. Indeed, the cost is even higher for those who require access to fertility treatments (at least in the United States). In one study, the average cost of successful medication-only treatment was between $5,894 and $61,377 for IVF, and the cost of successful donor egg IVF was even higher, at $72,642.[18] It is true that adoption can sometimes be quite costly, especially if it involves international adoption, which can cost as much as $40,000.[19] However, this figure is at the higher end of the spectrum. Also, in the United States there are federal tax credits for those who adopt a child, which would offset the additional cost of adoption.[20] If adoption will not cost much more for an individual who is already planning to have a child, then, according to this line of thought, this individual can adopt rather than have a biological child without sacrificing anything of substantial significance.

Regarding the point that children who are adopted at an older age tend to have special needs, advocates of the Easy Rescue view may say that they have in mind the adoption of infants without special needs. Indeed, Friedrich says that "I shall therefore limit my focus and ask whether there is a duty to adopt healthy children without any signs of long term special needs."[21]

Finally, with respect to the point that people prefer to have biological children, advocates of the Easy Rescue view may respond in a weak, strong, or moderate way. The weak response says that people's preference to have biological children is often based on false beliefs.[22] For example, people may be concerned that they will not love an adopted child or that they will not love an adopted child as much as a biological child. However, studies have found that the level of parental investment is similar between two-adoptive-parent families and two-biological-parent families.[23] Other people may worry that the biological parents could take back an adopted child. However, at least in the United States, adoptions are legally binding agreements that do not occur until the rights of all parents have been legally terminated by a court of law. Once this takes place, it is very rare for an adoption to be challenged legally. According to proponents of the weak response, once these false beliefs are corrected, some people would no longer prefer to have biological children over adoption.

The strong response says that people's preference to have biological children is irrational and normatively unjustified. For instance, some people prefer to have a biological child because they want to have someone who bears physical and psychological similarities to them. However, this preference seems irrational since there is no guarantee that one's biological child would be physically and psychologically similar to one. Other people prefer to have a biological child because they believe that having a biological child with a loved one is a unique way for the couple to express their love for one another. Against this thought, it might be argued that a couple can also express this love by adopting a child together. Still others believe that having a biological child would allow one to continue one's name.[24] In response, it might be pointed out that an adopted child can also continue one's name. Hence, so the argument goes, it seems that people are motivated to have biological children for all sorts of irrational and normatively unjustified reasons. On the strong response, since the preference to have biological children is irrational and normatively unjustified, requiring people to give up this preference and adopt is not asking them to give up anything of substantial significance.

Finally, on the moderate response, people's preference to have biological children can be rational and normatively justified, but preventing serious harm to a child who is not adopted is more important than having a biological child. According to this line of thought, if an individual who wants to have children does not have a biological child, a possible biological child is not harmed by not coming into existence. However, if that individual does not adopt a child who needs to be adopted, then a child will suffer serious harm. On the moderate response, it seems more important to perform an act that would prevent a serious harm than a different act the omission of which would not harm a possible biological child.

3. Why Adoption Is Not Easy Rescue

What should we think of the Easy Rescue view? There is something to the idea that if someone is already planning to have children, then the *financial* cost of adoption will not be much more than the *financial* cost of having a biological child. The data is more mixed on whether having an adopted child might be more burdensome in other ways than having a biological child, *even in cases of infant adoption.* It is true that some studies have found that adoption is not a risk factor for adjustment problems.[25] However, other, more recent, studies have found that parents and children reported more conflict in adoptive families when compared with nonadoptive families.[26] For instance, in one study in which all the adopted children were placed for adoption prior to two years of age, it was found that adopted adolescents were less warm and, in families with two adopted children, more conflict-prone than nonadopted adolescents.[27] Be that as it may, there are at least two problems with the Easy Rescue view.

First, the duty to adopt generated from this view seems to be of limited use. As we have seen, at best, the duty would be applicable to the adoption of healthy infants, since healthy infants are, other things being equal, easier to adopt. However, there is no real shortage of people wanting and waiting to adopt infants who are healthy. Since the 1970s, many countries have seen a large drop in the number of children available for adoption domestically.[28] In Italy, for example, there are fifteen couples who wish to adopt for every local child available for adoption.[29] In the United States, only one out of three women who seek to adopt actually succeed in adoption.[30] Factors that contribute to this decline in the number of children available for adoption include effective birth controls; the fact that abortion is legal in many countries; the fact that single parenthood is more acceptable today than in the past; the fact that the stigma of having a child out of wedlock has diminished; and so on.[31] At the same time, prospective adoptive parents often prefer adopting younger, healthier children. For instance, in the United States, women seeking to adopt would prefer to adopt a child younger than two years old, without disability, and a single child rather than two or more siblings.[32] Since there is no real shortage of people wanting and waiting to adopt healthy infants, even if there were a duty to adopt these infants, this duty would seem to be of limited use because these infants would be adopted anyway.

At the same time, children who do need to be adopted tend to be older and/or not as healthy. UNAIDS et al. estimate that close to 90 percent of the world's orphans are over the age of five.[33] Earlier we saw that over a hundred thousand children in foster care are eligible for adoption in the United States, but nearly 40 percent of these children will wait over three years in foster care before being adopted. Since adopting these children would, other things being equal, be much more work, the Easy Rescue view would not apply. In other words, the duty to adopt generated from the Easy Rescue view would at best apply in cases in which adoption is already taking place and would not apply in cases in which adoption is needed the most.

Second, the various responses addressing people's preference to have biological children are not convincing. For instance, consider the weak response, according to which people sometimes prefer to have biological children because they have certain false beliefs. Even if this is true, this response leaves open the possibility that some people who prefer to have biological children do not have these false beliefs. If so, those who take this line would have to accept that these people would not have a duty to adopt, as indeed Friedrich does.[34]

Or, consider the strong response, according to which people's preference to have biological children is irrational and normatively unjustified. This view seems too strong. We can grant that people may be motivated by all kinds of seemingly unjustified factors in wanting to have a biological child. But their doing so should not detract from the value of biological parenting as such. As we have seen in Chapter Six, the value of biological parenting comes from the fact that one is (a) creating a new life; (b) a rightholder; (c) with one's genetic material which in part determines the genetic identity of this new individual; (d) and one has the opportunity to see and shape the growth of this new individual. As I have argued, these factors together explain why biological parenting is a basic activity, that is, an activity that is important to human beings qua human beings' life as a whole. Suppose that this is so. The preference to have biological children can be rational and normatively justified.[35] Indeed, consider an analogy. People may want to have an education for all kinds of seemingly unjustified reasons—for instance, they may want to conquer the world, show off to their neighbors, and so on. Even so, their doing so should not detract from the value of education as such.

Finally, consider the moderate response, according to which preventing serious harm to a child who is not adopted is more important than having a biological child. As we have said in Chapter Six, people have human rights to the fundamental conditions for pursuing biological parenting; and, at least in normal circumstances, morality does not require one to sacrifice one's fundamental conditions for the sake of others. This means that, at least in normal circumstances, morality does not require one to sacrifice one's fundamental conditions for pursuing biological parenting in order to adopt a child, even if it is the case that preventing serious harm to a child who is not adopted is a very good and praiseworthy thing.

Some may reply that we are not in normal circumstances. Instead we are in an emergency situation in which there are millions of children who need to be adopted and where the rights that we ordinarily have should be suspended. I doubt that we are currently in an emergency situation where our ordinary rights should be suspended. But if we were in an emergency situation, then morality can require much more from us than just easy rescue. In an emergency situation, even those who do not want to have children can be required to adopt. In other words, once one appeals to the idea of an emergency situation, one has already moved away from the Easy Rescue view, which presupposes that we are in normal circumstances.

4. Adoption as a Human Right

Still, I do think that there is a duty to adopt children without adequate parents. I shall now show that we can derive this duty straightforwardly from the right of children to be loved and I shall argue that this way of justifying the duty to adopt is better than the Easy Rescue view.

In Chapter Five, we said that the right of children to be loved means that every able person in appropriate circumstances has a duty to love every child, and that for coordination reasons, biological parents should have the primary duty to love a child and everyone else has an associate duty to help the biological parents carry out their primary duty. We also said that if and when the biological parents became unavailable, then someone else would have the duty to step in and become the primary dutybearer. A child without adequate parents is a child whose biological parents are not available. Given this, someone else has the duty to step in and become the primary dutybearer for this child. In other words, someone has the duty to adopt this child.

As with the duty to love, the duty to adopt also belongs to every able person in appropriate circumstances. And as with the duty to love, since what a child needs is for a few individuals to adopt them rather than for everyone to do so, it is also helpful to distinguish between the primary and associate dutybearers of this duty. The primary dutybearers would be those who would adopt a child and the associate dutybearers would be those who would support the primary dutybearers in discharging the duty to adopt.

How should we determine who should be assigned the primary duty to adopt a child? When assigning the primary duty to love a child, I proposed four factors: responsibility, proximity, ability, motivation. Of these four factors, motivation and ability are probably the two most important factors when considering who should have the primary duty to adopt. Indeed, the ideal individual to adopt a child is someone who wants to adopt a child and who has the ability adequately to love and take care of the child. Proximity could also be a relevant factor. For instance, it could function as a tie-breaker in deciding between two people who are equally motivated to adopt a child and who have equal abilities to love and take care of a child. Responsibility probably does not play much of a role in determining who should be assigned this duty. Someone who accidentally caused the biological parents of a particular child to die might feel that he has the responsibility to adopt the child. However, such a scenario is likely to be rare.

In addition to these four factors, there are other factors that could also be relevant in determining who should be assigned the primary duty to adopt. For instance, those who have special relationships with the child and/or the child's biological parents, such as the grandparents, aunts, and uncles, may be assigned the primary duty to adopt, because in many instances, they are already motivated to love and take care of the child and may also have had a certain history with the child. However, not all relatives of a particular child are motivated and/or have the ability to adopt the child. In these cases, it may be preferable to assign someone else the duty to adopt. Culture and language could also be important, especially with respect to children who are older, since a child who is adopted into a new culture with a new language would have to learn the new language and/or assimilate into the new culture.

At the same time, everyone else has the associate duty to help the new primary dutybearers discharge their duty. As with the duty to love, this may mean supporting tax breaks for those who have adopted. It may also mean supporting the financing of free childcare and medical care for some adopted children. We can call this the Human Right view.

This way of justifying the duty to adopt is better than the Easy Rescue view in many respects. First, on the Human Right view, there is a duty to adopt even if a child is older and/or not as healthy. As we have seen, on the Easy Rescue view, the duty to adopt is applicable primarily in cases of healthy infants.

Second, on the Human Right view, the duty to adopt belongs to everyone and not just to those who are already planning to have children. This means that even people who do not want to have children would have this duty. Assuming that there are enough other people who would adopt, people who do not want to have children would themselves then not have to adopt. But they would still have associate duties to support those who have adopted. I shall shortly consider practical policies that could encourage more people who are motivated to adopt actually to do so.

Finally, the Human Right view is fully compatible with the idea that the preference to have a biological child can be rational and normatively justified. On the Human Right view, the ideal people to be assigned the primary duty to adopt are those with the motivation and the ability. As we have seen, the Easy Rescue view targets those who want to have children as subject to a duty to adopt. However, while those who want to have children may have, for example, the financial ability to adopt, many of them do not have the motivation to adopt, as they are motivated instead to have a biological child. Given this, on the Human Right view, they would not be the most ideal people to be assigned the primary duty to adopt. Still, those who want to have biological children can be required to assist those who have adopted, if they have, for example, the financial ability to do so, since, on the Human Right view, the duty to adopt belongs to all able persons in appropriate circumstances.

In short, the Human Right view is a better way of justifying a duty to adopt than the Easy Rescue view because it is applicable to all children without adequate parents, not just healthy infants, and it regards every able person as subject to the duty to adopt, not just those who want to have children.

5. How Can We Encourage More Adoptions?

As we have seen, there is an urgent need to make sure that many children without adequate parents, including those who are older and not as healthy, are adopted. Also, ideally, we should assign the primary duty to adopt to people who want to adopt and who have the ability to do so, other things being equal. What kind of policy can we enact to encourage more adoptions generally and more such adoptions in particular? Here I would like to suggest a possible way forward.

At present, we subscribe to what might be called a Single-Family Adoption (SFA) scheme, which aims to place a child in a single family, typically consisting of a married couple or a single parent. I suggest that we explore the possibility of supplementing the SFA scheme with what might be called a Multi-Family Adoption (MFA) scheme, which would allow a child to be adopted by individuals from different families who are not biologically related and who are not romantically or sexually involved with one another.[36] The co-adopters would all be parents of the child and would all share a significant portion of the childcare responsibility. By childcare responsibility, I mean providing love, housing, nurturance, and care for the child; making sure that the child has health insurance coverage and that the child visits health-care providers regularly; ensuring that the child receives adequate education; and so on—in short, providing for the general welfare of the child. The co-adopters could all be primary parents to the child and have what is akin to a joint custody of the child. Or, as another possible arrangement, some of the co-adopters may be designated as the primary parents and would have the primary responsibility of housing the child and providing for the general welfare of the child, while the other co-adopters may be designated as the secondary parents and would supplement the child-caring efforts of the primary parents. If the primary parents died, the secondary parents would take on their responsibilities.

Other details of the MFA scheme would depend on the particular circumstances of the parents and the legal arrangements of particular countries. For example, in the United States, there is at present no universal health care coverage. So, the primary parents would typically be the ones responsible for insuring the children. However, one might also make it the case that the secondary parents could cover the adopted child through their health insurance plan. This would be akin to some divorce cases where the Qualified Medical Child Support Order enables a custodial parent to obtain health insurance coverage for the children through the noncustodial parent's group health insurance plan.[37] Also, typically the primary parents might claim the child for a dependent deduction on their tax forms. However, perhaps there could be ways to divide the deduction so that both sets of parents could claim some amount of the deduction.

The MFA scheme is inspired by the "extended family" model, found in many parts of the world, where grandparents, aunts, and uncles sometimes share a significant portion of the childcare responsibility with the biological parents, including providing love for the children. The MFA scheme seeks to extend this model to adoption so that children without adequate parents might also be able to thrive by being raised by non-biologically related individuals from different families, provided that these individuals can give these children, among other things, the kind of love that children need. The MFA scheme also has some affinity with "open adoption," which allows the biological parents to have some contact with their children and the adoptive family.[38] Although some prospective adoptive parents worry that the biological parents might try to reclaim their child in an open adoption—a worry that need not apply to the MFA scheme assuming that only non-biologically related individuals are involved—many of the individuals who have participated in open adoption have found the experience to be satisfying.[39]

The MFA scheme could enable more children, including those who are older and not as healthy, to be adopted by people who want to adopt them. As we have seen, there are over four hundred thousand children without permanent families in foster care. On average, these children spend about two years in foster care.[40] Ten percent of these children stay in care for five or more years.[41] About 30 percent of these children have severe emotional, behavioral, or developmental problems as a result of the fact that they spend long periods of time in care awaiting adoption or other permanent arrangements.[42] At the same time, nearly four in ten Americans (39 percent), or about 81.5 million adults, have considered adopting at some time in their lives.[43] To be sure, many of these people are interested in adoption in order to create a family for themselves. But there is evidence that some of them would adopt in order to provide a home for children who need one. In a Harris Survey of 1,416 Americans eighteen and older with diverse ethnic backgrounds, 11 percent say that they would be very likely, and 36 percent say that they would be somewhat likely, to consider adopting a child with behavioral problems.[44] Fourteen percent say that they would be very likely, and 42 percent say that they would be somewhat likely, to consider adopting a child with medical problems.[45] The survey found that African Americans and Hispanics are more willing than whites to considering adopting children with characteristics that may concern prospective parents, such as a child out of foster care or a child with medical or behavioral problems.[46]

Even so, no more than 2 percent of Americans have actually adopted.[47] In the Harris Survey, it was found that a major concern for 49 percent of the individuals interviewed is having the time to raise a child.[48] In addition, the cost of adoption concerns 45 percent of the middle-income individuals (those earning from $25,000 to $99,000), and 52 percent of the lower income individuals. Moreover, 50 percent of the individuals would like to have counseling services and support groups for the adoptive parents.

The MFA scheme may be able to help here. By allowing individuals who are not biologically related to co-adopt, the MFA scheme could be especially attractive to those who are motivated to adopt a child, but who may not have the time and resources fully to do so, since the time and cost required to raise an adopted child would be shared. It would also allow the co-adopters to form their own support group, much like an extended family. The Harris Survey also found that the highest percentages of Americans who had considered adopting a child were those ages thirty-five to fifty-four, married, and female.[49] So, the MFA scheme could enable, for example, a working woman in her forties—who wants to adopt a child but who may not have the time to do so—to adopt a child with, for example, some of her close friends. Moreover, if all of us have associate duties to see to it that primary dutybearers can successfully discharge their duty to love their children, some people might find the MFA scheme to be a preferred way of fulfilling these associate duties, because they have the motivation and are willing to partake in such a scheme.

Some people will be concerned that the MFA scheme will not provide a stable family arrangement for children without adequate parents. To alleviate this concern, before implementing the MFA scheme, it will be important to conduct studies to see whether children will in fact receive adequate love under such a scheme, how one would delineate and enforce responsibilities among primary and secondary parents, whether people in fact would be willing to participate in such a scheme, and how the likely confusion for a child owing to the diffusion of parental responsibility might affect a child's development. This said, it is worth remembering that over twenty thousand children in the United States alone age out of foster care each year. If the MFA scheme can promote more adoption of children without adequate parents, including those who are older and not as healthy, and can make it more likely that these children would receive the kind of love and care that they need, then it may be worth the effort to explore it further.

6. Conclusion

There are millions of children in the world today who do not have someone to provide them with the kind of love and care necessary for healthy development. In this chapter, I examined the idea that there is a duty to adopt many of these children.

Some people believe that there is a duty to adopt and that this duty belongs to those who want to have children. The rationale is that morality says that if one can prevent a great harm to another by doing something without sacrificing anything of substantial significance, then one has a duty to do that thing; and those who want to have children are already prepared to meet many of the costs of parenting, and therefore adoption will not cost much more for these individuals, at least financially speaking, and especially if these individuals adopt a healthy infant. Against this Easy Rescue view, I argued that the children who need to be adopted the most tend to be older and not as healthy; many of those who want to have children prefer to have biological children; and our having a human right to pursue biological parenting means that in normal circumstances, we are permitted to pursue biological parenting rather than to adopt.

Nevertheless, I agreed that there is a duty to adopt, and I argued that we can derive this duty straightforwardly from the right of children to be loved. As I explained, this right entails, among other things, that if and when the biological parents became unavailable, then someone else would have the duty to step in and become the primary dutybearer. Since a child without adequate parents is a child whose biological parents are not available, someone else has the duty to step in and adopt this child.

This Human Right view is better than the Easy Rescue view, I argued, because on the Human Right view, there can be a duty to adopt older and/or not as healthy children, and the duty to adopt belongs to everyone, not just those who want to have children.

If there is a duty to adopt, how can we encourage more people to fulfill this duty? As a matter of policy, I suggested that we consider supplementing our current adoption practices with the Multi-Family Adoption scheme, which would allow a child to be adopted by individuals from different families who are not biologically related and who are not romantically or sexually involved with one another. Whether the Multi-Family Adoption scheme can be effective requires further investigation. However, given the vast number of children who continue not to be adopted and who suffer as a result of not having adequate parents who love them and who take care of them, there is an urgent need to put matters relating to adoption at the forefront of public consciousness and public policy.

Conclusion

1. How Should We Prioritize the Right to Be Loved?

In Chapter Five, I mentioned that there are issues regarding how we should prioritize the right to be loved. For instance, what priority should we give to this right vis-à-vis such rights as children's right to education, the right to be cared for, and the right to food? Also, other people have other rights that may conflict with children's right to be loved. Parents, as autonomous adults, have rights to pursue their own life plans. How should their rights be balanced against the right of children to be loved? Before drawing this book to a close, it may be useful to comment on these issues.

Generally, my view is that we have an obligation to structure our society and political institutions in such a way that every right of every individual is respected and promoted. In a world in which this is not possible, we need a theory of distributive justice to determine how resources can be allocated fairly and in such a way as to ensure that as many people's rights are respected and promoted as possible. It is beyond the scope of this book to provide such a theory. But it may be worthwhile keeping the following remarks in mind when developing public policies regarding how children's right to be loved should be prioritized.

One might think that the right of children to be loved is simply not as urgent as some of the other rights that children and others may have. To support this idea, one might appeal, for instance, to Alan Gewirth's "criterion of degrees of needfulness for action," which is roughly the idea that when two rights-claims conflict, one should promote the right that is more needed for action.[1] Using this criterion, one might argue that children's being loved is not as urgent as, for example, the poor's being fed, since being fed is more necessary for an individual's action.

First, even if we grant that being fed is more urgent than being loved, children's being loved is still very urgent. As we have seen in Chapter Three, despite being well-fed, children have died or have suffered serious physical, social, and cognitive harms as a result of lack of love. Indeed, as we have said, being loved is a fundamental condition for children to pursue a good life. Hence, even if we do not consider being loved to be more urgent than being fed, we should still give the right of children to be loved a very high priority. Indeed, being fed is also typically more urgent (in terms of necessity for action) than receiving basic education. Yet few would question the importance of promoting children's right to basic education.

Second, it is important to point out that governments do not in fact give absolute priority to whatever is most necessary for action. To see this, consider the value of life. As a precondition for action, life is obviously very important. Still, governments do not always promote life above other values. For example, governments build schools even though they could use that money to build even more hospitals to ensure that even more people's lives would be saved. This seems morally permissible, particularly in a society that already has very low mortality rates. If so, this suggests that even though life is very important, we do not give it an absolute priority over all other values. Hence, even if one grants that being loved is not as urgent as being fed, this does not mean that being fed has absolute priority over being loved, especially since both are fundamental conditions for children to pursue a good life.

Third, to develop institutional arrangements that can adequately provide for children's various fundamental conditions, it is important to take into account all of their fundamental conditions, including their need for love. Otherwise, the kind of institutional arrangements developed may be inadequate. Consider the real-world example of trying to help children orphaned as a result of HIV/AIDS in Africa. The US government has funded a global initiative known as the President's Emergency Plan for AIDS Relief (PEPFAR) to combat the HIV/AIDS epidemic. Suppose that we were asked to make recommendations to PEPFAR regarding the kind of institutional arrangements that they should set up and develop.[2] If we focused solely on children's rights to food and shelter, the kind of institutional arrangements that we would recommend and develop could be very different from ones in which we also took into account children's right to be loved. The reason is that children can be fed and sheltered adequately in large and efficiently run institutions that pay no attention to their need for love. Given this, if we only focused on children's rights to food and shelter, we might recommend setting up such large institutions, with the result that children's need for love are not met. By taking into account children's need for love, we would recognize from the very start the importance of smaller institutions that can provide not only food and shelter but also love for children. Indeed, a touted success story of PEPFAR involves a hospice in Nairobi under the leadership of Father Angelo D'Agostino, which brought together 750 children who lost their parents and 250 elders who lost their children to create the Nyumbani Village. According to the Office of the US Global AIDS Coordinator, the village offered "what every child needs most—love." Hence, to develop adequate institutional arrangements for children, it is essential to take into account all of their fundamental conditions, including their need for love, from the very beginning.

2. Conclusion

Many international declarations, bills of rights, and the mission statements of various charitable foundations have proclaimed that children have a right to be loved. In this book, I argued that this proclamation is not merely empty rhetoric and that in fact this right can be justified in the same way as other rights. Children have a human right to be loved, because, as rightholders (in virtue of the fact that they have the genetic basis for moral agency), human beings have human rights to the fundamental conditions for pursuing a good life, and being loved is a fundamental condition for children to pursue a good life. A duty to love is conceptually possible because contrary to popular perception, one can bring about the emotional aspect of love at will.

Since children's right to be loved is a human right, everyone has a duty to love every child *even when the biological parents are available*. This does not mean that everyone has a duty to love every child *directly*, but it does mean that everyone has at least associate duties to help primary dutybearers carry out their duty to love. The duty to love does not require that we sacrifice our fundamental conditions for pursuing the basic activities, but it may require that we sacrifice more than what common sense morality supposes. Some associate duties include supporting better childcare programs and more flexible workplace policies for men and women that would make it easier for primary dutybearers to discharge their duty to love their children.

Arguably, these policies are necessary in any case, but this right further underwrites their normativity.

Even though children have a right to be loved, this does not mean that biological parenting should therefore be licensed, since biological parenting is a fundamental human right and fundamental human rights should not be licensed. To address the problem of possibly inadequate parents, we could introduce mandatory basic parenting education so that middle- to high schoolers would acquire basic scientific knowledge about childhood development; the nature of parenting; and how society can influence the parent/child relationship. Moreover, the right to be loved implies that there is a duty to adopt the millions of children without adequate parents. To encourage more adoptions, I proposed that we consider and explore the Multi-Family Adoption scheme, which would allow a child to be adopted by individuals from different families who are not biologically related and who are not romantically or sexually involved with one another.

As one can see, the arguments for the right of children to be loved can and do hang together as a coherent whole. For instance, the fact that human beings have human rights to the fundamental conditions for pursuing a good life explains not just why there is a right to be loved, but also why biological parenting should not be licensed (because there is a fundamental right to pursue biological parenting). The fact that these arguments mutually support each other should go some ways toward satisfying those who are concerned about the proliferation of rights claims and who might have questioned whether the right to be loved can be justified. Rights are a very important part of our modern political, legal, and moral discourse. As such, there is no doubt many more rights will be claimed and asserted. If I have been successful, this book offers a blueprint for how other purported rights claims can and should be justified.

Notes

Introduction

1. http://www.bbc.com/news/uk-27693587.

2. Neil MacCormick, "Children's Rights: A Test-Case for Theories of Right," *Archiv für Rechts- und Sozialphilosophie* LXII, no. 3 (1976).

3. James Griffin, *On Human Rights* (Oxford: Oxford University Press, 2008); L. W. Sumner, *The Moral Foundation of Rights* (Oxford: Clarendon Press, 1987); Carl Wellman, *The Proliferation of Rights: Moral Progress or Empty Rhetoric?* (Boulder, CO: Westview Press, 1999).

4. Sumner, *The Moral Foundation of Rights*, pp. 1, 15.

5. Griffin, *On Human Rights*, p. 92.

6. Ibid., Chapter 4; Carl Wellman, *Real Rights* (Oxford: Oxford University Press, 1995).

7. Wellman, *Real Rights*, pp. 107, 113.

8. Griffin, *On Human Rights*, p. 95.

9. Wesley Hohfeld, *Fundamental Legal Conceptions*, ed. W. W. Cook (New Haven, CT: Yale University Press, 1919).

10. Immanuel Kant, *The Metaphysics of Morals*, trans. Mary Gregor (Cambridge: Cambridge University Press, 1996), p. 161.

11. Francis Schrag, "Children: Their Rights and Needs," in *Whose Child?*, ed. William Aiken and H. LaFollette (Totowa, NJ: Littlefield, Adams, & Co., 1980), pp. 243–44.

12. Bernard Williams, "Persons, Character, and Morality," in *Moral Luck*, ed. Bernard Williams (Cambridge: Cambridge University Press, 1981).

13. US Department of Health and Human Services, "Child Maltreatment," (Washington, DC: US Department of Health and Human Services, 2011), p. viii.

14. UNICEF, "Progress for Children: A Report Card on Child Protection," (2009).

15. Ibid.

16. US Department of Health and Human Services, "The AFCARS Report, No. 19," (2012).

17. Mhairi Cowden, "What's Love Got to Do with It? Why a Child Does Not Have a Right to Be Loved," *Critical Review of International Social and Political Philosophy* 15, no. 3 (2012).

18. Daniel Friedrich, "A Duty to Adopt?," *Journal of Applied Philosophy* 30, no. 1 (2013).

Chapter 1

1. James Griffin, *On Human Rights* (Oxford: Oxford University Press, 2008), p. 95; Carl Wellman, *Real Rights* (Oxford: Oxford University Press, 1995), pp. 107, 113.

2. Peter Singer, *Practical Ethics*, 2nd ed. (Cambridge: Cambridge University Press, 1993). There is conceptual space for a position, according to which all human beings as well as some other animals are rightholders. Such a position would not necessarily be speciesist. In fact, the account I shall develop may be an example of such a position. As far as I am aware, such a position has not been advanced in the literature.

3. Joel Feinberg and Barbara. B. Levenbook, "Abortion," in *Matters of Life and Death*, ed. Tom Regan (New York: McGraw-Hill, 1993).

4. Wellman, *Real Rights*, pp. 107, 113.

5. Griffin, *On Human Rights*, p. 95.

6. Gregory Vlastos, "Justice and Equality," in *Theories of Rights*, ed. Jeremy Waldron (Oxford: Oxford University Press, 1984); Ronald Dworkin, *Life's Dominion: An Argument About Abortion, Euthanasia, and Individual Freedom* (New York: Alfred A. Knopf, 1993).

7. H. J. McCloskey, "Respect for Human Moral Rights Versus Maximizing Good," in *Utility and Rights*, ed. R. G. Frey (Oxford: Basil Blackwell, 1985); Bernard Williams, "The Human Prejudice," in *Philosophy as a Humanistic Discipline*, ed. A. W. Moore (Princeton: Princeton University Press, 2008).

8. John Finnis, "A Philosophical Case against Euthanasia," in *Euthanasia Examined: Ethical, Clinical, and Legal Perspectives*, ed. J. Keown (Cambridge: Cambridge University Press, 1995), p. 48. Readers will notice that Finnis is talking about persons, whereas I have been discussing rightholders. In this chapter, I understand the terms "rightholding" and "personhood" interchangeably. Some people who equate rightholding with personhood also hold a particular conception of personhood, namely, all and only those who are actual moral agents are persons. Consequently, they believe that all and only those who are actual moral agents are rightholders. I do not hold this view. Others equate personhood with actual moral agency, but not with rightholding. As many of them also believe that some non-moral agents, e.g., animals, can also be rightholders, these people argue that personhood is only a sufficient but not a necessary condition for rightholding. Since my equating rightholding with personhood is a stipulation, nothing substantive follows from it. If animals are rightholders, then, as I understand these terms, they would be persons, even if they are not actual moral agents.

9. T. M. Scanlon, *What We Owe to Each Other* (Cambridge, MA: Belknap Press, 1998), p. 186.

10. McMahan used the term "species-norm account" to describe something different, namely, a view about the nature of fortune and misfortune. This term is useful, though, for capturing the ideas advanced by writers such as Finnis and Scanlon. See Jeff McMahan, *The Ethics of Killing: Problems at the Margins of Life* (Oxford: Oxford University Press, 2002).

11. Ibid., pp. 146–49. Some might question whether the Superchimp would still be a chimpanzee if in fact it has rational capacities. This is a difficult issue as it involves knowing the nature of being a chimpanzee. For the sake of argument, let us allow that a being can have rational capacities and be a chimpanzee at the same time.

12. G. E. Moore has cautioned that we should not try to derive an Ought from an Is (G. E. Moore, *Principia Ethica* (Cambridge: Cambridge University Press, 1959)). It is not possible to do justice to this important question here, but arguably, empirical attributes in the world play some role in giving moral agents certain moral reasons for action (whether these empirical attributes do so directly, as, for example, when one derives an Ought directly from an Is, or indirectly via some other means, seems to be another matter). For example, it seems that an empirical phenomenon such as pain does play some role in giving moral agents

moral reasons to avoid causing it and to alleviate it if and when they can. If the empirical phenomenon of pain did not exist, there would not be a moral reason to alleviate it. If this is right, we can begin to understand how internal, empirical attributes can play some role in determining what we ought to do. See, e.g., James Griffin, *Value Judgement: Improving Our Ethical Beliefs* (Oxford: Clarendon Press, 1996) for this point.

13. See, e.g., Singer, *Practical Ethics*.

14. For discussions about whether we are numerical identical to an embryo, see, e.g., S. Matthew Liao, "Twinning, Inorganic Replacement, and the Organism View," *Ratio* 23, no. 1 (2010); ———, "The Organism View Defended," *The Monist* 89, no. 3 (2006).

15. Judith Jarvis Thomson, "A Defense of Abortion," *Philosophy and Public Affairs* 1, no. 1 (1971). In S. Matthew Liao, "Rescuing Human Embryonic Stem Cell Research: The Blastocyst Transfer Method," *American Journal of Bioethics* 5, no. 6 (2005). I argue that even if embryos were rightholders, there are still permissible ways of pursuing embryonic stem cell research.

16. Some might think that one could understand rightholding in a narrow or a wide way, and that if one understood rightholding in a wide way, turtles could, for instance, also be rightholders. Given this, it might be asked, why not understand rightholding in a wide way? In response, it is useful to point out that most philosophers do not understand rightholding in a wide way. There is a good reason for this. In particular, if we understood rightholding in a wide way, we would lose some important moral distinctions. For instance, if we understood rightholding in a wide way, then a normal functioning adult human being and a turtle would both be rightholders. But suppose that it remains the case that confronted with the choice between saving a turtle's limb or a human being's limb, one should save the human being's limb. In such a case, it seems that we would have lost an important way of distinguishing the moral status of a turtle and a human being by regarding both as rightholders and we would still need some other moral concept to explain why the turtle and the human being have different moral status.

17. See Wellman, *Real Rights*, p. 113.

18. Piaget's work in human cognitive development, for example, supports the idea that rationality develops according to a fairly predictable

schedule. For the claim that the development of empathy in human beings also follows certain prescribed progression, see Martin L. Hoffman, "Moral Development," in *Developmental Psychology: An Advanced Textbook*, ed. M. H. Bornstein and M. E. Lamb (Hillsdale, NJ: Erlbaum, 1988), pp. 497–548.

19. I thank David Wasserman for this point.

20. CDC, "Effectiveness in Disease and Injury Prevention: Use of Folic Acid for Prevention of Spina Bifida and Other Neural Tube Defects, 1983–1991," *Morbidity and Mortality Weekly Report* 40, no. 513–16 (1991).

21. About 3–4 percent of the mentally impaired population is severely impaired, and only 1–2 percent of the mentally impaired population is classified as profoundly impaired. See, e.g., Mark L. Batshaw and Bruce K. Shapiro, "Mental Retardation," in *Children with Disabilities*, ed. Mark L. Batshaw (Baltimore, MD: Paul H. Brookes, 1997).

22. There are other kinds of genetic defects that involve more than a single gene. As far as I know, either those defects are so severe that the fetuses typically die before birth, or individuals with these defects typically only have mild mental impairments. See, e.g., American College of Obstetricians and Gynecologists, "Prenatal Diagnosis of Fetal Chromosomal Abnormalities," *ACOG Practice Bulletin* 27 (2001).

23. I thank Jeff McMahan for this suggestion.

24. S. Matthew Liao, "The Genetic Account of Moral Status: A Defense," *Journal of Moral Philosophy* 9, no. 2 (2012).

25. A. I. Melden, "Do Infants Have Moral Rights?" in *Whose Child?*, ed. William Aiken and Hugh LaFollette (Totowa, NJ: Littlefield, Adams & Co., 1980), pp. 210–11.

26. See, e.g., John Harris, *The Value of Life* (London: Routledge & Kegan Paul, 1985), pp. 11–12; L. W. Sumner, "Abortion," in *Health Care Ethics: An Introduction*, ed. D. Van DeVeer and T. Regan (Philadelphia: Temple University Press, 1987), p. 174; Mary Warnock, "Do Human Cells Have Rights?," *Bioethics* 1, no. 1 (1987), p. 12.

27. See Jonathan Glover, *Causing Death and Saving Lives* (Harmondsworth: Penguin, 1977).

28. See Massimo Reichlin, "The Argument from Potential: A Reappraisal," *Bioethics* 11, no. 1 (1997).

29. Feinberg and Levenbook, "Abortion."

30. See, e.g., Sumner, "Abortion," p. 173, who makes a similar point.

31. Some might suggest that perhaps infants are given preference because they are smaller. However, this cannot be the explanation, since if someone were to have a small turtle, and assuming that turtles are not rightholders, we would not give the turtle preference over an adult male just because it is smaller.

32. See, e.g., Don Marquis, "Why Abortion Is Immoral," *Journal of Philosophy* 86 , no. 4 (1989), p. 189.

33. S. Matthew Liao, "The Embryo Rescue Case," *Theoretical Medicine and Bioethics* 27, no. 2 (2006).

34. The concept of time-relative interest comes from McMahan, *The Ethics of Killing: Problems at the Margins of Life*, pp. 80, 170–74, 183–88. See also S. Matthew Liao, "Time-Relative Interests and Abortion," *Journal of Moral Philosophy* 4, no. 2 (2007).

35. I develop this point in greater detail in Liao, "The Embryo Rescue Case."

36. Joel Feinberg, "The Rights of Animals and Unborn Generations," in *Rights, Justice, and Bounds of Liberty* (Princeton, NJ: Princeton University Press, 1980).

37. Singer, *Practical Ethics*, Chs. 2 and 4.

38. For philosophers who have argued that Feinberg's notion of interest is too narrow and that some nonsentient entities such as plants can also have interests, see Gary Varner, *In Nature's Interests? Interests, Animal Rights, and Environmental Ethics* (New York: Oxford University Press, 1998); Kenneth Goodpaster, "On Being Morally Considerable," *Journal of Philosophy* 75, no. 6 (1978).

39. See Varner, *In Nature's Interests? Interests, Animal Rights, and Environmental Ethics*; Goodpaster, "On Being Morally Considerable."

40. Feinberg, "The Rights of Animals and Unborn Generations."

41. I thank Agnieszka Jaworska for this point. For similar examples, see Christopher Grau, "Moral Status, Speciesism, and Liao's Genetic Account," *Journal of Moral Philosophy* 7, no. 3 (2010). For my response to Grau, see Liao, "The Genetic Account of Moral Status: A Defense."

42. Ying Chen et al., "Embryonic Stem Cells Generated by Nuclear Transfer of Human Somatic Nuclei into Rabbit Oocytes," *Cell Research* 13, no. 4 (2003).

Chapter 2

1. James Griffin, "Towards a Substantive Theory of Rights," in *Utility and Rights*, ed. Raymond G. Frey (Oxford: Blackwell, 1984).

2. ———, *On Human Rights* (Oxford: Oxford University Press, 2008).

3. Martha C. Nussbaum, "Capabilities and Human Rights," *Fordham Law Review* 66, no. 2 (1997); ———, "Capabilities as Fundamental Entitlements: Sen and Social Justice," *Feminist Economics* 9, no. 2–3 (2003); ———, *Frontiers of Justice: Disability, Nationality, Species Membership* (Cambridge: Belknap Press, 2006); ———, *Creating Capabilities: The Human Development Approach* (Cambridge: Belknap Press, 2011).

4. What I am calling the Naturalistic Conception has, among other things, also been called the "orthodox" view (Charles R. Beitz, "Human Rights and the Law of Peoples," in *The Ethics of Assistance: Morality and the Distant Needy*, ed. Deen Chatterjee (Cambridge: Cambridge University Press, 2004); John Tasioulas, "Taking Rights out of Human Rights," *Ethics* 120, no. 4 (2010)).

5. John Rawls, *The Law of Peoples: With "The Idea of Public Reason Revisited"* (Harvard: Harvard University Press, 1999).

6. Charles R. Beitz, *The Idea of Human Rights* (Oxford: Oxford University Press, 2009).

7. Joseph Raz, "Human Rights without Foundations," in *The Philosophy of International Law*, ed. Samantha Besson and John Tasioulas (Oxford: Oxford University Press, 2010); ———, "Human Rights in the Emerging World Order," *Transnational Legal Theory* 1, no. 1 (2010).

8. Beitz, "Human Rights and the Law of Peoples," p. 197.

9. Ibid., p. 198.

10. Jan Narveson, *The Libertarian Idea* (Philadelphia: Temple University Press, 1988).

11. See, e.g., Henry Shue, *Basic Rights: Subsistence, Affluence, and U.S. Foreign Policy (Second Edition)* (Princeton, NJ: Princeton University Press, 1996).

12. See, e.g., James Griffin, "Welfare Rights," *The Journal of Ethics* 4, no. 1–2 (2000); Nussbaum, *Frontiers of Justice: Disability, Nationality, Species Membership*, p. 286.

13. A way to identify what the basic activities are is through a mixture of empirical research from, e.g., anthropological and sociological studies, and normative theorizing, using something like the method of reflective equilibrium.

14. John Rawls, *A Theory of Justice* (Oxford: Oxford University Press, 1971).

15. Ibid., p. 62.

16. Rights could also have non-instrumental importance in addition to having instrumental importance.

17. See, e.g., Ronald Dworkin, *Taking Rights Seriously* (London: Duckworth, 1977); Robert Nozick, *Anarchy, State and Utopia* (Oxford: Blackwell, 1974).

18. Joel Feinberg, "The Nature and Value of Rights," in *Bioethics and Human Rights : A Reader for Health Professionals*, ed. Elsie L. Bandman and Bertram Bandman (Boston: Little, Brown, 1970).

19. Griffin, *On Human Rights*; ———, "Welfare Rights"; ———, "Discrepancies between the Best Philosophical Account of Human Rights and the International Law of Human Rights," *Proceedings of the Aristotelian Society* 101, no. 1 (2001); ———, "First Steps in an Account of Human Rights," *European Journal of Philosophy* 9, no. 3 (2001). This sections draws on S. Matthew Liao, "Agency and Human Rights," *Journal of Applied Philosophy* 27, no. 1 (2010).

20. Griffin, "Discrepancies between the Best Philosophical Account of Human Rights and the International Law of Human Rights," p. 4.

21. ———, "First Steps in an Account of Human Rights," p. 311.

22. Ibid., p. 313.

23. See ———, *On Human Rights*, Chs. 12 and 13.

24. For an excellent discussion of some of the problems that Griffin's approach faces, see John Tasioulas, "Human Rights, Universality and the Values of Personhood: Retracing Griffin's Steps," *European Journal of Philosophy* 10, no. 1 (2002).

25. Lest this lead to confusion, let me note that Griffin does mention a second ground for human rights, what he calls practicalities, which, as he explains, help to make the content of a particular human right "determinate enough to be an effective guide to behaviour" (*Griffin, On Human Rights*, pp. 37–39). For my purpose, we can leave this aside,

because I am interested in standalone grounds for human rights, that is, grounds that are not parasitic on other grounds for human rights. For example, since the role of practicalities is to make human rights that are grounded in some other way, e.g., agency, more determinate, practicalities are parasitic on other grounds for human rights, and are therefore not standalone grounds for human rights. In fact, the requirement of practicalities seems to be a reasonable requirement for any standalone ground for human rights, since any standalone ground for human rights should be determinate enough to be an effective guide to behavior. Hence, when I claim that Griffin believes that "agency is the sole ground for human rights," I am taking him to be holding the view that agency is the sole standalone ground for human rights, which I believe he does hold. Also, when I investigate whether there could be other grounds for human rights, I am interested in whether there could be other standalone grounds for human rights. To save words, though, I shall leave out the word "standalone" throughout the rest of the chapter.

26. Ibid., p. 36.

27. Ibid., pp. 52–53.

28. As another example, while education is important for autonomy, it seems that the value of understanding is also sufficiently important to a human life that it could provide its own independent contribution to the existence of a human right to education. If so, it could also be asked whether Griffin's notion of agency should be the sole explanation for such human right as the right to education.

29. Griffin, *On Human Rights*, p. 52.

30. Ibid., p. 52.

31. Ibid., p. 53.

32. Ibid., p. 53.

33. It might be thought that offering someone a large sum of money so that she would do something she does not want to do or is even resolved not to do does not undermine her agency, since she has chosen to accept the offer. Two comments. First, this is not how Griffin understands what it means to undermine someone's agency. As said earlier, for Griffin, getting someone to do what she does not want to do or is even resolved not to do is sufficient to undermine that person's agency. Second, there are numerous examples in which it seems that a person's agency has been undermined even though the person has chosen to

accept an offer. For instance, the practice of paying subjects a large sum of money so that they would sell body parts, for instance, oocytes or organs, or participate in medical research, arguably undermines their agency even though these individuals have chosen to accept the offer. This may explain why a number of people believe that such a practice is a form of undue inducement.

34. Or, consider another example suggested by an anonymous reviewer: Suppose I decorate your work environment with images of enticing sweets, none of which you notice, but together they give you the idea that you would like a donut break and this prompts you to go to the cafeteria. It seems that I have undermined your agency, but it does not seem that I have violated your human rights.

35. Griffin, *On Human Rights*, p. 34.

36. Nussbaum, *Creating Capabilities: The Human Development Approach*, pp. 20–26.

37. Ibid., p. 28.

38. Ibid., pp. 33–34.

39. Ibid., p. 62.

40. Ibid., p. 36.

41. Ibid., p. 168.

42. Ibid., p. 169.

43. One could also quibble with Nussbaum's list of central capabilities. For instance, is being able to live with concern for and in relation to animals and plants really a central human capability without which a human life would be undignified? Suppose that it were possible for human beings to live on Mars (or some other planet). Suppose that Mars did not have other animals and plants. Suppose, further, that some human beings were to migrate to Mars. Would the lives of these human beings be undignified because these human beings would not be able to live with concern for and in relation to animals and plants? It does not seem so. Moreover, if human rights were grounded in capabilities, it does not seem that these human beings would be deprived of key human rights.

44. Nussbaum, *Frontiers of Justice: Disability, Nationality, Species Membership*, p. 172.

45. Ibid., p. 172.

46. Ibid., p. 172.

47. This section draws on S.Matthew Liao and Adam Etinson, "Political and Naturalistic Conceptions of Human Rights: A False Polemic?," *Journal of Moral Philosophy* 9, no. 3 (2012).

48. Rawls, *The Law of Peoples: With "The Idea of Public Reason Revisited,"* p. 79.

49. Ibid., p. 80.

50. Ibid., p. 68.

51. Ibid., p. 81.

52. Raz, "Human Rights without Foundations," p. 328.

53. Ibid., p. 329.

54. Ibid., pp. 330–32.

55. Beitz, *The Idea of Human Rights*, p. 101.

56. ———, "Human Rights and the Law of Peoples," p. 198; ———, *The Idea of Human Rights*, p. 57.

57. Raz, "Human Rights in the Emerging World Order," p. 40.

58. Beitz, *The Idea of Human Rights*, pp. 56–57.

59. Raz, "Human Rights in the Emerging World Order," p. 41.

60. http://www.survivalinternational.org/uncontactedtribes.

61. D. D. Raphael, "Human Rights, Old and New," in *Political Theory and the Rights of Man*, ed. D. D. Raphael (London: Macmillan, 1967), p. 65.

62. Beitz, *The Idea of Human Rights*, p. 109.

63. Raz, "Human Rights without Foundations," p. 336.

64. Ibid., p. 330.

Chapter 3

1. Mhairi Cowden, "What's Love Got to Do with It? Why a Child Does Not Have a Right to Be Loved," *Critical Review of International Social and Political Philosophy* 15, no. 3 (2012). I respond to Cowden in S. Matthew Liao, "Why Children Need to Be Loved," *Critical Review of International Social and Political Philosophy* 15, no. 3 (2012). I shall present and elaborate on some of those reponses shortly.

2. The United Nations Convention on the Rights of the Child 1989, Article 1.

3. U. K. Children Act 1989, s. 105(1).

4. David Archard, *Children: Rights and Childhood* (London: Routledge, 2004).

5. This account of parental love is a minimal account of love and the elements in this account are not exclusive to parental love. They are, for instance, also applicable to romantic love and friendship. The difference among the various kinds of love may be explained in part by differences in the physical and psychological proximity achievable (e.g., romantic love would be very proximate) and differences in the way one promotes the well-being of the beloved (e.g., parental love may involve restricting the autonomy of one's children, which would usually be inappropriate in other kinds of love).

6. Mia Kellmer Pringle, *The Needs of Children*, 3 ed. (London: Routledge, 1986), p. 35.

7. Erik H. Erikson, *Children and Society* (New York: Norton, 1950); John Bowlby, *Loss, Sadness and Depression*, 3 vols., vol. 3, Attachment and Loss (New York: Basic Books, 1980).

8. Jean Piaget, *The Origins of Intelligence in Children* (New York: International Universities Press, 1952).

9. Howard Miller and Paul S. Siegel, *Loving: A Psychological Approach* (New York: John Wiley and Sons, 1972), p. 14.

10. Pringle, *The Needs of Children*, p. 35.

11. Susan Harter, "Processes Underlying Adolescent Self-Concept Formation," in *From Childhood to Adolescence: A Transitional Period?*, ed. Raymond Montemayor, Gerald R. Adams, and Thomas P. Gullotta (Newbury Park, CA: Sage, 1990).

12. Miller and Siegel, *Loving: A Psychological Approach*, p. 4.

13. Ibid., p. 5.

14. Ibid., pp. 14–15.

15. Ibid., pp. 19–20.

16. Ross D. Parke and Richard H. Walters, "Some Factors Determining the Efficacy of Punishment for Inducing Response Inhibition," *Monographs of the Society for Research in Child Development* 32, no. 1 (1967).

17. William H. Redd, Edward K. Morris, and Jerry Martin, "Effects of Positive and Negative Adult-Interaction on Children's Social Preferences," *Journal of Experimental Child Psychology* 19, no. 1 (1975).

18. Susan Harter, "Developmental Perspectives on the Self-System," in *Handbook of Child Psychology*, ed. E. Mavis Hetherington (New York: Wiley, 1983).

19. Diana Baumrind, "Child Care Practices Anteceding Three Patterns of Preschool Behavior," *Genetic Psychology Monographs* 75, no. 1 (1967); Eleanor Maccoby and John Martin, "Socialization in the Context of the Family: Parent-Child Interaction," in *Handbook of Child Psychology*, ed. E. Mavis Hetherington (New York: Wiley, 1983).

20. Baumrind, "Child Care Practices Anteceding Three Patterns of Preschool Behavior."

21. Diana Baumrind and Allen Black, "Socialization Practices Associated with Dimension of Competence in Preschool Boys and Girls," *Child Development* 38 (1967).

22. Michael Boyes and Sandra Allen, "Styles of Parent-Child Interaction and Moral Reasoning in Adolescence," *Merrill-Palmer Quarterly* 39, no. 4 (1993); Lawrence Kohlberg, "Stage and Sequence: The Cognitive-Developmental Approach to Socialization," in *Handbook of Socialization Theory and Research*, ed. David A. Goslin (Chicago: Rand McNally, 1969).

23. Baumrind, "Child Care Practices Anteceding Three Patterns of Preschool Behavior."

24. Diana Baumrind, "Current Patterns of Parental Authority," *Developmental Psychology Monograph* 4, no. 1 (1971).

25. Ibid.

26. Maccoby and Martin, "Socialization in the Context of the Family: Parent-Child Interaction."

27. Advances in brain imaging techniques may enable scientists to study love directly. See, e.g., Thomas R. Insel and Larry J. Young, "The Neurobiology of Attachment," *Nature Reviews Neuroscience* 2, no. 2 (2001); S. Zeki, "The Neurobiology of Love," *FEBS Letters* 581, no. 14 (2007).

28. Liao, "Why Children Need to Be Loved."

29. William Goldfarb, "Effects of Psychological Deprivation in Infancy and Subsequent Stimulation," *American Journal of Psychiatry* 102, no. 1 (1945), p. 18.

30. René Spitz and Katherine M. Wolf, "Anaclitic Depression: An Inquiry into the Genesis of Psychiatric Conditions in Early Childhood," *The Psychoanalytic Study of the Child* 2 (1946), p. 320.

31. Jill Hodges and Barbara Tizard, "Social and Family Relationships of Ex-Institutional Adolescents," *Journal of Child Psychology and Psychiatry* 30, no. 1 (1989).

32. Sandra Kaler and B. J. Freeman, "Analysis of Environmental Deprivation: Cognitive and Social Development in Romanian Orphans," *Journal of Child Psychology and Psychiatry* 35, no. 4 (1994).

33. Karen Bos et al., "Psychiatric Outcomes in Young Children with a History of Institutionalization," *Harvard Review of Psychiatry* 19, no. 1 (2011).

34. NFTT has sometimes also been called "environmental retardation," "masked deprivation," or "environmental failure to thrive." See, e.g., Rose Coleman and Sally Provence, "Environmental Retardation (Hospitalism) in Infants Living in Families," *Pediatrics* 19, no. 2 (1957).

35. PSD has sometimes also been called "deprivation dwarfism," "abuse dwarfism," "psychological dwarfism," or "linear growth retardation." See, e.g., Henry K. Silver and Marcia Finkelstein, "Deprivation Dwarfism," *Journal of Pediatrics* 70, no. 3 (1967).

36. Donald. M. Berwick, Janice C. Levy, and Ruth Kleinerman, "Failure to Thrive: Diagnostic Yield of Hospitalization," *Archives of Diseases in Children* 57, no. 5 (1982).

37. Bengt Kristiansson and Sven P. Fallstrom, "Growth at the Age of 4 Years Subsequent to Early Failure to Thrive," *International Journal of Child Abuse and Neglect* 11, no. 1 (1987).

38. R. Kim Oates, Anthony Peacock, and Douglas Forest, "Long-Term Effects of Nonorganic Failure to Thrive," *Pediatrics* 75, no. 1 (1985).

39. Laura M. Mackner, J. Raymond Starr, and Maureen Black, "The Cumulative Effect of Neglect and Failure to Thrive on Cognitive Functioning," *Child Abuse and Neglect* 21, no. 7 (1997).

40. Oates, Peacock, and Forest, "Long-Term Effects of Nonorganic Failure to Thrive."

41. Helen H. Glaser et al., "Physical and Psychological Development of Children with Early Failure to Thrive," *Journal of Pediatrics* 73, no. 5 (1968).

42. E. Elmer, G. S. Gregg, and Patricia Ellison, "Late Results of the Failure to Thrive Syndrome," *Clinical Pediatrics* 8, no. 10 (1969).

43. Oates, Peacock, and Forest, "Long-Term Effects of Nonorganic Failure to Thrive."

44. Norman S. Ellerstein and Barbara E. Ostrov, "Growth Patterns in Children Hospitalized Because of Caloric-Deprivation Failure to Thrive," *American Journal of Disease in Children* 139, no. 2 (1985).

45. Harry F. Harlow, Robert O. Dodsworth, and Margaret K. Harlow, "Total Social Isolation in Monkeys," *Proceedings of the National Academy of Sciences* 54, no. 1 (1965).

46. Henry A. Cross and Harry F. Harlow, "Prolonged and Progressive Effects of Partial Isolation on the Behavior of Macque Monkeys," *Journal of Experimental Research in Personality* 1, no. 1 (1965).

47. Harry F. Harlow, "The Nature of Love," *American Psychologist* 13 (1958).

48. Harry F. Harlow, "Age-Mate or Peer Affectional System," in *Advances in the Study of Behavior*, ed. Daniel S. Lehrman, Robert A. Hinde, and Evelyn Shaw (New York: Academic Press, 1969).

49. Michael W. Andrews and L. A. Rosenblum, "Attachment in Infants Raised in Variable- and Low-Demand Environments," *Child Development* 62, no. 4 (1991).

50. Ibid.

51. Michael W. Andrews and L. A. Rosenblum, "The Development of Affiliative and Agonistic Social Patterns in Differentially Reared Monkeys," *Child Development* 65, no. 5 (1994).

52. Andrea Jackowski et al., "Early-Life Stress, Corpus Callosum Development, Hippocampal Volumetrics, and Anxious Behavior in Male Nonhuman Primates," *Psychiatry Research: Neuroimaging* 192, no. 1 (2011).

53. "Surrogate peer rearing" involves placing the infant monkeys with a cloth-covered inanimate surrogate mother for a certain amount of time during the day and with like-aged peers for the remaining amount of time.

54. Gabriella Conti et al., "Primate Evidence on the Late Health Effects of Early-Life Adversity," *Proceedings of the National Academy of Sciences* 109, no. 23 (2012).

55. Marie Åsberg, Lil Träskman, and Peter Thorén, "5-HIAA in the Cerebrospinal Fluid: A Biochemical Suicide Predictor," *Archives of General Psychiatry* 33, no. 10 (1976).

56. Gerald L. Brown et al., "Aggression, Suicide, and Serotonin: Relationships of CSF Amine Metabolites," *The American Journal of Psychiatry* 139, no. 6 (1982).

57. Courtney Shannon et al., "Interindividual Differences in Neonatal Serotonin Functioning: Stability of Interindividual Differences and Behavioral Correlates," *American Journal of Primatology* 36 (1995).

58. J. Dee Higley, Stephen J. Suomi, and Markku Linnoila, "A Longitudinal Assessment of CSF Monoamine Metabolite and Plasma Cortisol Concentrations in Young Rhesus Monkeys," *Biological Psychiatry* 32, no. 2 (1992).

59. Stephen J. Suomi and Christopher Ripp, "A History of Mother-Less Mother Monkey Mothering at the University of Wisconsin Primate Laboratory," in *Child Abuse: The Nonhuman Primate Data*, ed. Martin Reite and Nancy Caine (New York: Alan R. Liss, 1983).

60. Robert M. Sapolsky, "The Physiological Relevance of Glucocorticoid Endangerment of the Hippocampus," *Annals of the New York Academy of Sciences* 746, no. 1 (1994).

61. D. Steven Kerr et al., "Chronic Stress-Induced Acceleration of Electrophysiologic and Morphometric Biomarkers of Hippocampal Aging," *Journal of Neuroscience* 11, no. 5 (1991).

62. Michael J. Meaney and David H. Aitken, "The Effects of Early Postnatal Handling on the Development of the Hippocampal Receptors: Temporal Parameters," *Developmental Brain Research* 22, no. 2 (1985).

63. Jeremy D. Coplan et al., "Cerebrospinal Fluid Concentrations of Somatostatin and Biogenic Amines in Growth Primates Reared by Mothers Exposed to Manipulated Foraging Conditions," *Archives of General Psychiatry* 55, no. 5 (1998).

64. M. Champoux et al., "Hormonal Effects of Early Rearing Conditions in the Infant Rhesus Monkey," *American Journal of Primatology* 19, no. 2 (1989).

65. Cynthia M. Kuhn and Saul M. Schanberg, "Responses to Maternal Separation: Mechanisms and Mediators," *International Journal of Developmental Neuroscience* 16, no. 3/4 (1998).

66. Champoux et al., "Hormonal Effects of Early Rearing Conditions in the Infant Rhesus Monkey."

67. Frank A. Scafidi et al., "Massage Stimulates Growth in Preterm Infants: A Replication," *Infant Behavior and Development* 13, no. 2 (1990).

68. Elizabeth A. Carlson and L. Alan Sroufe, "Contribution of Attachment Theory to Developmental Psychopathology," in *Developmental Psychopathology*, ed. Dante. Cicchetti and Donald K. Cohen (New York: Wiley, 1995).

69. Shyamala Nada Raja, Rob McGee, and Warren R. Stanton, "Perceived Attachments to Parents and Peers and Psychological Well-Being in Adolescence," *Journal of Youth and Adolescence* 21, no. 4 (1992).

70. Catherine S. Tamis-LeMonda and Marc H. Bornstein, "Habituation and Maternal Encouragement of Attention in Infancy as Predictors of Toddler Language, Play, and Representational Competence," *Child Development* 60, no. 3 (1989).

71. Kathryn E. Barnard et al., "Measurement and Meaning of Parent-Child Interaction," in *Applied Developmental Psychology*, ed. Frederick J. Morrison, Catherine Lord, and Daniel P. Keating (San Diego: Academic Press, 1989).

72. Marian Radke-Yarrow and Carolyn Zahn-Waxler, "Roots, Motives, and Patterns in Children's Prosocial Behavior," in *The Development and Maintenance of Prosocial Behaviors*, ed. Ervin Staub, et al. (New York: Plenum, 1984).

73. Bonnie Klimes-Dougan and Janet Kistner, "Physically Abused Preschoolers' Responses to Peers' Distress," *Developmental Psychology* 26, no. 4 (1990).

74. Joan L. Luby et al., "Maternal Support in Early Childhood Predicts Larger Hippocampal Volumes at School Age," *Proceedings of the National Academy of Sciences* 109, no. 8 (2012).

Chapter 4

1. Immanuel Kant, *The Metaphysics of Morals*, trans. Mary Gregor (Cambridge: Cambridge University Press, 1996), p. 161.

2. Richard Taylor, *Good and Evil* (New York: Macmillan, 1970), pp. 252–53.

3. Stephen Leighton, "Unfelt Feelings in Pain and Emotion," *Southern Journal of Philosophy* 24, no. 1 (1986).

4. Joseph Raz, *Ethics in the Public Domain: Essays in the Morality of Law and Politics* (Oxford: Clarendon Press, 1994), p. 11.

5. William James, "What Is an Emotion?," in *The Emotions*, ed. Knight Dunlap (New York: Hafner, 1967).

6. B. F. Skinner and James G. Holland, *The Analysis of Behavior* (New York: McGraw-Hill, 1961), pp. 213–14.

7. Robert C. Solomon, "The Logic of Emotion," *Nous* 11, no. 1 (1977).

8. Stuart Hampshire, "Sincerity and Single-Mindedness," in *Freedom of the Mind and Other Essays* (Princeton, NJ: Princeton University Press, 1971), p. 239.

9. Iris Murdoch, *The Sovereignty of Good* (London: Routledge and Kegan Paul, 1970), pp. 17–18.

10. Rick Hanson, *Hardwiring Happiness: The New Brain Science of Contentment, Calm, and Confidence* (New York: Harmony, 2013).

11. Aristotle, *The Nicomachean Ethics*, trans. David Ross (Oxford: Oxford University Press, 1980), bk II, ch. 1, 1103a33–b25.

12. Augustine, *De Cura Pro Mortuis*, trans. H. Chadwick (Oxford: Oxford University Press, 1998), p. 57.

13. For some similar ideas from child psychologists, see, e.g., Susan Goodwyn and Linda Acredolo, *Baby Hearts: A Guide to Giving Your Child an Emotional Head Start* (New York: Bantam, 2007).

14. See also Daniel J. Siegel and Mary Hartzell, *Parenting from the Inside Out: How a Deeper Self-Understanding Can Help You Raise Children Who Thrive* (New York: Tarcher, 2004).

15. See, e.g., what Jeffrey Bernstein calls "toxic thoughts" (Jeffrey Bernstein, *Liking the Child You Love: Build a Better Relationship with Your Kids—Even When They're Driving You Crazy* (Cambridge, MA: Da Capo Press, 2009)).

16. Joseph Raz, *The Morality of Freedom* (Oxford: Clarendon Press, 1986), p. 166.

17. Advances in mood enhancement technologies may in the near future enable such an individual to feel love for her child. Such technologies raise ethical issues of their own, however. See, e.g., S. Matthew Liao, "Parental Love Pills: Some Ethical Considerations," *Bioethics* 25, no. 9 (2011).

18. Bernard Williams, "Deciding to Believe", in *Problems of the Self* (Cambridge: Cambridge University Press, 1973).

19. S. Matthew Liao, "Why Children Need to Be Loved," *Critical Review of International Social and Political Philosophy* 15, no. 3 (2012).

20. Laurel J. Trainor, "Infant Preferences for Infant-Directed Versus Noninfant-Directed Playsongs and Lullabies," *Infant Behavior and Development* 19, no. 1 (1996).

21. I thank an anonymous reviewer for this suggestion.

22. Immanuel Kant, *Groundwork of the Metaphysic of Morals*, trans. H. J. Paton (New York: Harper & Row, 1964).

23. Michael Stocker, "The Schizophrenia of Modern Ethical Theories," *The Journal of Philosophy* 73, no. 14 (1976).

24. Bernard Williams, "Persons, Character, and Morality," in *Moral Luck*, ed. Bernard Williams (Cambridge: Cambridge University Press, 1981), p. 18.

Chapter 5

1. Immanuel Kant, *The Metaphysics of Morals*, trans. Mary Gregor (Cambridge: Cambridge University Press, 1996), p. 64.

2. Frederick Olafson, "Rights and Duties in Education," in *Educational Judgments: Papers in the Philosophy of Education*, ed. James F. Doyle (London: Routledge & Kegan Paul, 1973).

3. Henry Sidgwick, *The Methods of Ethics*, 7 ed. (Chicago: University of Chicago, 1962), p. 249.

4. Robert Goodin, "What Is So Special About Our Fellow Countrymen?," *Ethics* 98, no. 4 (1988), p. 684.

5. Maurice Cranston, *What Are Human Rights?* (London: Bodley Head, 1973), p. 69.

6. Alan Gewirth, *The Community of Rights* (Chicago: University of Chicago, 1996), p. 63.

7. Jeffrey Blustein, *Parents and Children: The Ethics of the Family* (Oxford: Oxford University Press, 1982), p. 142.

8. Peter Hobson, "Some Reflections on Parents' Rights in the Upbringing of Their Children," *Journal of Philosophy of Education* 18, no. 1 (1984), p. 64.

9. Jean-Jacques Rousseau, *Émile*, trans. Barbara Foxley (London: J. M. Dent and Sons, Ltd., 1974), p. 16.

10. Carl Wellman, *Welfare Rights* (Totowa, NJ: Rowman & Littlefield, 1982), p. 162.

11. Judith Jarvis Thomson, "A Defense of Abortion," *Philosophy and Public Affairs* 1, no. 1 (1971), pp. 61-62.

12. John Arthur, "Rights and the Duty to Bring Aid," in *Ethics in Practice*, ed. Hugh LaFollette (Oxford: Blackwell, 1997), p. 603.

13. Peter Singer, "Famine, Affluence, and Morality," in *Ethics in Practice*, ed. H. LaFollette (Oxford: Blackwell, 1997), pp. 591–92.

14. Ibid., p. 592.

15. The term "deeply partial" comes from James Griffin, *Value Judgement: Improving Our Ethical Beliefs* (Oxford: Clarendon Press, 1996), p. 86. This objection is often also called the "integrity objection." See Bernard Williams, "Persons, Character, and Morality," in *Moral Luck*, ed. Bernard Williams (Cambridge: Cambridge University Press, 1981).

16. John Locke, *Two Treatises of Government*, ed. Peter Laslett (Cambridge: Cambridge University Press, 1988), p. 271.

Chapter 6

1. US Department of Health and Human Services, "Child Maltreatment," (Washington, DC: US Department of Health and Human Services, 2011), p. viii.

2. Ibid., p. ix.

3. Ibid., p. ix.

4. Ibid., p. x.

5. David W. Brown et al., "Adverse Childhood Experiences and the Risk of Premature Mortality," *American Journal of Preventive Medicine* 37, no. 5 (2009).

6. Fight Crime, "New Hope for Preventing Child Abuse and Neglect: Proven Solutions to Save Lives and Prevent Future Crime," (Washington, DC: Fight Crime: Invest in Kids, 2006).

7. US Department of Health and Human Services, "Long-Term Consequences of Child Abuse and Neglect," (Washington, DC: US Department of Health and Human Services, 2008).

8. US Department of Health and Human Services, "Child Maltreatment."

9. Richard J. Gelles and Staci Perlman, *Estimated Annual Cost of Child Abuse and Neglect* (Chicago, IL: Prevent Child Abuse America, 2012).

10. I also set aside the issue of parents who do not have a history of abusing and/or neglecting their children, but who are about to do so imminently. If my arguments below are successful, we may be able to

treat these cases using something like a "clear and present danger" (Schenk v. United States) or "imminent lawless action" test (Brandenburg v. Ohio).

11. John Stuart Mill, *On Liberty*, ed. Elizabeth Rapaport (Indianapolis/ Cambridge: Hackett Publishing, 1978); Hugh LaFollette, "Licensing Parents," *Philosophy and Public Affairs* 9, no. 2 (1980); ———, "Licensing Parents Revisited," *Journal of Applied Philosophy* 27, no. 4 (2010); Robert S. Taylor, "Children as Projects and Persons: A Liberal Antinomy," *Social Theory and Practice* 35 (2009); Jack C. Westman, *Licensing Parents: Can We Prevent Child Abuse and Neglect?* (Cambridge, MA: Perseus, 1994); Michael McFall, *Licensing Parents: Family, State, and Child Maltreatment* (Lanham, MD: Lexington Books, 2009); Peg Tittle, ed., *Should Parents Be Licensed? Debating the Issues* (Amherst, NY: Prometheus, 2004).

12. LaFollette, "Licensing Parents"; ———, "Licensing Parents Revisited."

13. LaFollette, "Licensing Parents."

14. ———, "Licensing Parents Revisited," p. 337. See also Claudia Pap Mangel, "Licensing Parents: How Feasible?," *Family Law Quarterly*, 22, no. 1 (1988), pp. 17–39.

15. ———, "Licensing Parents," p. 196.

16. Some, such as William Irvine and Robert Taylor, have proposed additional requirements for the licensing scheme, such as requiring prospective parents to demonstrate financial stability. William Irvine, *The Politics of Parenting* (St. Paul, MN: Paragon House, 2003); Taylor, "Children as Projects and Persons: A Liberal Antinomy." Others, such as Michael McFall, have argued for universal mandatory reversible sterilization that would be reversed when one receives a parental license. McFall, *Licensing Parents: Family, State, and Child Maltreatment.*

17. Michael W. Austin, *Conceptions of Parenthood: Ethics and the Family* (Aldershot: Ashgate, 2007); Jurgen De Wispelaere and Daniel Weinstock, "Licensing Parents to Protect Our Children?," *Ethics and Social Welfare* 6, no. 2 (2012); Daniel Engster, "The Place of Parenting within a Liberal Theory of Justice," *Social Theory and Practice* 36, no. 2 (2010); Lawrence E. Frisch, "Licentious Parenting: A Reply to Hugh LaFollette," *Philosophy and Public Affairs* 11, no. 2 (1982); Michael J. Sandmire and Michael S. Wald, "Licensing Parents—a Response to Claudia Mangel's Proposal," *Family Law Quarterly* 24, no. 1 (1990).

18. Sandmire and Wald, "Licensing Parents—a Response to Claudia Mangel's Proposal."

19. Engster, "The Place of Parenting within a Liberal Theory of Justice."

20. See, e.g., Taylor, "Children as Projects and Persons: A Liberal Antinomy."

21. Engster, "The Place of Parenting within a Liberal Theory of Justice."

22. Ibid.

23. Ibid., p. 248.

24. Ibid., p. 236.

25. In my view, the values of biological parenting discussed below are negated when the pursuit of biological parenting is non-consensual, as in the case of rape. The relevance of consent makes my account of parental rights a normative one rather than a purely biological one, as, for example, a genetic account of parental rights appears to be.

26. For good overviews of various accounts of parental rights, see, e.g., Elizabeth Brake and Joseph Millum, "Parenthood and Procreation," http://plato.stanford.edu/archives/fall2014/entries/parenthood/; Tim Bayne and Avery Kolers, "Toward a Pluralistic Account of Parenthood," *Bioethics* 17, no. 3 (2003). In the ensuing discussion, I try to avoid repeating the objections that these authors have made against genetic, intentional, and causal accounts of parental rights. I also attempt to focus my attention on accounts that are more likely to generate a robust account of parental rights in order to explain how the human rights account differs from these accounts.

27. I thank an anonymous reviewer for this point.

28. See, though, Jan Narveson, *Respecting Persons in Theory and Practice* (Lanham, MD: Rowman and Littlefield, 2002), which defends such a view.

29. LaFollette, "Licensing Parents Revisited."

30. Harry Brighouse and Adam Swift, "Parents' Rights and the Value of the Family," *Ethics* 117, no. 1 (2006). See also Ferdinand Schoeman, "Rights of Children, Rights of Parents, and the Moral Basis of the Family," *Ethics* 91, no. 1 (1980).

31. Brighouse and Swift, "Parents' Rights and the Value of the Family."

32. Ibid.

33. See also Anca Gheaus, "The Right to Parent One's Biological Baby," *Journal of Political Philosophy* 20, no. 4 (2012).

34. Norvin Richards, *The Ethics of Parenthood* (New York: Oxford University Press, 2010).

35. Ibid., p. 22.

36. Wesley Hohfeld, Fundamental Legal Conceptions, ed. W. W. Cook (New Haven, CT: Yale University Press, 1919).

37. Ibid., pp. 23–24.

38. Barbara K. Rothman, *Recreating Motherhood: Ideology and Technology in a Patriarchal Society* (New York: W. W. Norton, 1989); Gheaus, "The Right to Parent One's Biological Baby."

39. Gheaus, "The Right to Parent One's Biological Baby," p. 15.

40. Ibid., p. 16. Gheaus is drawing on Amy Mullin's work here. Amy Mullin, *Reconceiving Pregnancy and Childcare: Ethics, Experience and Reproductive Labor* (Cambridge: Cambridge University Press, 2005).

41. Gheaus, "The Right to Parent One's Biological Baby," p. 18.

42. Ibid., p. 18.

43. Ibid., p. 17.

44. Gheaus, p. 17.

45. Joseph Millum, "How Do We Acquire Parental Rights?," *Social Theory and Practice* 36, no. 1 (2010).

46. Ibid., p. 114.

47. Ibid., p. 120.

48. I thank an anonymous reviewer for this point.

49. As I shall discuss in the next chapter, in one study, the average cost of successful medication-only treatment was between $5,894 and $61,377 for IVF, and the cost of successful donor egg IVF was even higher, at $72,642. See, e.g., Patricia Katz et al., "Costs of Infertility Treatment: Results from an 18-Month Prospective Cohort Study," *Fertility and Sterility* 95, no. 3 (2011). Also, as we shall see, UNICEF estimates that there are over 150 million orphans in the world, where an orphan is defined as a child who has lost one or both parents (UNICEF, UNAIDS, and WHO, "Children and AIDS: Fifth Stocktaking Report," (2010)).

50. A good source for those in the United States who are advocating mandatory parenting education is the Parenting Project. http://www.parentingproject.org/. I shall shortly explain how the parenting education I have in mind differs from their proposal.

51. Chris Collins, Priya Alagiri, and Todd Summers, *Abstinence Only Vs. Comprehensive Sex Education: What Are the Arguments? What Are the Evidence?*, Policy Monograph Series (San Francisco: AIDS Policy Research Center & Center for AIDS Prevention Studies, University of California, 2002).

52. I thank an anonymous reviewer for this point.

53. Carolyn T. Halpern et al., "Smart Teens Don't Have Sex (or Kiss Much Either)," *Journal of Adolescent Health* 26, no. 3 (2000).

54. Heather Paradis, Guillermo Montes, and Peter G. Szilagyi, "A National Perspective on Parents' Knowledge of Child Development, Its Relation to Parent-Child Interaction, and Associated Parenting Characteristics," in *Pediatrics Academic Society* (Honolulu, 2008).

55. For an example of this kind of education, see Judith Schiffer et al., *Preparing Tomorrow's Parents Today: How to Bring Parenting Education for Children and Teens to Your Schools* (The Parenting Project, 2002).

56. Rosemary Chalk and Patricia A. King, eds., *Violence in Families: Assessing Prevention and Treatment Programs* (Washington, DC: National Academy Press, 1998); N. Dickon Reppucci, Preston A. Britner, and Jennifer L. Woolard, *Preventing Child Abuse and Neglect through Parent Education* (Baltimore, MD: Paul H. Brookes Publishing Co., 1997).

57. Elizabeth Cutting and Lynne Tammi, *Understanding Parents, Understanding Parenthood: An Education for Parenthood Course Piloted at Monifeith High School* (Edinburgh: Save the Children Scotland, 1999); Philip Hope and Penny Sharland, *Tomorrow's Parents: Developing Parenthood Education in Schools* (London: Calouste Gulbenkian Foundation, 1997). See also Elizabeth McFarlane et al., "The Importance of Early Parenting in At-Risk Families and Children's Social-Emotional Adaptation to School," *Academic Pediatrics* 10, no. 5 (2010).

Chapter 7

1. UNICEF, UNAIDS, and WHO, "Children and AIDS: Fifth Stocktaking Report" (2010).

2. Ibid.

3. UNICEF, "Progress for Children: A Report Card on Child Protection," (2009).

4. Ibid.

5. US Department of Health and Human Services, "The AFCARS Report, No. 19," (2012).

6. Elizabeth Bartholet, "International Adoption: Thoughts on the Human Rights Issue," *Buffalo Human Rights Law Review* 13 (2007).

7. Marinus H. van IJzendoorn, Maartje Luijk, and Femmie Juffer, "IQ of Children Growing up in Children's Homes: A Meta-Analysis on IQ Delays in Orphanages," *Merrill-Palmer Quarterly* 54, no. 3 (2008).

8. US Department of Health and Human Services, "The AFCARS Report, No. 19."

9. Mark Courtney et al., *Midwest Evaluation of the Adult Functioning of Former Foster Youth: Outcomes at Age 19* (Chicago, IL: Chapin Hall, 2005).

10. Thom Reilly, "Transition from Care: Status and Outcomes of Youth Who Age out of Foster Care," *Child Welfare* 82, no. 6 (2003).

11. UNICEF, UNAIDS, and WHO, "Children and AIDS: Fifth Stocktaking Report."

12. United Nations Department of Economic and Social Affairs/Population Division, "Child Adoption: Trends and Policies," (2009).

13. US Department of Health and Human Services, "The AFCARS Report, No. 19."

14. Daniel Friedrich, "A Duty to Adopt?," *Journal of Applied Philosophy* 30, no. 1 (2013).

15. Ibid.

16. US Department of Agriculture, "Expenditure on Children by Families, 2012," (2013).

17. US Department of Health and Human Services, "Children Adopted from Foster Care: Child and Family Characteristics, Adoption Motivation, and Well-Being," ed. Office of the Assistant Secretary for Planning and Evaluation (2011).

18. Patricia Katz et al., "Costs of Infertility Treatment: Results from an 18-Month Prospective Cohort Study," *Fertility and Sterility* 95, no. 3 (2011).

19. Child Welfare Information Gateway, "Costs of Adopting," (Washington, DC: US Department of Health and Human Services, 2011).

20. The credit in the United States is a maximum amount of $12,650 per child in 2012.

21. Friedrich, "A Duty to Adopt?," p. 28.

22. Ibid., p. 28.

23. Laura Hamilton, Simon Cheng, and Brian Powell, "Adoptive Parents, Adaptive Parents: Evaluating the Importance of Biological Ties for Parental Investment," *American Sociological Review* 72, no. 1 (2007).

24. Christine Overall, *Why Have Children?: The Ethical Debate* (Cambridge, MA: MIT Press, 2012).

25. Jeffrey J. Haugaard, "Is Adoption a Risk Factor for the Development of Adjustment Problems?," *Clinical Psychology Review* 18, no. 1 (1998).

26. Martha A. Rueter et al., "Family Interactions in Adoptive Compared to Nonadoptive Families," *Journal of Family Psychology* 23, no. 1 (2009); Nicole Bimmel et al., "Problem Behavior of Internationally Adopted Adolescents: A Review and Meta-Analysis," *Harvard Review of Psychiatry* 11, no. 2 (2003).

27. Rueter et al., "Family Interactions in Adoptive Compared to Nonadoptive Families."

28. United Nations Department of Economic and Social Affairs/Population Division, "Child Adoption: Trends and Policies."

29. Ibid.

30. Ibid.

31. Ibid.

32. Jo Jones, "Adoption Experiences of Women and Men and Demand for Children to Adopt by Women 18–44 Years of Age in the United States, 2002," ed. US Department of Health and Human Services, Vital Health Statistics, Series 23 (2008).

33. UNAIDS, UNICEF, and USAID, "Children on the Brink: A Joint Report of New Orphan Estimates and a Framework for Action," (2004).

34. Friedrich, "A Duty to Adopt?," p. 28.

35. A reviewer has helpfully pointed out that even if biological parenting were a non-basic activity, the preference to have biological children can be rational and normatively justified, since we have many rational and reasonable preferences for non-basic activities.

36. See also Angela Mae Kupenda et al., "Aren't Two Parents Better Than None: Contractual and Statutory Basics for a 'New' African American Coparenting Joint Adoption Model," *9 Temple Political and Civil Rights Law Review* 59 (1999), for a similar idea applied to the African American context.

37. See, e.g., Employee Retirement Income Security Act (ERISA) §§ 4(b), 609(a), and 607(1).

38. Harold D. Grotevant and Ruth G. McRoy, *Openness in Adoption: Exploring Family Connections* (Thousand Oaks, CA: Sage Publications, 1998).

39. Marianne Berry et al., "The Role of Open Adoption in the Adjustment of Adopted Children and Their Families," *Children and Youth Services Review* 20, no. 1–2 (1998).

40. US Department of Health and Human Services, "The AFCARS Report, No. 19."

41. Ibid.

42. American Academy of Child and Adolescent Psychiatry, "Facts for Families: Foster Care (No. 64)," (2002).

43. Harris Interactive, *National Adoption Attitudes Survey* (The Evan B. Donaldson Adoption Institute, 2002).

44. Ibid.

45. Ibid.

46. Ibid.

47. Jones, "Adoption Experiences of Women and Men and Demand for Children to Adopt by Women 18–44 Years of Age in the United States, 2002."

48. Harris Interactive, *National Adoption Attitudes Survey*.

49. Ibid.

Conclusion

1. Alan Gewirth, *The Community of Rights* (Chicago: University of Chicago, 1996).

2. A government agency conducting an independent, expert-based study evaluating the effectiveness of PEPFAR asked me to comment on their report pertaining to orphans and vulnerable children (OVC). One of my recommendations was precisely that PEPFAR should ensure that these children are not only cared for but also loved, for reasons outlined below.

Bibliography

American Academy of Child and Adolescent Psychiatry. "Facts for Families: Foster Care (No. 64)." 2002.

American College of Obstetricians and Gynecologists. "Prenatal Diagnosis of Fetal Chromosomal Abnormalities." *ACOG Practice Bulletin* 27 (2001).

Andrews, Michael W., and L. A. Rosenblum. "Attachment in Infants Raised in Variable- and Low-Demand Environments." *Child Development* 62, no. 4 (1991): 686–93.

———. "The Development of Affiliative and Agonistic Social Patterns in Differentially Reared Monkeys." *Child Development* 65, no. 5 (1994): 1398–404.

Archard, David. *Children: Rights and Childhood.* London: Routledge, 2004.

Aristotle. *The Nicomachean Ethics.* Translated by David Ross. Oxford: Oxford University Press, 1980.

Arthur, John. "Rights and the Duty to Bring Aid." In *Ethics in Practice,* edited by Hugh LaFollette, 596–604. Oxford: Blackwell, 1997.

Åsberg, Marie, Lil Träskman, and Peter Thorén. "5-HIAA in the Cerebrospinal Fluid: A Biochemical Suicide Predictor." *Archives of General Psychiatry* 33, no. 10 (1976): 1193–97.

Augustine. *De Cura Pro Mortuis.* Translated by H. Chadwick. Oxford: Oxford University Press, 1998.

Austin, Michael W. *Conceptions of Parenthood: Ethics and the Family.* Aldershot: Ashgate, 2007.

Barnard, Kathryn E., M. A. Hammond, C. L. Booth, H. L. Bee, S. K. Mitchell, and S. J. Spieker. "Measurement and Meaning of Parent-Child

Interaction." In *Applied Developmental Psychology*, edited by Frederick J. Morrison, Catherine Lord, and Daniel P. Keating, 40–81. San Diego: Academic Press, 1989.

Bartholet, Elizabeth. "International Adoption: Thoughts on the Human Rights Issue." *Buffalo Human Rights Law Review* 13 (2007): 151–203.

Batshaw, Mark L., and Bruce K. Shapiro. "Mental Retardation." In *Children with Disabilities*, edited by Mark L. Batshaw. Baltimore, MD: Paul H. Brookes, 1997.

Baumrind, Diana. "Child Care Practices Anteceding Three Patterns of Preschool Behavior." *Genetic Psychology Monographs* 75, no. 1 (1967): 43–88.

———. "Current Patterns of Parental Authority." *Developmental Psychology Monograph* 4, no. 1 (1971).

Baumrind, Diana, and Allen Black. "Socialization Practices Associated with Dimension of Competence in Preschool Boys and Girls." *Child Development* 38, no. 2 (1967): 291–327.

Bayne, Tim, and Avery Kolers. "Toward a Pluralistic Account of Parenthood." *Bioethics* 17, no. 3 (2003): 221–42.

Beitz, Charles R. "Human Rights and the Law of Peoples." In *The Ethics of Assistance: Morality and the Distant Needy*, edited by Deen Chatterjee. Cambridge: Cambridge University Press, 2004.

———. *The Idea of Human Rights*. Oxford: Oxford University Press, 2009.

Bernstein, Jeffrey. *Liking the Child You Love: Build a Better Relationship with Your Kids—Even When They're Driving You Crazy*. Cambridge, MA: Da Capo Press, 2009.

Berry, Marianne, Debora J. Cavazos Dylla, Richard P. Barth, and Barbara Needell. "The Role of Open Adoption in the Adjustment of Adopted Children and Their Families." *Children and Youth Services Review* 20, no. 1–2 (1998): 151–71.

Berwick, Donald. M., Janice C. Levy, and Ruth Kleinerman. "Failure to Thrive: Diagnostic Yield of Hospitalization." *Archives of Diseases in Children* 57, no. 5 (1982): 347–51.

Bimmel, Nicole, Femmie Juffer, Marinus H. van IJzendoorn, and Marian J. Bakermans-Kranenburg. "Problem Behavior of Internationally Adopted Adolescents: A Review and Meta-Analysis." *Harvard Review of Psychiatry* 11, no. 2 (2003): 64–77.

Blustein, Jeffrey. *Parents and Children: The Ethics of the Family*. Oxford: Oxford University Press, 1982.

Bos, Karen, Charles H. Zeanah, Nathan A. Fox, Stacy. S. Drury, Katie A. McLaughlin, and Charles A. Nelson. "Psychiatric Outcomes in Young Children with a History of Institutionalization." *Harvard Review of Psychiatry* 19, no. 1 (2011): 15–24.

Bowlby, John. *Loss, Sadness and Depression*. 3 vols. Vol. 3, Attachment and Loss. New York: Basic Books, 1980.

Boyes, Michael, and Sandra Allen. "Styles of Parent-Child Interaction and Moral Reasoning in Adolescence." *Merrill-Palmer Quarterly* 39, no. 4 (1993): 551–70.

Brake, Elizabeth, and Joseph Millum. "Parenthood and Procreation." http://plato.stanford.edu/archives/fall2014/entries/parenthood/.

Brighouse, Harry, and Adam Swift. "Parents' Rights and the Value of the Family." *Ethics* 117, no. 1 (2006): 80–108.

Brown, David W., Robert F. Anda, Henning Tiemeier, Vincent J. Felitti, Valerie J. Edwards, Janet B. Croft, and Wayne H. Giles. "Adverse Childhood Experiences and the Risk of Premature Mortality." *American Journal of Preventive Medicine* 37, no. 5 (2009): 389–96.

Brown, Gerald L., Michael H. Ebert, Peter F. Goyer, David C. Jimerson, William J. Klein, William E. Bunney, and Frederick K. Goodwin. "Aggression, Suicide, and Serotonin: Relationships of CSF Amine Metabolites." *The American Journal of Psychiatry* 139, no. 6 (1982): 741–46.

Carlson, Elizabeth A., and L. Alan Sroufe. "Contribution of Attachment Theory to Developmental Psychopathology." In *Developmental Psychopathology*, edited by Dante. Cicchetti and Donald K. Cohen, 581–617. New York: Wiley, 1995.

CDC. "Effectiveness in Disease and Injury Prevention: Use of Folic Acid for Prevention of Spina Bifida and Other Neural Tube Defects, 1983–1991." *Morbidity and Mortality Weekly Report* 40, no. 513–16 (1991).

Chalk, Rosemary, and Patricia A. King, eds. *Violence in Families: Assessing Prevention and Treatment Programs*. Washington, DC: National Academy Press, 1998.

Champoux, M., C. L. Coe, S. M. Schanberg, C. M. Kuhn, and S. J. Suomi. "Hormonal Effects of Early Rearing Conditions in the Infant Rhesus Monkey." *American Journal of Primatology* 19, no. 2 (1989): 111–17.

Chen, Ying, Zhi Xu He, Ailian Liu, and Kai Wang. "Embryonic Stem Cells Generated by Nuclear Transfer of Human Somatic Nuclei into Rabbit Oocytes." *Cell Research* 13, no. 4 (2003): 251–63.

Child Welfare Information Gateway. "Costs of Adopting." Washington, DC: US Department of Health and Human Services, 2011.

Coleman, Rose, and Sally Provence. "Environmental Retardation (Hospitalism) in Infants Living in Families." *Pediatrics* 19, no. 2 (1957): 285–92.

Collins, Chris, Priya Alagiri, and Todd Summers. *Abstinence Only Vs. Comprehensive Sex Education: What Are the Arguments? What Are the Evidence?*, Policy Monograph Series. San Francisco: AIDS Policy Research Center & Center for AIDS Prevention Studies, University of California, 2002.

Conti, Gabriella, Christopher Hansman, James J. Heckman, Matthew F. X. Novak, Angela Ruggiero, and Stephen J. Suomi. "Primate Evidence on the Late Health Effects of Early-Life Adversity." *Proceedings of the National Academy of Sciences* 109, no. 23 (2012): 8866–71.

Coplan, Jeremy D., Ronald C. Trost, Michael J. Owens, Thomas B. Cooper, Jack M. Gorman, Charles B. Nemeroff, and Leonard A. Rosenblum. "Cerebrospinal Fluid Concentrations of Somatostatin and Biogenic Amines in Growth Primates Reared by Mothers Exposed to Manipulated Foraging Conditions." *Archives of General Psychiatry* 55, no. 5 (1998): 473–77.

Courtney, Mark, Amy Dworsky, Gretchen Ruth, Tom Keller, Judy Havlicek, and Noel Bost. *Midwest Evaluation of the Adult Functioning of Former Foster Youth: Outcomes at Age 19*. Chicago, IL: Chapin Hall, 2005.

Cowden, Mhairi. "What's Love Got to Do with It? Why a Child Does Not Have a Right to Be Loved." *Critical Review of International Social and Political Philosophy* 15, no. 3 (2012): 325–45.

Cranston, Maurice. *What Are Human Rights?* London: Bodley Head, 1973.

Cross, Henry A., and Harry F. Harlow. "Prolonged and Progressive Effects of Partial Isolation on the Behavior of Macaque Monkeys." *Journal of Experimental Research in Personality* 1, no. 1 (1965): 39–49.

Cutting, Elizabeth, and Lynne Tammi. *Understanding Parents, Understanding Parenthood: An Education for Parenthood Course Piloted at Monifeith High School*. Edinburgh: Save the Children Scotland, 1999.

De Wispelaere, Jurgen, and Daniel Weinstock. "Licensing Parents to Protect Our Children?" *Ethics and Social Welfare* 6, no. 2 (2012): 195–205.

Dworkin, Ronald. *Life's Dominion: An Argument About Abortion, Euthanasia, and Individual Freedom*. New York: Alfred A. Knopf, 1993.

———. *Taking Rights Seriously*. London: Duckworth, 1977.

Ellerstein, Norman S., and Barbara E. Ostrov. "Growth Patterns in Children Hospitalized Because of Caloric-Deprivation Failure to Thrive." *American Journal of Disease in Children* 139, no. 2 (1985): 164–66.

Elmer, E., G. S. Gregg, and Patricia Ellison. "Late Results of the Failure to Thrive Syndrome." *Clinical Pediatrics* 8, no. 10 (1969): 584–88.

Engster, Daniel. "The Place of Parenting within a Liberal Theory of Justice." *Social Theory and Practice* 36, no. 2 (2010): 233–62.

Erikson, Erik H. *Children and Society*. New York: Norton, 1950.

Feinberg, Joel. "The Nature and Value of Rights." In *Bioethics and Human Rights: A Reader for Health Professionals*, edited by Elsie L. Bandman and Bertram Bandman, 19–31. Boston: Little, Brown, 1970.

———. "The Rights of Animals and Unborn Generations." In *Rights, Justice, and Bounds of Liberty*, 159–84. Princeton, NJ: Princeton University Press, 1980.

Feinberg, Joel, and Barbara. B. Levenbook. "Abortion." In *Matters of Life and Death*, edited by Tom Regan, 195–234. New York: McGraw-Hill, 1993.

Fight Crime. "New Hope for Preventing Child Abuse and Neglect: Proven Solutions to Save Lives and Prevent Future Crime." Washington, DC: Fight Crime: Invest in Kids, 2006.

Finnis, John. "A Philosophical Case against Euthanasia." In *Euthanasia Examined: Ethical, Clinical, and Legal Perspectives*, edited by J. Keown, 23–35. Cambridge: Cambridge University Press, 1995.

Friedrich, Daniel. "A Duty to Adopt?" *Journal of Applied Philosophy* 30, no. 1 (2013): 25–39.

Frisch, Lawrence E. "On Licentious Parenting: A Reply to Hugh LaFollette." *Philosophy and Public Affairs* 11, no. 2 (1982): 173–80.

Gelles, Richard J. and Staci Perlman. *Estimated Annual Cost of Child Abuse and Neglect*. Chicago, IL: Prevent Child Abuse America, 2012.

Gewirth, Alan. *The Community of Rights*. Chicago: University of Chicago, 1996.

Gheaus, Anca. "The Right to Parent One's Biological Baby." *Journal of Political Philosophy* 20, no. 4 (2012): 432–55.

Glaser, Helen H., Margaret C. Heagarty, Dexter M. Bullard, and Elizabeth Pivchik. "Physical and Psychological Development of Children with Early Failure to Thrive." *Journal of Pediatrics* 73, no. 5 (1968): 690–98.

Glover, Jonathan. *Causing Death and Saving Lives*. Harmondsworth: Penguin, 1977.

Goldfarb, William. "Effects of Psychological Deprivation in Infancy and Subsequent Stimulation." *American Journal of Psychiatry* 102, no. 1 (1945): 18–33.

Goodin, Robert. "What Is So Special About Our Fellow Countrymen?" *Ethics* 98, no. 4 (1988): 663–86.

Goodpaster, Kenneth. "On Being Morally Considerable." *Journal of Philosophy* 75, no. 6 (1978): 308–25.

Goodwyn, Susan, and Linda Acredolo. *Baby Hearts: A Guide to Giving Your Child an Emotional Head Start*. New York: Bantam, 2007.

Grau, Christopher. "Moral Status, Speciesism, and Liao's Genetic Account." *Journal of Moral Philosophy* 7, no. 3 (2010): 387–96.

Griffin, James. "Discrepancies between the Best Philosophical Account of Human Rights and the International Law of Human Rights." *Proceedings of the Aristotelian Society* 101, no. 1 (2001): 1–28.

———. "First Steps in an Account of Human Rights." *European Journal of Philosophy* 9, no. 3 (2001): 306–27.

———. *On Human Rights*. Oxford: Oxford University Press, 2008.

———. "Towards a Substantive Theory of Rights." In *Utility and Rights*, edited by Raymond G. Frey, 137–60. Oxford: Blackwell, 1984.

———. *Value Judgement: Improving Our Ethical Beliefs*. Oxford: Clarendon Press, 1996.

———. "Welfare Rights." *The Journal of Ethics* 4, no. 1–2 (2000): 27–43.

Grotevant, Harold D., and Ruth G. McRoy. *Openness in Adoption: Exploring Family Connections*. Thousand Oaks, CA: Sage Publications, 1998.

Halpern, Carolyn T., Kara Joyner, J. Richard Udry, and Chirayath Suchindran. "Smart Teens Don't Have Sex (or Kiss Much Either)." *Journal of Adolescent Health* 26, no. 3 (2000): 213–25.

Hamilton, Laura, Simon Cheng, and Brian Powell. "Adoptive Parents, Adaptive Parents: Evaluating the Importance of Biological Ties for Parental Investment." *American Sociological Review* 72, no. 1 (2007): 95–116.

Hampshire, Stuart. "Sincerity and Single-Mindedness." In *Freedom of the Mind and Other Essays*. Princeton, NJ: Princeton University Press, 1971.

Hanson, Rick. *Hardwiring Happiness: The New Brain Science of Contentment, Calm, and Confidence*. New York: Harmony, 2013.

Harlow, Harry F. "Age-Mate or Peer Affectional System." In *Advances in the Study of Behavior*, edited by Daniel S. Lehrman, Robert A. Hinde and Evelyn Shaw, 333–83. New York: Academic Press, 1969.

———. "The Nature of Love." *American Psychologist* 13 (1958): 673–85.

Harlow, Harry F., Robert O. Dodsworth, and Margaret K. Harlow. "Total Social Isolation in Monkeys." *Proceedings of the National Academy of Sciences* 54, no. 1 (1965): 90–96.

Harris Interactive. *National Adoption Attitudes Survey*: The Evan B. Donaldson Adoption Institute, 2002.

Harris, John. *The Value of Life*. London: Routledge & Kegan Paul, 1985.

Harter, Susan. "Developmental Perspectives on the Self-System." In *Handbook of Child Psychology*, edited by E. Mavis Hetherington, 275–385. New York: Wiley, 1983.

———. "Processes Underlying Adolescent Self-Concept Formation." In *From Childhood to Adolescence: A Transitional Period?*, edited by Raymond Montemayor, Gerald R. Adams, and Thomas P. Gullotta, 205–39. Newbury Park, CA: Sage, 1990.

Haugaard, Jeffrey J. "Is Adoption a Risk Factor for the Development of Adjustment Problems?" *Clinical Psychology Review* 18, no. 1 (1998): 47–69.

Higley, J. Dee, Stephen J. Suomi, and Markku Linnoila. "A Longitudinal Assessment of CSF Monoamine Metabolite and Plasma Cortisol Concentrations in Young Rhesus Monkeys." *Biological Psychiatry* 32, no. 2 (1992): 127–45.

Hobson, Peter. "Some Reflections on Parents' Rights in the Upbringing of Their Children." *Journal of Philosophy of Education* 18, no. 1 (1984): 63–74.

Hodges, Jill, and Barbara Tizard. "Social and Family Relationships of Ex-Institutional Adolescents." *Journal of Child Psychology and Psychiatry* 30, no. 1 (1989): 77–97.

Hoffman, Martin L. "Moral Development." In *Developmental Psychology: An Advanced Textbook*, edited by M. H. Bornstein and M. E. Lamb, 497–548. Hillsdale, NJ: Erlbaum, 1988.

Hohfeld, Wesley. *Fundamental Legal Conceptions*. Edited by W. W. Cook. New Haven, CT: Yale University Press, 1919.

Hope, Philip, and Penny Sharland. *Tomorrow's Parents: Developing Parenthood Education in Schools*. London: Calouste Gulbenkian Foundation, 1997.

Insel, Thomas R., and Larry J. Young. "The Neurobiology of Attachment." *Nature Reviews Neuroscience* 2, no. 2 (2001): 129–36.

Irvine, William. *The Politics of Parenting*. St. Paul, MN: Paragon House, 2003.

Jackowski, Andrea, Tarique D. Perera, Chadi G. Abdallah, Griselda Garrido, Cheuk Y. Tang, Jose Martinez, Sanjay J. Mathew, Jack M. Gorman, Leonard A. Rosenblum, Eric L. P. Smith, Andrew J. Dwork, Dikoma C. Shungu, Arie Kaffman, Joel Gelernter, Jeremy D. Coplan, and Joan Kaufman. "Early-Life Stress, Corpus Callosum Development, Hippocampal Volumetrics, and Anxious Behavior in Male Nonhuman Primates." *Psychiatry Research: Neuroimaging* 192, no. 1 (2011): 37–44.

James, William. "What Is an Emotion?" In *The Emotions*, edited by Knight Dunlap. New York: Hafner, 1967.

Jones, Jo. "Adoption Experiences of Women and Men and Demand for Children to Adopt by Women 18–44 Years of Age in the United States, 2002." edited by US Department of Health and Human Services, 1–36, 2008.

Kaler, Sandra, and B. J. Freeman. "Analysis of Environmental Deprivation: Cognitive and Social Development in Romanian Orphans." *Journal of Child Psychology and Psychiatry* 35, no. 4 (1994): 769–81.

Kant, Immanuel. *Groundwork of the Metaphysic of Morals*. Translated by H. J. Paton. New York: Harper & Row, 1964.

————. *The Metaphysics of Morals*. Translated by Mary Gregor. Cambridge: Cambridge University Press, 1996.

Katz, Patricia, Jonathan Showstack, James F. Smith, Robert D. Nachtigall, Susan G. Millstein, Holly Wing, Michael L. Eisenberg, Lauri A. Pasch, Mary S. Croughan, and Nancy Adler. "Costs of Infertility Treatment: Results from an 18-Month Prospective Cohort Study." *Fertility and sterility* 95, no. 3 (2011): 915–21.

Kerr, D. Steven, Lee W. Campbell, Michael D. Applegate, Alvin Brodish, and Philip W. Landfield. "Chronic Stress-Induced Acceleration of Electrophysiologic and Morphometric Biomarkers of Hippocampal Aging." *Journal of Neuroscience* 11, no. 5 (1991): 1316–24.

Klimes-Dougan, Bonnie, and Janet Kistner. "Physically Abused Preschoolers' Responses to Peers' Distress." *Developmental Psychology* 26, no. 4 (1990): 599–602.

Kohlberg, Lawrence. "Stage and Sequence: The Cognitive-Developmental Approach to Socialization." In *Handbook of Socialization Theory and Research*, edited by David A. Goslin, 347–480. Chicago: Rand McNally, 1969.

Kristiansson, Bengt, and Sven P. Fallstrom. "Growth at the Age of 4 Years Subsequent to Early Failure to Thrive." *International Journal of Child Abuse and Neglect* 11, no. 1 (1987): 35–40.

Kuhn, Cynthia M., and Saul M. Schanberg. "Responses to Maternal Separation: Mechanisms and Mediators." *International Journal of Developmental Neuroscience* 16, no. 3/4 (1998): 261–70.

Kupenda, Angela Mae, Angelia Wallace, Jamie Deon Travis, Brandon Issac Dorsey, and Bryant Guy. "Aren't Two Parents Better Than None: Contractual and Statutory Basics for A 'New' African American Coparenting Joint Adoption Model." *9 Temple Political and Civil Rights Law Review* 59 (1999): 59–64.

LaFollette, Hugh. "Licensing Parents." *Philosophy and Public Affairs* 9, no. 2 (1980): 182–97.

———. "Licensing Parents Revisited." *Journal of Applied Philosophy* 27, no. 4 (2010): 327–43.

Leighton, Stephen. "Unfelt Feelings in Pain and Emotion." *Southern Journal of Philosophy* 24, no. 1 (1986): 69–79.

Liao, S. Matthew. "Agency and Human Rights." *Journal of Applied Philosophy* 27, no. 1 (2010): 15–25.

———. "The Embryo Rescue Case." *Theoretical Medicine and Bioethics* 27, no. 2 (2006): 141–47.

———. "The Genetic Account of Moral Status: A Defense." *Journal of Moral Philosophy* 9, no. 2 (2012): 265–77.

———. "The Organism View Defended." *The Monist* 89, no. 3 (2006).

———. "Parental Love Pills: Some Ethical Considerations." *Bioethics* 25, no. 9 (2011): 489–94.

———. "Rescuing Human Embryonic Stem Cell Research: The Blastocyst Transfer Method." *American Journal of Bioethics* 5, no. 6 (2005): 8–16.

———. "Time-Relative Interests and Abortion." *Journal of Moral Philosophy* 4, no. 2 (2007): 242–56.

———. "Twinning, Inorganic Replacement, and the Organism View." *Ratio* 23, no. 1 (2010): 59–72.

———. "Why Children Need to Be Loved." *Critical Review of International Social and Political Philosophy* 15, no. 3 (2012): 347–58.

Liao, S. Matthew, and Adam Etinson. "Political and Naturalistic Conceptions of Human Rights: A False Polemic?" *Journal of Moral Philosophy* 9, no. 3 (2012): 327–52.

Locke, John. *Two Treatises of Government.* Edited by Peter Laslett. Cambridge: Cambridge University Press, 1988.

Luby, Joan L., Deanna M. Barch, Andy Belden, Michael S. Gaffrey, Rebecca Tillman, Casey Babb, Tomoyuki Nishino, Hideo Suzuki, and Kelly N. Botteron. "Maternal Support in Early Childhood Predicts Larger Hippocampal Volumes at School Age." *Proceedings of the National Academy of Sciences* 109, no. 8 (2012): 2854–59.

Maccoby, Eleanor, and John Martin. "Socialization in the Context of the Family: Parent-Child Interaction." In *Handbook of Child Psychology*, edited by E. Mavis Hetherington, 1–101. New York: Wiley, 1983.

MacCormick, Neil. "Children's Rights: A Test-Case for Theories of Right." *Archiv für Rechts- und Sozialphilosophie* LXII, no. 3 (1976): 305–16.

Mackner, Laura M., J. Raymond Starr, and Maureen Black. "The Cumulative Effect of Neglect and Failure to Thrive on Cognitive Functioning." *Child Abuse and Neglect* 21, no. 7 (1997): 691–700.

Mangel, Claudia Pap. "Licensing Parents: How Feasible?" *Family Law Quarterly*, 22, no. 1 (1988): pp. 17–39.

Marquis, Don. "Why Abortion Is Immoral." *Journal of Philosophy* 86, no. 4 (1989): 183–203.

McCloskey, H. J. "Respect for Human Moral Rights Versus Maximizing Good." In *Utility and Rights*, edited by R. G. Frey, 121–36. Oxford: Basil Blackwell, 1985.

McFall, Michael. *Licensing Parents: Family, State, and Child Maltreatment*: Lanham, MD: Lexington Books, 2009.

McFarlane, Elizabeth, Rachel A. B. Dodge, Lori Burrell, Sarah Crowne, Tina L. Cheng, and Anne K. Duggan. "The Importance of Early Parenting in at-Risk Families And children's Social-Emotional Adaptation to School." *Academic Pediatrics* 10, no. 5: 330–37 (2010).

McMahan, Jeff. *The Ethics of Killing: Problems at the Margins of Life.* Oxford: Oxford University Press, 2002.

Meaney, Michael J., and David H. Aitken. "The Effects of Early Postnatal Handling on the Development of the Hippocampal Receptors: Temporal Parameters." *Developmental Brain Research* 22, no. 2 (1985): 301–04.

Melden, A. I. "Do Infants Have Moral Rights?" In *Whose Child?*, edited by William Aiken and Hugh LaFollette, 199–220. Totowa, N.J.: Littlefield, Adams & Co., 1980.

Mill, John Stuart. *On Liberty.* Edited by Elizabeth Rapaport. Indianapolis/Cambridge: Hackett Publishing, 1978.

Miller, Howard, and Paul S. Siegel. *Loving: A Psychological Approach.* New York: John Wiley and Sons, 1972.

Millum, Joseph. "How Do We Acquire Parental Rights?" *Social Theory and Practice* 36, no. 1 (2010): 112–32.

Moore, G. E. *Principia Ethica.* Cambridge: Cambridge University Press, 1959.

Mullin, Amy. *Reconceiving Pregnancy and Childcare: Ethics, Experience and Reproductive Labor.* Cambridge: Cambridge University Press, 2005.

Murdoch, Iris. *The Sovereignty of Good.* London: Routledge and Kegan Paul, 1970.

Narveson, Jan. *The Libertarian Idea.* Philadelphia: Temple University Press, 1988.

———. *Respecting Persons in Theory and Practice.* Lanham, MD: Rowman and Littlefield, 2002.

Nozick, Robert. *Anarchy, State and Utopia.* Oxford: Blackwell, 1974.

Nussbaum, Martha C. "Capabilities and Human Rights." *Fordham Law Review* 66, no. 2 (1997): 273–300.

———. "Capabilities as Fundamental Entitlements: Sen and Social Justice." *Feminist Economics* 9, no. 2–3 (2003): 33–59.

———. *Creating Capabilities: The Human Development Approach.* Cambridge: Belknap Press, 2011.

———. *Frontiers of Justice: Disability, Nationality, Species Membership.* Cambridge: Belknap Press, 2006.

Oates, R. Kim, Anthony Peacock, and Douglas Forest. "Long-Term Effects of Nonorganic Failure to Thrive." *Pediatrics* 75, no. 1 (1985): 36–40.

Olafson, Frederick. "Rights and Duties in Education." In *Educational Judgments: Papers in the Philosophy of Education*, edited by James F. Doyle, 173–95. London: Routledge & Kegan Paul, 1973.

Overall, Christine. *Why Have Children?: The Ethical Debate.* Cambridge, MA: MIT Press, 2012.

Paradis, Heather, Guillermo Montes, and Peter G. Szilagyi. "A National Perspective on Parents' Knowledge of Child Development, Its Relation to Parent-Child Interaction, and Associated Parenting Characteristics." In *Pediatrics Academic Society.* Honolulu, HI, 2008.

Parke, Ross D., and Richard H. Walters. "Some Factors Determining the Efficacy of Punishment for Inducing Response Inhibition." *Monographs of the Society for Research in Child Development* 32, no. 1 (1967): 1–45.

Piaget, Jean. *The Origins of Intelligence in Children*. New York: International Universities Press, 1952.

Pringle, Mia Kellmer. *The Needs of Children*. 3rd ed. London: Routledge, 1986.

Radke-Yarrow, Marian, and Carolyn Zahn-Waxler. "Roots, Motives, and Patterns in Children's Prosocial Behavior." In *The Development and Maintenance of Prosocial Behaviors*, edited by Ervin Staub, Daniel Bar-Tal, Jerzy Karylowski, and Janusz Reykowski, 81–99. New York: Plenum, 1984.

Raja, Shyamala Nada, Rob McGee, and Warren R Stanton. "Perceived Attachments to Parents and Peers and Psychological Well-Being in Adolescence." *Journal of Youth and Adolescence* 21, no. 4 (1992): 471–85.

Raphael, D. D. "Human Rights, Old and New." In *Political Theory and the Rights of Man*, edited by D. D. Raphael, 54–67. London: Macmillan, 1967.

Rawls, John. *The Law of Peoples: With "The Idea of Public Reason Revisited."* Harvard: Harvard University Press, 1999.

———. *A Theory of Justice*. Oxford: Oxford University Press, 1971.

Raz, Joseph. *Ethics in the Public Domain: Essays in the Morality of Law and Politics*. Oxford: Clarendon Press, 1994.

———. "Human Rights in the Emerging World Order." *Transnational Legal Theory* 1, no. 1 (2010): 31–47.

———. "Human Rights without Foundations." In *The Philosophy of International Law*, edited by Samantha Besson and John Tasioulas, 321–38. Oxford: Oxford University Press, 2010.

———. *The Morality of Freedom*. Oxford: Clarendon Press, 1986.

Redd, William H., Edward K. Morris, and Jerry Martin. "Effects of Positive and Negative Adult Interaction on Children's Social Preferences." *Journal of Experimental Child Psychology* 19, no. 1 (1975): 153–64.

Reichlin, Massimo. "The Argument from Potential: A Reappraisal." *Bioethics* 11, no. 1 (1997): 1–23.

Reilly, Thom. "Transition from Care: Status and Outcomes of Youth Who Age out of Foster Care." *Child Welfare* 82, no. 6 (2003): 727–46.

Reppucci, N. Dickon, Preston A. Britner, and Jennifer L. Woolard. *Preventing Child Abuse and Neglect through Parent Education*. Baltimore, MD: Paul H. Brookes Publishing Co., 1997.

Richards, Norvin. *The Ethics of Parenthood*. New York: Oxford University Press, 2010.

Rothman, Barbara K. *Recreating Motherhood: Ideology and Technology in a Patriarchal Society.* New York: W. W. Norton, 1989.

Rousseau, Jean-Jacques. *Émile.* Translated by Barbara Foxley. London: J. M. Dent and Sons, Ltd., 1974.

Rueter, Martha A., Margaret A. Keyes, William G. Iacono, and Matt McGue. "Family Interactions in Adoptive Compared to Nonadoptive Families." *Journal of Family Psychology* 23, no. 1 (2009): 58–66.

Sandmire, Michael J, and Michael S. Wald. "Licensing Parents—a Response to Claudia Mangel's Proposal." *Family Law Quarterly* 24, no. 1 (1990): 53–76.

Sapolsky, Robert M. "The Physiological Relevance of Glucocorticoid Endangerment of the Hippocampus." *Annals of the New York Academy of Sciences* 746, no. 1 (1994): 294–307.

Scafidi, Frank A., Tiffany M. Field, Saul M. Schanberg, Charles R. Bauer, Karen Tucci, Jacqueline Roberts, Connie Morrow, and Cynthia M. Kuhn. "Massage Stimulates Growth in Preterm Infants: A Replication." *Infant Behavior and Development* 13, no. 2 (1990): 167–88.

Scanlon, T. M. *What We Owe to Each Other.* Cambridge, MA: Belknap Press, 1998.

Schiffer, Judith, Cynthia Cooper, Suzy Garfinkle Chevrier, and Andrea Schuver. *Preparing Tomorrow's Parents Today: How to Bring Parenting Education for Children and Teens to Your Schools.* The Parenting Project, 2002.

Schoeman, Ferdinand. "Rights of Children, Rights of Parents, and the Moral Basis of the Family." *Ethics* 91, no. 1 (1980): 6–19.

Schrag, Francis. "Children: Their Rights and Needs." In *Whose Child?*, edited by William Aiken and H. LaFollette, 237–53. Totowa, NJ: Littlefield, Adams, & Co., 1980.

Shannon, Courtney, M. Champoux, J. D. Higley, A. Dodson, S. B. Higley, S. J. Suomi, and M. Linnoila. "Interindividual Differences in Neonatal Serotonin Functioning: Stability of Interindividual Differences and Behavioral Correlates." *American Journal of Primatology* 36 (1995): 155.

Shue, Henry. *Basic Rights: Subsistence, Affluence, and U.S. Foreign Policy (Second Edition).* Princeton: NJ: Princeton University Press, 1996.

Sidgwick, Henry. *The Methods of Ethics.* 7 ed. Chicago: University of Chicago, 1962.

Siegel, Daniel J., and Mary Hartzell. *Parenting from the inside Out: How a Deeper Self-Understanding Can Help You Raise Children Who Thrive.* New York: Tarcher, 2004.

Silver, Henry K., and Marcia Finkelstein. "Deprivation Dwarfism." *Journal of Pediatrics* 70, no. 3 (1967): 317–24.

Singer, Peter. "Famine, Affluence, and Morality." In *Ethics in Practice*, edited by H. LaFollette, 585–95. Oxford: Blackwell, 1997.

———. *Practical Ethics*. 2nd ed. Cambridge: Cambridge University Press, 1993.

Skinner, B. F., and James G. Holland. *The Analysis of Behavior*. New York: McGraw-Hill, 1961.

Solomon, Robert C. "The Logic of Emotion." *Nous* 11, no. 1 (1977): 41–49.

Spitz, René, and Katherine M. Wolf. "Anaclitic Depression: An Inquiry into the Genesis of Psychiatric Conditions in Early Childhood." *The Psychoanalytic Study of the Child* 2 (1946): 313–42.

Stocker, Michael. "The Schizophrenia of Modern Ethical Theories." *The Journal of Philosophy* 73, no. 14 (1976): 453–66.

Sumner, L. W. "Abortion." In *Health Care Ethics: An Introduction*, edited by D. Van DeVeer and T. Regan, 162–83. Philadelphia: Temple University Press, 1987.

———. *The Moral Foundation of Rights*. Oxford: Clarendon Press, 1987.

Suomi, Stephen J., and Christopher Ripp. "A History of Mother-Less Mother Monkey Mothering at the University of Wisconsin Primate Laboratory." In *Child Abuse: The Nonhuman Primate Data*, edited by Martin Reite and Nancy Caine. New York: Alan R. Liss, 1983.

Tamis-LeMonda, Catherine S., and Marc H. Bornstein. "Habituation and Maternal Encouragement of Attention in Infancy as Predictors of Toddler Language, Play, and Representational Competence." *Child Development* 60, no. 3 (1989): 738–51.

Tasioulas, John. "Human Rights, Universality and the Values of Personhood: Retracing Griffin's Steps." *European Journal of Philosophy* 10, no. 1 (2002): 79–100.

———. "Taking Rights out of Human Rights." *Ethics* 120, no. 4 (2010): 647–78.

Taylor, Richard. *Good and Evil*. New York: Macmillan, 1970.

Taylor, Robert S. "Children as Projects and Persons: A Liberal Antinomy." *Social Theory and Practice* 35 (2009): 555–76.

Thomson, Judith Jarvis. "A Defense of Abortion." *Philosophy and Public Affairs* 1, no. 1 (1971): 47–66.

Tittle, Peg. *Should Parents Be Licensed? Debating the Issues*. Amherst, NJ: Prometheus, 2004.

Trainor, Laurel J. "Infant Preferences for Infant-Directed Versus Noninfant-Directed Playsongs and Lullabies." *Infant Behavior and Development* 19, no. 1 (1996): 83–92.

US Department of Health and Human Services. " The AFCARS Report, No. 19." 2012.

UNAIDS, UNICEF, and USAID. "Children on the Brink: A Joint Report of New Orphan Estimates and a Framework for Action." 2004.

UNICEF. "Progress for Children: A Report Card on Child Protection." 2009.

UNICEF, UNAIDS, and WHO. "Children and Aids: Fifth Stocktaking Report." 2010.

United Nations Department of Economic and Social Affairs/Population Division. "Child Adoption: Trends and Policies." 2009.

United States Department of Agriculture. "Expenditure on Children by Families, 2012." 2013.

US Department of Health and Human Services. "Child Maltreatment." Washington, DC: US Department of Health and Human Services, 2011.

———. " Children Adopted from Foster Care: Child and Family Characteristics, Adoption Motivation, and Well-Being." edited by Office of the Assistant Secretary for Planning and Evaluation, 2011.

———. " Long-Term Consequences of Child Abuse and Neglect." Washington, DC: US Department of Health and Human Services, 2008.

van IJzendoorn, Marinus H., Maartje Luijk, and Femmie Juffer. "IQ of Children Growing up in Children's Homes: A Meta-Analysis on IQ Delays in Orphanages." *Merrill-Palmer Quarterly* 54, no. 3 (2008): 341–66.

Varner, Gary. *In Nature's Interests? Interests, Animal Rights, and Environmental Ethics.* New York: Oxford University Press, 1998.

Vlastos, Gregory. "Justice and Equality." In *Theories of Rights*, edited by Jeremy Waldron, 41–76. Oxford: Oxford University Press, 1984.

Warnock, Mary. "Do Human Cells Have Rights?" *Bioethics* 1, no. 1 (1987): 1–14.

Wellman, Carl. *The Proliferation of Rights: Moral Progress or Empty Rhetoric?* Boulder, CO: Westview Press, 1999.

———. *Real Rights.* Oxford: Oxford University Press, 1995.

———. *Welfare Rights.* Totowa, NJ: Rowman & Littlefield, 1982.

Westman, Jack C. *Licensing Parents: Can We Prevent Child Abuse and Neglect.* Cambridge, MA: Perseus, 1994.

Williams, Bernard. "Deciding to Believe." In *Problems of the Self*. Cambridge: Cambridge University Press, 1973.

———. "The Human Prejudice." In *Philosophy as a Humanistic Discipline*, edited by A. W. Moore, 135–54. Princeton: Princeton University Press, 2008.

———. "Persons, Character, and Morality." In *Moral Luck*, edited by Bernard Williams. Cambridge: Cambridge University Press, 1981.

Zeki, S. "The Neurobiology of Love." *FEBS Letters* 581, no. 14 (2007): 2575–79.

Index